TREE
MAGIC

© Jessica Weiser

About the Author

Sandra Kynes is a Reiki practitioner and a member of the Bards, Ovates and Druids. She likes to develop creative ways to explore the world and integrate them with her spiritual path and everyday life. Her unique views and methods form the basis of her books, which serve as reference material for Wiccans, Pagans, and anyone who wants to experience their spirituality in a different way.

Sandra has lived in New York City, Europe, England, and now Mid-Coast Maine where she lives with her family and cats in an 1850's farmhouse surrounded by meadows and woods. She loves connecting with nature through gardening, hiking, bird watching, and kayaking. Visit her website at www.kynes.net.

SANDRA KYNES

TREE MAGIC

Connecting with the
Spirit & Wisdom of Trees

Llewellyn Publications
Woodbury, Minnesota

FIRST EDITION
First Printing, 2021

Book design by Donna Burch-Brown
Cover design by Shannon McKuhen
Editing by Marjorie Otto
Interior illustrations by Eugene Smith

Portions of this book were previously published in *Whispers from the Woods: The Lore and Magic of Trees* by Sandra Kynes, 2006.

Llewellyn is a registered trademark of Llewellyn Worldwide Ltd.

Library of Congress Cataloging-in-Publication Data
Names: Kynes, Sandra, author.
Title: Tree magic : connecting with the spirit & wisdom of trees / by Sandra Kynes.
Description: First edition. | Woodbury : Llewellyn Publications, [2021] | Includes bibliographical references and index. | Summary: "A guide on trees and their magical correspondences, history, lore, and uses"— Provided by publisher.
Identifiers: LCCN 2021011600 (print) | LCCN 2021011601 (ebook) | ISBN 9780738761930 (paperback) | ISBN 9780738761985 (ebook)
Subjects: LCSH: Plants—Miscellanea. | Witchcraft. | Magic.
Classification: LCC BF1572.P43 K963 2021 (print) | LCC BF1572.P43 (ebook) | DDC 133.4/3—dc23
LC record available at https://lccn.loc.gov/2021011600
LC ebook record available at https://lccn.loc.gov/2021011601

Llewellyn Publications
A Division of Llewellyn Worldwide Ltd.
2143 Wooddale Drive
Woodbury, MN 55125-2989
www.llewellyn.com

Printed in the United States of America

Other Books by Sandra Kynes

Beginner's Guide to Herbal Remedies (2020)

Magical Symbols and Alphabets (2020)

Llewellyn's Complete Book of Essential Oils (2019)

365 Days of Crystal Magic (2018)

Crystal Magic (2017)

Plant Magic (2017)

Bird Magic (2016)

Herb Gardener's Essential Guide (2016)

Star Magic (2015)

Mixing Essential Oils for Magic (2013)

Llewellyn's Complete Book of Correspondences (2013)

Change at Hand (2009)

Sea Magic (2008)

Your Altar (2007)

Whispers from the Woods (2006)

A Year of Ritual (2004)

Gemstone Feng Shui (2002)

"I don't believe this wood is a world at all.
I think it's just a sort of in-between place."
—C. S. LEWIS, *THE MAGICIAN'S NEPHEW* [1]

1. C. S. Lewis, *The Magician's Nephew*. New York: HarperCollins, 2005, 39.

Contents

PART TWO: THE TREE PROFILES

Acknowledgments

Many thanks to my editor Elysia Gallo
for the opportunity to return to the forest.

INTRODUCTION

In this era of climate change, trees are one of our greatest allies because they help moderate the climate by giving off water and oxygen and taking in carbon dioxide. For city dwellers, trees are especially important because they act as filters absorbing pollutants from the air, including carbon monoxide, sulfur dioxide, and ozone. They also clean the air by filtering out small particles of dust and pollen. A large tree can produce enough oxygen for four people per day and provide the cooling equivalent of ten room air conditioners.[2] While trees cool the surrounding area during the day, the soil around them radiates heat at night. Trees protect rivers and streams and conserve water by securing the ground from erosion and reducing runoff.

We are intimately connected with trees because they are largely responsible for creating Earth's atmosphere. We breathe in oxygen and breathe out carbon dioxide; trees take in carbon dioxide and give off oxygen. In addition to this symbiotic relationship, we are

2. Erv Evans, "Benefits of Trees," North Carolina State University, Department of Horticulture Science, Raleigh, NC. Accessed May 24, 2019. https://projects.ncsu.edu/project/treesofstrength/benefits.htm.

strongly connected with trees because they made it possible for civilization to develop. After humans first attached sharpened stones to the ends of sticks to extend their reach as hunters and kindled fires for warmth and cooking, there was no going back.

Although people relied on trees as a source of food, shelter, and raw material, they also regarded them as something more, something mystical. Trees were an integral part of spiritual and cultural traditions as well as one of the most powerful symbols the psyche could summon. Trees served as vivid reminders of the cycle of life, death, and rebirth. They seemed imbued with magic because they simultaneously dwelled in the three realms of heaven, earth, and the underworld providing access to the wisdom of the ancestors and the Divine.

The forest was an enticing place of mystery and deep transformation. People could sense the subtle energy that moved through the trees because it also moved through them. The connection between humans and trees was real and central to everyday life. However, for a time we lost our way through the woods along the road to scientific discovery and industrialization. We forgot that we, too, are part of the natural world. But people have been rediscovering the power of trees and the mystical beauty of the arboreal world. In fact, people are turning to the forest for health reasons and not just for the cardio workout of a brisk hike. Called *forest therapy* and *forest bathing*, taking in the atmosphere of a forest has been found to have positive physiological and psychological effects. In studies, people have been shown to have a decrease in blood pressure and a relaxed but focused state of mind. And perhaps, people may also be finding a sense of awe and magic as they walk through the woods.

While it may make us feel good, a walk in the forest or a wooded park makes it easy to understand the reverence our ancestors had for trees. Trees evoke majesty and power with soaring trunks that can hold a huge protective canopy of leaves and branches aloft. As Pagans, we seek ways to honor the natural world and live more closely with the rhythm and spirit of the land. Establishing more than a gossamer connection with the green world helps us access different levels of energy and awareness that can bring deeper meaning to our lives. Functioning as a gateway to these different levels of being, trees enhance our spiritual practices and provide a better understanding of the world and our place in it.

In the woods, you can't help but feel part of the natural world. With that feeling comes the self-realization of returning to Source, to the Divine. Nature is not out there and separate from us; we are part of it. How we regard the world is how we live in it. As

Pagans, we understand that the integrity of our spiritual and magical lives is intimately bound to the integrity of the natural world and, of course, trees.

The Wood Wide Web

While this book focuses on the magical and sacred aspect of trees, there is an interesting phenomenon in the forest to think about. Although all plants vie with one another for light and water, trees work together to create an environment that is protective and nurturing through a network of underground fungi. Depending on trees (and other plants) for photosynthesis and nourishment, fungi return the favor by enabling trees to communicate via chemical and electrical signals.

A fine, cottony web of fungi throughout the soil grows into the soft root hairs of trees creating a massive interconnection. Suzanne Simard, professor of forest ecology at the University of British Columbia, Canada, dubbed this the *wood wide web*. Trees share nutrients and communicate through this web and not just with their own species. Studies have also shown that large, dominant trees nurture younger ones by creating the ideal environment for slow growth, which is necessary for long life. The wisdom of the forest passes beneath our feet. Perhaps this is part of the reason many indigenous forest-dwelling peoples, past and present, believe that their habitats possess awareness.

About This Book

Trees provide a gateway into a wider world of spirit and magic. This book is intended to help you explore their timeless mysteries and work with their power. While some of the material contained here was previously published in my book *Whispers from the Woods* (2006), almost all of it has been completely revised. In addition, this new book includes expanded tree profiles and focuses on magical practices.

Part one of this book contains a brief history of beliefs regarding trees, their associations with deities, and their importance from sacred forest to mundane gathering place. Other chapters provide information on working with tree energy, how to use it in ritual and magic, and how to make various tools from parts of trees. Of course, the Celtic ogham is also explored along with several tree calendars and the runic half months.

The tree profiles in part two include sixty-five types of trees. Although not all of them are trees, per se, some have been added to accommodate the Celtic ogham, plus a few others that are of magical interest. In addition to descriptions and seasonal details, each profile includes historical and magical background information, associated deities, and items to purchase when the tree is not available. Each entry also includes suggestions for magical and ritual use.

This book will serve as a guide to bring the magic, spirit, and wisdom of trees into your life. Like music, trees speak to something deep and primal within us. Working with trees enriches our lives and provides unique access to the power and spirit that surrounds us.

PART ONE

CHAPTER 1
LIVING HISTORY

Because of tree rings, we know that many types of trees can live for hundreds of years and sometimes over a thousand. With trees such as the yew and olive that can live over two thousand years, it's no wonder that early civilizations regarded them as immortal. The oldest of all are the bristlecone pines, which grow in one of the harshest climates on earth. Dubbed *Methuselah*, the oldest bristlecone is close to five thousand years old.[3]

While some trees are impressive in size, most are remarkable, as they seem to defy gravity by holding aloft heavy loads of branches and leaves. Like mythological heroes, trees are larger than life. Their beauty evokes wonder, and so it is no surprise that they occupy a central place in folklore, myth, and religion. A tree may have been considered sacred because of an association with a deity, a spiritual practice or event, the location where it grew, or what it came to represent. For example, the yew may have become sacred because people noticed its longevity that spanned many generations. Veneration

---

3. James Balog, *Tree: A New Vision of the American Forest* (New York: Sterling Publishing Co., Inc. 2004), 152.

of the oak may have pre-Celtic roots with the hunter-gatherer peoples of Ireland and Gaul and their survival in the dense oak forests that were abundant at that time. Trees may have seemed like deities or magical in their ability to sprout new growth appearing to return from the dead, breakdown rocks with their roots, and like a slow motion river of living wood encompass objects in their growth path.

Life and Creation

In many ancient cultures, the tree held a two-fold symbolic purpose as a world tree and as a tree of life. Celestial and chthonic, a world tree connected the three realms of heaven, earth, and underworld (deities, the living, the dead). As a tree of life, it represented the source of life and abundance for ongoing vitality.

The most famous world tree is the ash called *Yggdrasil*. Connecting the nine realms of Norse mythology, it was upon this tree that Odin suspended himself in a shamanic trance and perceived the runes. In Finland, the tree of life also functioned as a cosmic sky pole that held the heavens in place. It was believed to extend from the North Star through the center of the earth. Some sources describe this tree as an oak, others as a pine.

The Hessian and Saxon Germanic tribes erected pillars of large tree trunks on hilltops to represent their universal tree. Called *Irminsul*, the pillars were named for the god Irmin of which little is known.[4] The great Irminsul at Eresburg, Germany, was the center of a ritual complex that was used into the eighth century. Similarly, the tree of life in ancient Egypt was usually depicted atop a sacred mound. As the *axis mundi* (axis of the world), its branches reached to the stars and its roots extended deep into the netherworld. Osiris, the god of the dead, was sometimes portrayed as the world tree. Likewise, in the eastern Mediterranean, the Canaanites used a wooden pillar to represent their revered mother goddess Asherah, whose name was most often translated as "grove."[5]

The Mesopotamian tree of life was associated with Enlil, the supreme god. This tree was a symbol of cosmic order and thought to have been either a date palm or pomegranate. Arabs believed that a great lote tree existed between the human and divine realms, functioning as a connection and a boundary. In the story of Muhammad's ascent, a lote

4. Alexander Porteous, *The Forest in Folklore and Mythology* (Mineola, NY: Dover Publications, Inc., 2002), 194.

5. Margaret Barker, *The Mother of the Lord: Volume 1 The Lady in the Temple* (New York: Bloomsbury T&T Clark, 2012), 80.

tree marked the point beyond which only Allah knew what existed. The lote tree was used to represent the manifestation of Allah as well as to symbolize the spiritual aspect of the self.

In the spirit landscape of the shaman, a tree represented the axis mundi and provided the means to travel between the realms. Stretching deep into the underworld, into the realm of departed spirits, tree roots could draw up the wisdom of those who have departed the earthly plane. And when deities needed to be consulted, tree branches reaching to the heavens provided access to their celestial realm.

Sometimes, even a single tree branch had great power and could provide access to the otherworld. In Celtic mythology, a silver branch from the mystical apple tree or a branch with leaves and fruit of gold and silver functioned as a passport between the worlds. In the epic *Aeneid,* written by Roman poet Virgil (70–19 BCE), a golden branch provided passage into and out of the underworld.

Trees are central in the creation stories of diverse cultures such as the Celts, Greeks, Indonesians, Scandinavians, Siberians, and Japanese. English historian and author Peter Berresford Ellis (1943–) provided a beautiful interpretation of a Celtic creation myth in which an oak tree represents Bilé, the consort of the Great Mother Goddess Danu.[6] Her divine water as rain and his seed produced the Dagda and other Tuatha Dé Danann gods and goddesses. Two of the Gaulish tribes of Central Europe were closely identified with trees. The tribal name *Ebutones* meant "yew tribe" and *Lemovices* "the people of the elm."[7] Well known for using ash for their ships and for magical purposes, the Vikings were called *Æseling*, "men of ash" from the Old English word *æsc*, "ash tree."[8] The Vikings themselves used the Old Norse word for ash, *askr*, to refer to their ships.[9]

Sacred Groves and Forests

The forest was sometimes perceived as a dark and mysterious place that seemed separate from the everyday world. The sense of it being a place apart from the rest of the world was bolstered by widely held beliefs that trees were dwelling places of deities and other spirits, and that trees had souls. The Druids are best known for worshipping in sacred

6. Peter Berresford Ellis, *The Chronicles of the Celts* (New York: Carrol and Graf Publishers Inc., 1999), 21.

7. Miranda Jane Green, *Celtic Myths,* 3rd ed. (Austin, TX: University of Texas Press, 1998), 50.

8. Della Hooke, *Trees in Anglo-Saxon England: Literature, Lore and Landscape* (Woodbridge, England: The Boydell Press, 2010), 200–201.

9. Ibid.

groves. Thanks to Pliny the Elder, it is popularly believed that the name *Druid* is based on the Greek *drys* meaning "oak" or *drus*, "sacred tree."[10] However, Peter Berresford Ellis takes issue with this. Although the Celts would have been familiar with the Greek language through their trade with merchants in the Mediterranean, Ellis questions why they would have overlooked their own root word *dru* meaning "immersed."[11] Combined with *wid*, "to know", a Dru-wid would be someone "immersed in knowledge" or someone with great knowledge.

The Celts were not the only people to worship in sacred groves and forests. The early religious sites of the Germanic tribes and Slavic people were also situated in forests. Third-century Roman writers noted that Germanic tribes of northern Germany and the Jutland peninsula of Denmark conducted rituals in sacred groves. In the German state of Prussia, the Teutonic Donar, god of thunder, continued to be worshipped in oak groves as late as the sixteenth century.

The Celts of Gaul called their forested place of worship *nemeton*; *nem* meaning "heaven," which comes from the same root as the Latin *nemus* "sacred wood."[12] In Bath, England, the goddess Nemetona was depicted on the side of an altar, and in Derbyshire the Roman spa was called *Aquae Amemetiae*, "the waters of the goddess of the sacred grove."[13]

In addition to worshipping in forests, archaeologists have found numerous Neolithic sites (c. 4000–2500 BCE) in England with a structure called a *woodhenge*. A woodhenge consisted of concentric circles of large wooden posts surrounded by a ditch with a break in the northeast sector; similar to the layout of Stonehenge. There is speculation that these structures may have been roofed. At Avebury circle in Wiltshire, England, not far from Stonehenge, there is evidence that a woodhenge consisted of 168 huge posts in six concentric oval rings. If it had a roof, walking through the dimly lit interior with all its columns may have been evocative of strolling through a dense forest. Remnants of woodhenges have also been found in Ireland and Germany.

---

10. Fred Hageneder, *The Meaning of Trees: Botany, History, Healing, Lore* (San Francisco: Chronicle Books, LLC, 2005), 177.

11. Peter Berresford Ellis, *A Brief History of the Druids* (New York: Carroll & Graf Publishers, 2002), 38.

12. Gaul encompassed an area that includes present day France and parts of Belgium, Germany, and Italy. Jean Markale, *Merlin Priest of Nature*, trans. Belle N. Burke (Rochester, VT: Inner Traditions, 1995), 119.

13. Michael Wood, *In Search of England: Journeys into the English Past* (Berkeley, CA: University of California Press, 2001), 233.

In 1998, a unique woodhenge was discovered on the Norfolk coast of England. Storms and beach erosion revealed a circle of fifty-six posts with part of a large inverted oak in the center. It is thought that the flattened remainder of its roots may have functioned as an altar. Dubbed *Seahenge*, dendrochronology dates the site to 2049 BCE.[14] Similarly in the Vedic text *Katha Upanishad* (c. 600–300 BCE), the Hindu cosmic tree was described as inverted. Solitary trees were sometimes regarded as holding significant power as evidenced by single trees situated in the centers of ceremonial circles in the Midlands and elsewhere in England.

Mundane Gathering Places

A tree often served as a community symbol and gathering place. The sacred tree of most Celtic tribes also functioned as a community talisman, providing continuity for a village or group's history. As a way to demoralize a rival tribe, one group would destroy the other's tree. In Ireland, a great tree in each of the five provinces was revered as a symbol of sovereignty. Centuries later, trees served as community symbols in Colonial America. Called *liberty trees*, they functioned as meeting and rallying points and remained potent symbols of freedom long after independence from England was won.

The ancient equivalent of a town hall meeting was held at assembly places usually designated with a standing stone or an earthen mound but quite often a tree. Recorded in 1086, the name of one such meeting place, *Ghidenetroi*, is thought to mean "tree of the goddess" from the Old English *gyden*, "goddess" indicating that it may have been a sacred place for worship in earlier times.[15] Trees are prominent in English documents as boundary markers, a practice that dates to Roman times. A replacement tree was commonly planted at a boundary marker when the original showed signs of dying.

Functioning as a symbol of power and wisdom, a large tree in front of a castle or royal residence often served as a place of judgment where courts of law were conducted. When execution was in the cards, the tree also served as gallows.

Sacred Trees and Holy Water

Wells and springs were believed to hold the power of local deities. The combination of a tree and sacred well was regarded as particularly potent to Celtic and Germanic peoples.

14. Timothy Darvill, *Prehistoric Britain*, 2nd ed. (New York: Routledge, 2010), 149.

15. Hooke, *Trees in Anglo-Saxon England*, 172.

The term *well* generally included springs and small pools but on occasion extended to the water that collected in the stump of a special tree. Even water that collected in a hollow created by the forked limbs of certain trees was considered magical.

Since Roman times, many sites in Europe were places of pilgrimage for physical healing as well as spiritual communion and cleansing. As part of the pilgrimage ritual to sacred water, it was customary to take a drink from, bathe in, or be anointed with the water, and then leave an offering. In addition to pilgrimage sites, it was common practice to tie a piece of cloth on a branch of a tree that was regarded as sacred or special. According to theory, by the time the cloth disintegrated, the healing or other request would materialize. This practice was also used to symbolically remove a burden. In the British Isles, these were called *clootie trees* or *rag trees*.

A similar practice in the British Isles and Europe involved driving a nail or coin into a tree trunk. One such tree on Innis Maree in Scotland was used during the eighteenth century to petition and leave offerings to St. Maree. However, this practice at that location may date to the veneration of the Celtic solar deity Magh Ruith. Another custom called *drawing the nail* was practiced in the British Isles and Europe. Driving a nail into a tree symbolically sealed a vow; removing the nail with all parties and a witness present was the only way to reverse it.

According to Norse legend, a spring bubbled up from deep within the earth at the roots of Yggdrasil. As Odin hung suspended upside down on the tree, he was eventually able to stretch far enough to take a sip of water. It was then that he began to receive wisdom. Some versions of the legend say that he saw the rune characters on the surface of the water. Perhaps a reflection of tree branches produced the images as his shamanic state of mind perceived related information. Although Yggdrasil was the Norse world tree, its name translates as "Odin's steed"; Ygg was another name for Odin.[16] Either as tree or horse, it was Odin's shamanic transport.

In Celtic mythology, nuts, especially hazelnuts, held concentrated wisdom. There are many legends about nine hazel trees surrounding a sacred well or spring. Because hazelnuts dropped into the water, anyone drinking it received wisdom. In similar legends, the salmon of knowledge that inhabited the water ate the hazelnuts and gained greater

16. John Lindow, *Norse Mythology: A Guide to Gods, Heroes, Rituals, and Beliefs* (New York: Oxford University Press, 2002), 201.

wisdom. This was transferred to a person who ate one of these salmon or even just the roasting juices as in the story of hunter and warrior Fionn Mac Cumhail.

Just as salmon and trees are linked in ancient legend, they also have an intertwined relationship that has been noted in British Columbia, Canada. According to environmentalist David Suzuki (1936–), as salmon return upriver to spawn, they bring valuable nutrients to the forest. This occurs when animals catch the fish and take them into the woods to get away from thieving competitors and leave parts of the carcasses on the forest floor. A correlation has been detected between the size of tree rings and the size of the annual salmon runs. The trees return the favor to the salmon by shielding the water from the sun and keeping it cool. In areas where trees have been clear-cut, the salmon population has dropped. The wisdom of trees and the salmon of knowledge are sending messages that we should heed.

CHAPTER 2
GETTING STARTED

While leaves and other parts of trees or tools made of wood can be used in ritual and magic, getting to know trees and working with their energy allows us to fully incorporate their power into our practices. Since we are such visually oriented creatures, observation is a good way to start tuning into and working with tree energy. To begin, study a tree's aura, and then zero in on its individual characteristics and details.

Working with Auras

The aura is an electromagnetic field that surrounds all living things. Although it can be expansive, it is easiest to see near a tree, animal, or human. It usually appears whitish or grayish and mostly transparent. Occasionally, it can appear yellowish or gold, which makes it easy to understand where Renaissance artists may have gotten the idea for halos.

Observing the aura is easier from a distance, especially if you can see the top of the tree against the sky. The fading light at dusk is the best time of day. Spring and summer are the best times of the year because trees have more active energy above ground during these seasons. In autumn and winter, energy becomes concentrated in the roots.

If you have tried seeing the image in a Magic Eye picture, the concept is basically the same. It's similar to daydreaming, too, when your eyes are not focusing on details. Sometimes, using peripheral vision can be easier; turn your head slightly instead of looking directly at the tree. Soften your gaze and look at the sky around the edge of the tree. An outline of the tree will seem to be repeated as a whitish shadow slightly above it. During the summer when the tree's vitality is at its height, the aura may seem to move and ripple like the aurora borealis.

When observing a group of trees, you may notice that their energy fields merge into one if they are close together. If the trees are not touching, you may be able to see wispy white or grayish strands between them connecting their energy. Don't get discouraged if you don't see auras right away; it takes practice and patience.

Getting to Know a Tree

The next step in observation is to select a tree in your yard, nearby park, or anywhere that is easily accessible for you. Be sure to have a notebook or digital device with you for taking notes. Begin by looking at the tree from a distance. Look at its aura, and then focus on its details. What is its overall shape? What are your initial feelings or impressions of the tree? How would you describe the tree? Noble, peaceful, wild; write it down. Look at the pattern of branches and how they intertwine or how they may be spaced apart. What type of leaves or needles does it have or are the branches bare right now? What are the nuances of its colors? Get to know the individual characteristics of the tree.

After visual observation, walk to within arm's length of the tree and note if your impressions or feelings change. Close your eyes. Visualize your energy expanding from your heart toward the tree. Send a greeting and tell the tree your name. Reach out and place your palms against its trunk. Send a welcoming flow of energy to the tree for a minute or two, and then remove your hands. Stand or sit next to it and note how you feel. Take notes about any physical sensations, thoughts, or emotions that you experience. Take time to just be with the tree, and then before leaving, thank it and say goodbye.

You may or may not sense the tree's energy the first couple of times that you visit it. Don't expect to hear a choir of angelic voices to herald your contact. However, while it is usually very subtle, on occasion you may be surprised to have a particular phrase or image suddenly pop into your mind.

One time when I visited a place that I hadn't been to for more than twenty years, as is my habit, I walked around putting my hands on the trees and enjoying the atmosphere of the place. Suddenly, the phrase "we remember your spirit" came into my mind. Needless to say, I was surprised. Of course, when something like this happens, it's normal to question one's sanity. It's good to be skeptical, but ultimately be honest with yourself and trust what your heart and intuition tell you.

Another example of communication came from an acquaintance, Elizabeth. She told me about the time she was walking in the woods on a summer's day and noticed a severe gash on the trunk of a tree. She thought it was odd because the gash was so far above the ground and she couldn't imagine what had hit the tree. The gash was mostly healed, but she stopped and put her hand on it. She was surprised to suddenly think about snowmobiles. A moment later, she remembered that we'd had an old-fashioned New England winter with lots of snow that would have raised the level of the trail to the height of the gash. When she realized that the tree had responded to her wondering about its wound, she spent time sending it loving, healing energy.

While such messages are not particularly common, the more you work with trees the more likely these experiences may occur. However, most communication is subtle, which is why we need to keep all of our senses open. We are so accustomed to widescreen, surround sound razzmatazz that we fail to detect the delicate, low-key signs. We need to slow down, empty our minds of useless clutter, and pay attention. Learn to listen with more than your ears and to see with more than your eyes. I think Elizabeth and I had these experiences because we were present to the moment with all of our senses.

After working with a tree for a few weeks, choose another and go through the same exercises. Afterwards, review your notes. Do your experiences vary with individual trees or different species of trees? You may also want to note how you felt before and after visiting each tree. After a time, you may find that your energy resonates at a different level when interacting with trees and that you may experience a shift in awareness.

As previously mentioned, studies are showing that spending time in the woods is healthy. It can lower blood pressure, reduce stress, aid mental focus, and contribute to general well-being. Trees give off phytoncides, which are a type of chemical for dealing with insects. For humans, phytoncides lower cortisol, a stress hormone. They also activate the vagus nerve, which is the longest cranial nerve that has sensory functions and helps regulate heart rate. Like meditation, being in a forest brings a relaxed but heightened state of awareness.

Feel the Energy

Our skin is the largest organ for sensing the world around us, and even if you are not able to see a tree's aura, you can feel its energy. If you're not sure what energy feels like, following is a simple exercise that is often used when getting started in reiki and other types of energy work.

In addition to the body's seven major chakras, we have secondary chakras located in the center of the palms through which we sense energy. Begin this exercise by sitting comfortably and closing your eyes. Spend a minute or two quieting your mind by focusing your attention on your breath. When you feel relaxed, rub the palms of your hands together until they feel warm. Separate your hands to about shoulder width apart; palms facing each other. Keeping your eyes closed, slowly bring your hands closer together until you can feel a little resistance. Open your eyes. You may be surprised at how far apart your hands are from each other, but don't be discouraged if your hands were close together. It takes a little time and practice to develop the ability to sense energy.

Also try this. Close your eyes and rub your hands together. Separate your hands with palms facing each other, and then quickly move them toward each other, and then away several times. It may feel as though there is a ball between your palms that keeps them from touching. After doing this several times, sit with your hands in your lap, palms up. Keep your eyes closed and focus your attention on the sensations in your hands. This is what energy feels like.

Move Inward

Another way to access tree energy is by meditating and focusing your attention on one tree. Meditation allows us to access the subconscious and can produce a shift in awareness. Start by choosing a tree; it doesn't have to be one that you worked with. Write the type of tree on a slip of paper, perhaps cut in the shape of a leaf. Alternatively, find a picture of that type of tree or take a picture of one.

When you are ready, light a candle and sit in front of your altar. Sit with your hands cupped in your lap, holding the piece of paper with the tree name. If you are using a picture, place it on your altar. Close your eyes and breathe deeply and slowly to help your mind shift from the outer world to your inner space. When you feel calm and grounded, allow your focus to move to the tree as you slowly open your eyes.

If you are using a picture, keep your focus soft as you look at it. Let your eyes rest on the nuances of color and form. If you are using a slip of paper with a tree name, you can rest your gaze on it or keep your eyes closed and visualize the tree. Allow yourself to be receptive to energy, thoughts, messages, and feelings.

Don't approach this meditation with expectations of great, earth-shattering revelations. Most information comes softly. And don't be disappointed if nothing seems to happen. Just relax and be receptive. If you are to learn something at this time, it will come.

Taking time after meditation is important even if you don't track your experiences in a journal. Having time for reflection allows information to settle. Things that may not be obvious during the meditation may come to the surface while you sit quietly afterwards. Or, it may take a day or two for you to understand information that may have come to you. Be patient and you will learn what you need to know.

When working with trees, use as many of your senses as possible, especially touch. When visiting a tree, put your hands on it or sit with your back against it. Get to know the feel of its bark. Pick up a fallen branch, leaf, nut, or fruit. How does it feel in your hands? Hold one of these items the next time you do a tree meditation.

Use a small twig, thorn, or nut as a talisman. Every part of the tree holds its spirit. Carry it with you as a reminder of your relationship with that tree. Keep it in your pocket or purse, in your car, or at your place of work. Pick it up occasionally and let your senses remind you about the tree and how you felt in its presence. Also think about the characteristics embodied by the tree and how they may relate to you.

Frequency is important. Whether you want to use tree energy in your magic or to deepen your spiritual life, it is the frequent contact or practice that brings about change. You don't have to do a tree meditation every day, but the more you do it or spend time in the presence of trees, the easier it becomes to work with their energy.

CHAPTER 3

TREES IN MAGIC
AND RITUAL

While holding rituals and conducting magic in forests or special groves is an obvious way to integrate the energy of trees with your practices, it is not the only one. A twig, leaf, nut, flower, fruit, piece of bark or anything from a tree embodies its energy and can be used to represent it. You may already incorporate trees into your practices with the Celtic ogham or for seasonal energy with flowers in the spring, fruit in summer, nuts and fallen leaves in autumn. A branch or other part of a tree can represent an associated deity or be used as an offering. In ancient Greece, branches were often used as offerings to gods and goddesses.

Sometimes, you may not have access to a particular type of tree, however, just as we use pictures of deities and other objects to represent them, we can do the same when working with trees. In addition to objects made from the wood of a tree, oils, essential oils, and flower essences can be used too. These and other items will be covered in the following chapters on tools. When using a picture, oil, or other object, take a few minutes to prepare it for magical and spiritual work. Refer to the section "Cleanse, Consecrate, and Charge an Item for Magic" at the end of chapter 4.

Tree energy can be incorporated into a candle spell by inscribing its name into the wax. When you give voice to your intention in a spell, call on the tree to add its energy to yours. For example, you can simply begin with "Soul of the _____ tree, I call on your power to aid me," and then continue with the rest of your spell. A short incantation works well because it's easy to memorize and repetition helps access the subconscious and emotions.

How to Incorporate the Power of Trees

Following are a few suggestions on how to bring the power of trees into your magic and ritual. These samples are intended to spark your imagination; expand upon them and make them your own. Where it is suggested to write something in ogham, you can use runes or whatever alphabet you want. When burning anything, be sure you have a cast iron cauldron or other fireproof container.

General Purpose

Gather strips of fallen birch bark. Write keywords for your intention on the bark as you keep your purpose in mind. When you conduct your spell or ritual, pass the piece of bark through a candle flame, and then drop it into your cauldron.

Balance and Harmony

At Yule, ivy and holly symbolize the struggle for balance between the light and dark halves of the year. When you are seeking to balance your energy or that of your household at any time of year, make a small holly wreath or use a small branch and lightly wind a length of ivy around it.

Use a reed or bamboo flute or a small piece from either plant to symbolically invite harmony into your life. Sing an incantation to it, and then place it somewhere in your home where you will see it frequently.

Banish and Release

The classic broom plants of gorse and heather work well but any type of pliant twig can be used. If you are working on a carpeted floor, you may want to put a protective cover over it. Bundle a handful of twigs to create a small ritual broom. Write the name of what you want to release from your life on a piece of paper, and then burn it. When the ashes are cool, scatter them on the floor around your altar. Use the broom to sweep the ashes from the center out to the edge of your circle. Gather the ashes and scatter them outside. Alternatively, if you don't want to scatter ashes around the floor, burn the paper and symbolically sweep the floor with the broom. Afterwards, burn a small piece of the broom. When all the ashes are cool, scatter them outside for final release.

Write the name of someone or a keyword for what you want to remove from your life on a small slip of paper. Place it in a cup and pour in enough witch hazel to cover it. Position the cup where it can stand overnight in the light of the waning moon, and then dispose of it outside on the ground.

Binding

A branch or piece of bark from a cypress tree and a strand of ivy can be used in a binding spell for protection against a negative person. Write the person's initials on a piece of paper and then wrap it around a small cypress branch. Tie it in place with a strand of ivy. Hold the branch between your hands as you visualize the person's energy unable to reach you. Because cypress is associated with protection and peace, think of binding the person with positive energy to counteract their negativity. When the situation improves, burn the branch along with the paper and ivy.

Blessings and Gratitude

Gather fir or pine needles and cones. Tie a small bundle of needles together with thread. Burn them in your cauldron as you think of the things for which you are grateful. Pass the cones through the smoke, and then place them in a location where you will see them frequently and be reminded of your blessings.

Divination, Communication, and Psychic Work

To improve communication with someone, gather two aspen leaves. Paint your initials in ogham on one leaf and their initials on the other. Wrap the leaves in a cloth and place it under your pillow for three consecutive nights.

According to legend, laurel leaves were burned in the temple at Delphi, Greece. Place several leaves on your altar and burn one as you engage in your favorite method of divination.

Create this charm prior to divination or psychic work: Place three sycamore seed balls in a pouch. Hang it from your belt or keep it in your pocket during sessions.

Fertility and Sexuality

Red holly berries symbolize the life-giving blood of the Mother Goddess. Take three holly berries to a body of water. As you say your incantation, drop the berries into the water. As you do this, visualize a circle of light surrounding you.

To boost male energy, empower a sprig of mistletoe with an incantation. Hang it near your bed or over the doorway into the bedroom.

Health and Healing

Use a piece of cedarwood or scent a symbolic object with cedar oil as you visualize recovery from an ailment. Keep it in your bedroom until the scent fades, and then bury it in the ground. If you use an object you want to keep, place it on a bed of salt and let it stand in the light of the waning moon for three nights to cleanse it.

Place a handful of dried rowan berries in the center of a square white or purple cloth. Gather the cloth over the berries and tie it into a bundle with white or purple ribbon. Hang this in your kitchen during flu season or keep it for the entire winter.

Love

If possible, use an apple that you have picked. Carve the initials of the one you desire and your own into a ring around the apple. Bury it in the ground or commit it to a body of water.

Do the following just before or on Valentine's Day if the catkins of the birch or hazel are available. Light a red or pink candle, and then place the catkins in a piece of pink or red tissue paper. Hold it over your heart as you recite your incantation. Continue to visualize your desired outcome as you burn the bundle.

Take three long, supple branches of willow, braid them together, and then fasten it into a circle with pink, red, or white ribbon. Place a picture or the name of the person you love in the center and keep it in your bedroom.

Protection

Carefully gather a few thorns from a blackthorn, hawthorn, or locust tree. Write the name of the person or situation from which you seek protection on a piece of paper, and then wrap it around the thorns. Bury the bundle in the ground. If possible, bury it near the tree from which the thorns were collected.

Cut a piece of paper in the shape of a holly leaf or use a picture of holly. Write what you seek protection from on it, and then burn it. When the ashes are cool, sprinkle them in front of your house.

Success

Use this for success in exams or any situation that requires knowledge. Prepare a candle with the ogham Coll (hazel) and a keyword for your situation. Using a sturdy sewing needle, string nine hazelnuts together to form a ring. Place it around the base of the candle. Ideally, keep the spell brief and perform it just before studying or when preparing for an event.

How to Use Tree Symbolism

Whenever possible, coordinate the symbolism of the part of a tree you use for magic or ritual with your purpose. While symbolism and purpose may not always align, when it does, it adds an extra boost of energy.

Residing under the earth, roots are the most natural plant part for grounding energy and providing stability to magic work. Roots can aid psychic or astral work as well as postritual grounding. As a symbol of longevity, roots encourage us to hold secrets when bidden. In addition, roots offer access to the underworld, making them useful for connecting with ancestors, spirits, and chthonic deities.

Sturdy wood and bark provide protective energy for rituals, spells, and charms. Wood and bark are also a gauge of growth and can aid in manifesting your growth on various levels: social, emotional, and spiritual. Within and encircling a tree, wood and bark symbolically provide balance and strength.

From the time they burst forth in the spring until the wind whisks them away in the autumn, leaves enfold the world with aerial enchantment. Personifying energy and growth, leaves give magic and personal endeavors an encouraging boost. Showy or subtle, flowers and catkins are often a crowning glory. They represent beauty with a goal: attraction, sex, and fertility. Using flowers can be especially potent when they add fragrance to magic work. Of course, leaves are often aromatic too.

With the base word *fruit*, fruition means completion or culmination, and so a piece of fruit symbolizes manifestation and success. Fruit represents an increase in power and energy. The feel and smell of fruit is the personification of abundance and freedom from want. Use fruit to increase what you have and to gain what you seek.

Seeds and nuts represent beginnings and the future. They can be instrumental when encouraging something new in your life. They also represent duality such as the alternation between life and death, light and dark. Seeds and nuts move between the worlds, carried on a breeze or snuggled into the earth, they represent beginnings, changes, and cycles.

CHAPTER 4
TOOLS FROM THE WOODS

Bringing parts of a tree into the home conveys their energy into our personal environments. The tools that we make with our own hands are imbued with our intentions and function with powerful purpose. When making your own tools, you may want to sing, chant, recite poetry, or meditate on the task at hand to begin your magical association with it.

Some parts of a tree, especially leaves and flowers, don't last long, but there are ways to preserve them. Wands, walking sticks, and magic staffs are easy to make and can be as simple or elaborate as you like. Don't make wreaths only for Yule; they can be used in other ways to bring tree energy to your magic and rituals any time of year.

When gathering material, only take what is needed. We don't need large pieces of bark, handfuls of flowers, or other parts of a tree for magical purposes. Keep in mind that we want to live in harmony with the natural world; walk softly and leave no trace.

Leaves and Flowers

Leaves contain a great deal of energy and embody the turning cycle of the wheel of the year. In the autumn, gather the most colorful fallen leaves and allow them to dry. They will curl into various shapes. Place them on your altar or in places around your home along with acorns, other nuts, or husks (the husk of the beechnut is rather interesting). These serve as a reminder of transition and change as the earth prepares for a winter's rest and we prepare for our journey through the dark of the year. Of course, you don't have to wait for autumn. A leaf from a tree that you are working with deepens your experience and connection with it.

The easiest way to preserve leaves and flowers is to press them. The goal of this method is to remove moisture and maintain shape. Although plant presses are available, it is not necessary to use one. Place leaves or flowers between two layers of paper towels on a table, and then position a large book or two on top to keep them flat. Autumn leaves only require a couple of days. Fresh leaves and flowers will take longer. Check them after a week, replace the paper towels with fresh ones, and continue pressing for two or three weeks.

Gather and press leaves throughout the year to create a seasonal wheel of the year for your altar. Autumn leaves have a fleeting moment of glory before they become brittle and crumble. Even in this state, they are useful and can be burned in ritual and spell work.

Another way to preserve leaves and flowers is to place their cut stems in a cup of glycerin, which is available at craft stores and online. Use one part glycerin and two parts boiling water to warm the solution before using. When the plant material becomes soft and flexible, remove it from the glycerin. Flowers and leaves remain supple because the glycerin replaces their water content. The process can take several days to several weeks. Small leaves or flowers can be immersed in the glycerin. Younger plants usually produce brighter colors than mature plants. Green leaves usually turn yellow or coppery. Glycerin will preserve them for up to a year and sometimes longer.

Waxing is a method that works well with leaves. Place a leaf between two pieces of waxed paper and gently iron it. Use the "wool" setting and be careful to not press too hard. Groups of leaves can be arranged together, or you can press one at a time. When waxed individually, the paper can be trimmed to the shape of the leaf or cut into any shape.

A method called *rubbing* is a way to save the image of a leaf, which can be incorporated into a journal or book of shadows. This can be done with fresh or dried leaves, although you will need to be especially careful with dried ones. Position the leaf underneath the page where you want its image, and then carefully rub with the side of a colored pencil or crayon over the paper. The details of the leaf will be captured.

The Leaf and Flower Altar Cloth

If you like to create unique cloths for your altar, you can imbue them with tree energy. This method requires fresh leaves and/or flowers, a sturdy flat surface, a hammer, and a small board. Since work is done on a small section at a time, the board only needs to be slightly larger than several leaves or flowers. Gentle tapping will transfer the image of the leaf or flower directly to the cloth. You may want to experiment with a scrap of fabric to get a feel for this technique before launching into the project.

If you are working on a good table, place a layer of cardboard or newspaper under the board. Begin by arranging a few leaves and/or flowers on the board, and then carefully place a section of cloth over it. Hold the cloth in place with one hand, and then tap repeatedly over the plant material with the hammer until an image of the flower or leaf bleeds through the fabric. Continue tapping until the colors reach the desired intensity. Details, embellishments, symbols, and text can be drawn on the cloth with fabric paint or markers.

Wands

I never thought about using a wand until one presented itself to me. I was taking a walk and noticed a fallen tree branch. As I looked at it, it seemed to change. It was as if I were looking at one image superimposed over another; the branch with a wand inside.

I picked up the branch and continued my walk, getting a feel for the future wand in my hand. There were no leaves attached to the branch and only a few tiny side twigs. When I returned home, I wasn't quite sure what to do with it. I didn't know anything about wand making, but I had a feeling this one would tell me what I needed to know. It did, and my first wand emerged into this world.

If you decide to make a wand, before going for a walk sit quietly, send out your intention, and ask for blessings and guidance. You may be surprised at what you find. Consider fallen branches as gifts and leave an offering to express your gratitude. Branches that come down in a storm are often regarded as holding extra power. As for the length of a wand, some people say it should measure from the elbow to the tip of the middle finger; others say shorter. Follow whatever feels right for you. Since it's rare to find a branch the exact length you need, look for one that is longer and thicker than you envision your finished wand.

The hard part begins when you get home because you need to set the branch aside for a couple of months to allow the wood to dry out. Remove any small side twigs, and then lay the branch flat. Turn it every couple of days to keep it from warping. If you plan on removing the bark, now is the time to do it so the wood will dry quicker.

While the wood is seasoning, make plans for your wand. You may want to carve or paint symbols, runes, or ogham characters. If you leave the bark on, anything carved on it will reveal the light inner bark and contrast with the darker outer layer. If you remove the bark, decide whether or not you will stain or paint the wood. Also think about any crystals or other objects that you may want to attach to it if you feel these will enhance your energy as it passes through the wand. Make it uniquely yours.

Most of the work can be done with an X-ACTO knife, however, a few basic, and I mean very basic, woodworking tools are useful. Most arts and crafts stores carry an inexpensive four- or five-piece set. There are two tools that I found most useful. One has a V-shaped blade and the other has a narrow, slightly U-shaped blade. The former is good for inscriptions, the latter for scooping out the tip to insert a crystal or to hollow out the handle if these are part of your plan.

To create a handle for the wand, strips of ribbon, yarn, or leather can be wrapped around one end, which can make it more comfortable to hold. The handle should be long enough to accommodate the width of your hand. Instead of wrapping the handle, you can differentiate it by leaving the bark on that end, or if you remove the bark, stain it a different color. You can carve a groove to mark where the handle ends or whittle the shaft of the wand to make it narrower than the handle.

Consider if you want to hollow out the handle to seal something inside. If you are good with power tools, use a drill to bore into the handle. I am not adept with such tools, nor do I want to damage a wand (or my hands) so I use a drill bit and manually twist it into the handle. Once you place whatever you want inside, use wood filler to seal the end. Use sandpaper to smooth the surface of the wood, especially where small twigs were removed. After carving symbols or words into the wand, lightly sand over the area.

If you plan to fit a crystal on the tip, you will need to scoop out the end. As you do this, it is important to constantly check the fit of the crystal and when it is snug, stop carving. Set the crystal aside until you finish staining or painting the wand. Use a tiny bit of jewelry glue to secure the crystal in the tip.

Walking Sticks and Magic Staffs

If you spend any time hiking, you know the value of a walking stick. It is worth the time and effort to create your own, which can be used for hiking and/or ritual and magic. Follow the same methods for creating a wand. Look for a branch that is longer and thicker than you envision your finished stick. To gauge its diameter and length, keep in mind that you should be able to wrap you fingers around it at a comfortable height. A stick that is too fat, short, or long will not be easy to use.

As with a wand, allow the wood to dry and decide if you will remove the bark, seal something inside, or attach a crystal. Whether you are hiking or leading a ritual, a wrist strap is helpful to prevent dropping the stick. Drill a hole through the stick near where you will hold it so the strap will be easy to slip around your wrist. Make the hole large enough to thread a strip of leather or a thin braided cord.

With a larger surface area than a wand, there is plenty of room to carve symbols or inscriptions. If you have a lot of sanding to do to shape the stick or if there are knotholes and stubs of removed twigs, you may want to use a rasp. Similar to a file, a rasp is specially designed for shaping wood. After attaining the shape you want, use sandpaper to smooth the surface. Even though this can be a lengthy process, I find that it gives me time to get to know the wood and all the details of the branch. It is also a good way to slow down and get into the rhythm of tree energy. We tend to expect immediate results and rush to get a job done but ignore these impulses and listen for the whispers from the wood to guide you. Put time and loving care into the project and you will be rewarded with a powerful tool.

Wreaths

The ancient Greeks used wreaths to wear as chaplets at festivals, to lay on graves to honor loved ones, to give as an award for achievement, and to place on statues of deities as offerings. A wreath embodies the power of the circle, one of humankind's oldest and most elemental symbols. The circle represents unity, completion, and endlessness. It echoes the turning cycles of life, of the seasons, of time and timelessness. As a circle, a wreath of branches brings a perpetual flow of tree energy into rituals and magic.

Evergreen branches are nice to make a winter wreath, but bare branches can be used for the base of a wreath that can be decorated according to season or occasion throughout the year. Look for branches that are slightly curved, and then arrange them in a circle to assess how the wreath may come together. You may need to snip off some smaller branchlets or secure them to the main branch with yarn or twine. Long, thin willow or birch branches can be easily bent into a circle. When working with conifers, arrange them with the needles pointing in the same direction to provide visual continuity and energy flow.

Use wire, twine, or yarn to attach the tip of one branch to the bottom of the next or to secure one long branch into shape. Once you have a basic circle, you may want to attach a couple of smaller branches to add volume or a strand of ivy can be wound around it. Experiment but don't overwork it; allow your wreath to develop organically to hold the integrity of the tree's energy.

A wreath can be placed above or on your altar to draw on the energy of the tree. Small wreaths can be placed around the base of candles or figurines of deities. A small wreath can be created for a specific purpose and used in a spell. For an esbat altar, bind a wreath with white yarn or strips of cloth to make it evocative of the moon. Let your magical imagination fly.

Cleanse, Consecrate, and Charge Items for Magic

Whether making or purchasing an item for magic and ritual, cleanse, consecrate, and charge it with your energy and willpower before using it. While there are many ways to cleanse an item for magical purposes, here's a quick and powerful way to use your energy for the job. Hold the object between your hands and close your eyes. Visualize your energy as white light glowing at your third eye chakra, between and slightly above your eyes. See and feel the light move to your heart, and then down your arms surrounding the object. Visualize that energy moving back up your arms, and then down through your body to the earth where any unneeded energy from the item will be neutralized.

To consecrate the object, pass it through the smoke of sage, mugwort, lavender, or any herb(s) of your choice. Of course, adding a crumbled dry tree leaf to the herbs enhances the energy. Use any incantation that you prefer or try something like this:

By water, earth, air, and fire; may this object bring my desire.
By north, south, east, and west; may its energy by spirit be blessed.
May this tree's magic work with me; so mote its purpose come to be.

To charge the object, stand in front of your altar with it. Again, visualize your energy as white light at your third-eye chakra. See and feel it move to your heart, and then down your arms surrounding the object as you think about its purpose. Visualize the light encompassing you and the object, and then allow the image to fade. Place the object on your altar for a day or two before using it. If you are not planning to use it right away, store it with your tools and other ritual gear.

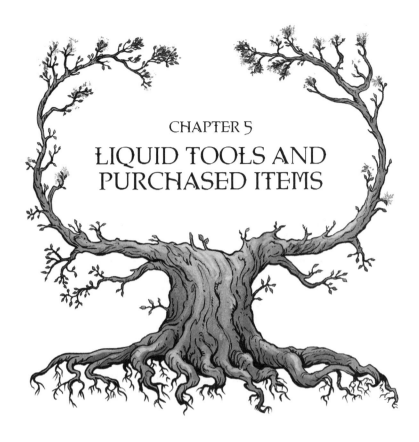

CHAPTER 5
LIQUID TOOLS AND PURCHASED ITEMS

In addition to using various parts of a tree, oils and waters are effective in magic and ritual. These include cooking oils, massage oils, essential oils, infused oils, flower essences, and floral waters, which are also called *hydrosols*. The use of oils and hydrosols provides a way to maintain tradition while giving our practices new depth.

Oils, Hydrosols, and Essences

Many cooking and massage oils are made from tree fruits, nuts, and seeds and work well for magic and ritual. Massage oils are also known as carrier and base oils. Select one that is unrefined and, whenever possible, buy organic. Refined oils are produced as cheaply as possible with the aid of chemical solvents that leech nutrients, aromas, and the life from the oil. Unrefined organic oils carry the energy of the tree they came from.

Unrefined oil may be labeled *cold pressed*, which means that it was not subjected to high temperatures. A similar method called *expeller pressed* employs hydraulic presses.

While the friction of a hydraulic press raises the temperature to 200°F (approximately 93°C), this amount of heat does not harm the oil.

Plant material is usually put through a press more than once to obtain as much oil as possible. Oil that is extracted from the first pressing is called *virgin*. The term *extra virgin* means that the oil is of the highest grade. However, when it comes to coconut oil, the unrefined oil is also known as virgin oil and the refined as fractionated oil.

Essential oils are also known as ethereal oils, volatile oils, and essences. Perhaps it's no coincidence that the word *essence* can mean fragrance or spirit. Derived from the Latin word *esse*, meaning "to be," the word *essence* can refer to the intrinsic nature of something or an extract from a plant; spirit and fragrance.[17] Essential oils are called *volatile* because they are not stable substances and easily evaporate at room temperature. The defining factor of an essential oil is the method used to extract the oil from plant material. Essential oils are obtained through the processes of distillation and expression. This differs from aromatic extracts, which are obtained using solvents.

In the distillation process, after the essential oil is separated from the water, the water itself is an aromatic byproduct called a *hydrosol*. Traditionally called *floral waters* (i.e. rosewater) a hydrosol can be made from other parts of a plant, not just flowers.

An infused oil is made by steeping plant material, usually leaves, seeds, and flowers, in oil. These are popular for cooking and herbal remedies.

The term *flower essence* may cause some confusion because these products are not fragrant, and they are not essential oils. They are simply infusions of flowers in water that is mixed (usually 50/50) with brandy, which acts as a preservative. While these are used for various healing purposes, we can attune them to our intentions for magic and use as we would an oil or hydrosol.

Uses in Magic and Ritual

Consecrating candles for ritual and magic is a common way that oils and essential oils have been used. Hydrosols and flower essences can be used this way too. Simply place a small amount of liquid on your fingertip and draw a line from the base of the candle to the top on four sides (think cardinal directions) to direct the energy outward. If a candle is for banishing or grounding purposes, go from top to bottom. Alternatively, you can

---

17. Angus Stevenson, ed., *Oxford Dictionary of English*, 3rd ed. (New York: Oxford University Press, 2010), 598.

draw a spiral up or down the candle or just create several circles around it. Instead of carving names, runes, numbers, oghams or other symbols into candles, draw them with oil or water.

Although essential oils are popular for consecrating objects, they can damage varnish, paint, plastic, and other surfaces. Since my altar is a wooden table, I dab the oil underneath the tabletop and visualize tree energy providing magical support. As an alternative to putting essential oil directly on tools, put a few drops on a cotton ball and place it where you store them. This will allow the tools to absorb the vibrational energy of the tree without the oil causing any damage.

If bathing before ritual is part of your practice, adding an oil or hydrosol to the water is a good way to amplify purification as well as focus energy. Essential oils need to be diluted in carrier oil before adding to the bath or used on the body because they can irritate the skin. A two to three percent dilution ratio with carrier oil (six to sixteen drops of essential oil per tablespoon of oil) works well. Hydrosols can be added directly to the water or used on the body.

Scenting an area with essential oil before and during ritual, magic, or psychic work is another way to harness the vibrational energy of trees. This is easily done with a diffuser. While electronic diffusers and all sorts of gadgets are available, the low-tech tea light candle lamp does the job nicely. Besides, candles enhance the ambiance of ritual and craft work. In addition to oils, hydrosols can be used to scent an area using a spray bottle to mist the air. The fragrance doesn't last as long as an essential oil, but it is a simple and quick way to purify and consecrate an area.

Just as the ancient Egyptians used incense as a scented offering to deities, we can use an oil or hydrosol for the same purpose. Place a few drops in a bowl on your altar and chant or recite an incantation to announce its purpose. An offering of this type can precede magic, divination, or psychic work to vibrationally set the tone. Oils and hydrosols can be used for anointing, for house blessings, and to boost the power of an amulet. While making an essential oil takes special equipment, expertise, and a great deal of plant material, hydrosols and infused oils are easy to make at home.

How to Make a Hydrosol

While a hydrosol is usually an aromatic byproduct of the essential oil distillation process, there are three methods for making a hydrosol at home. These include hot infusion, cold infusion, and steam distillation. All methods require fresh flowers or leaves.

For a hot infusion, preheat a large glass jar with hot tap water, which will prevent it from cracking or shattering when boiled water is poured into it. After drying the jar, fill it half or two-thirds with plant material. Boil some water and let it sit for a moment before pouring it into the jar. Use enough water to cover the plant material. Put the lid on and let it stand for three to four hours, and then strain out the plant material.

For a cold infusion, simply place the plant material in the jar and add enough water to cover it. Put the lid on and let it stand for about twenty-four hours before straining out the plant material.

The steam distillation method takes a little more work, but it's fun to experiment with. You will need a big stainless-steel pot (a stock pot or lobster pot works well) and two small glass or ceramic bowls. Place one bowl upside down in the middle of the pot to serve as a pedestal for the second bowl. Set that bowl right side up to act as a catch basin for the condensation. Add the flowers and/or leaves and water to the pot. The water level should be below the catch basin (top) bowl; you don't want it to float around. Put the lid on the pot upside down. This will direct the condensation to the center of the pot and into the catch basin. When the water begins to boil, turn down the heat to a low simmer. To quicken the condensation process, place ice cubes on top of the upside-down lid.

To make it less messy, put the ice cubes in a plastic bag. Place a tea towel on the lid of the pot and the bag of ice cubes on top. The ice cubes may need to be replaced a few times during the process. After thirty or forty minutes, turn off the heat and let the pot cool before removing the lid and retrieving the catch basin. After the hydrosol cools, store it in a jar with a tight-fitting lid.

Hydrosols made with either infusion method will keep for a few days, even if stored in the refrigerator. When made by the steam method, they can last several months. However, even when stored in the fridge, being mostly water a hydrosol can go bad. If it becomes cloudy or smells off, throw it away.

How to Make Infused Oil

Infused oils are popular for cooking and herbal remedies and work well for ritual and magic. Plus, we can make a special oil for magic with plant material from any tree that we want to work with. There are two methods for making infused oils: cold and hot. A cold infusion is an easier but slower process. It works best for leaves and flowers, which tend to be more heat sensitive. The hot infused method works best with the tougher parts of a plant such as roots, fruit, and seeds.

Whether using dried or fresh plant material, prepare it by crumbling or chopping it into small pieces. Choose any cooking or carrier oil as a base. As mentioned, buy an organic and unrefined oil, as these are not treated with chemicals and retain their natural properties.

For a cold infusion, fill a jar half or two-thirds with the plant material, and then add enough oil to cover it. Gently poke around with a butter knife to release any air pockets. Leave the jar open for several hours to allow additional air to escape. If most of the oil gets absorbed, add a little more to cover the plant material. After you put the lid on, gently swirl the contents. Place the jar where it will stay at room temperature for four to six weeks. Strain the oil into a dark glass bottle for storage.

Plant material left in the oil longer than four to six weeks may turn moldy. When using fresh plants, check for any condensation in the bottle after it is stored. The moisture content of fresh material is released into the oil and can foster bacteria growth.

For a hot infused oil, use half to two-thirds cup of dried or fresh plant material and one cup of oil. Place them in a double boiler and cover. With the heat as low as possible, warm the oil for thirty minutes to an hour. Remove the pot from the heat and allow the oil to cool completely. Strain it into a dark glass bottle for storage.

A double boiler is a set of saucepans that fit together; the larger bottom pan is used to boil water to create steam to warm the smaller upper pan. The upper saucepan has a lid. In place of a double boiler, a stainless-steel mixing bowl can be placed over a large saucepan of water. You will need a lid to cover the bowl. The bottom of the bowl should not touch the water in the pan because the contents may overheat.

When a Tree Is Not Available for Magic

As is often the case, we may want to work with a tree that does not grow where we live. As mentioned, essential oils, flower essences, and some tree oils are available. Fruit can be purchased and from it seeds or pits can be obtained and dried for future use. Some tree seeds are available at garden centers but check that they have not been treated with chemicals. Of course, there are many types of edible nuts that can be purchased. All of these can be used to make an infused oil too.

In addition to objects made from wood, sample pieces of wood can be purchased. These are often three by six inches wide and long, and half an inch thick. You can make something with these or use them as they are.

Follow the information at the end of chapter 4 for cleansing, consecrating, and charging an object. Suggestions for specific items are included in the tree profiles.

CHAPTER 6
THE CELTIC OGHAM

Also known as the tree alphabet, the Celtic ogham is a popular way to work with the wisdom of trees. Although it is associated with a limited number of trees, the ogham can be used for writing the name of any tree as you work with it in magic and ritual.

For centuries, almost everything about the ogham, its name, origin, and characters, has been disputed. Also spelled *ogam* and *ogum*, even the simple fact of how to pronounce the word has variations ranging from "OH-umm" to "OH-wam" to "OH-yam."[18] Take your pick.

Like spelling and pronouncing the word *ogham*, there are several theories concerning the origin of the name itself. According to Celtic myth, it was created by and named for Ogma. Known as Ogma the Eloquent, he was the god of learning, poetry, and speech. According to researchers, another contender for the origin of the name is the

---

18. Editorial Staff, *Webster's Third New International Dictionary*, vol. 3. (Chicago: Encyclopedia Britannica, Inc., 1981), 1569.

Greek word *ogmos*, which means "furrow" or "groove."[19] This refers to the straight lines of the first twenty characters that resemble little furrows when carved into rock or wood.

Although the ogham was written in stone, it was not a static alphabet, and over time, some of the characters were replaced or modified. After centuries of obscurity, the Celtic Revival in the late nineteenth and early twentieth centuries brought the ogham to light where it captivated the attention of the world and became an integral part of some Pagan and Wicca practices.

The main source of information about the ogham comes from the *Book of Bally-mote*, which was compiled around 1391 for the McDonagh family of Ballymote Castle in County Sligo, Ireland.[20] This "book" is a collection of documents containing history, lore, legal, medical, and religious writings. Other books that contain information on the ogham include the *Yellow Book of Lecan* (fourteenth century), the *Book of Lismore* (late fourteenth or early fifteenth century), and the *Book of Leinster* (twelfth century). Like the *Book of Ballymote*, these are manuscript collections of prose, poetry, and other documents. The grammatical handbook *Auraicept na n-Éces*, "Scholar's Primer" (c. eighth century) also contains ogham tracts that are similar to the ones found in the *Book of Ballymote* and the *Yellow Book of Lecan*.

The problem with these multiple sources is that some of the details vary widely from one to another. In addition, scholars believe that several of these documents were copied from much earlier sources. Any time a manuscript was copied, the information was open to mistranslation, reinterpretation, and embellishment. To err and tinker is human.

Ogham Inscriptions

Despite a plethora of tangled theories and information, what we know for certain is that there are almost four hundred ogham stone inscriptions. Most of these are located in Ireland, particularly the southwest, with a smattering in Scotland, Wales, the Isle of Man, and southwestern England. While there is still some disagreement about the age of the ogham writing on these stones, many scholars place their time frame from the fourth to sixth centuries CE during the early spread of Christianity.

---

19. Ruth P. M. Lehmann, "Ogham: The Ancient Script of the Celts." *The Origins of Writing*, ed. Wayne M. Senner (Lincoln, NE: University of Nebraska Press, 1989), 160.

20. Steven L. Danver, ed., *Popular Controversies in World History: Investigating History's Intriguing Questions. Prehistory and Early Civilizations,* vol. 1 (Santa Barbara, CA: ABC-CLIO, LLC, 2011), 56.

Most ogham stones are near ring forts, earthen mounds, cairns (mounds of stones built as landmarks or memorials), single standing stones, stone circles, and Christian churches. Many of the inscriptions contain names and kinship lineages. While some of the stones are thought to have been boundary markers that laid claim to the land, others may have been grave markers because a few of the inscriptions resemble funerary prayers. Although burials have not been found beneath ogham stones, some of them appear to have been moved or repurposed, which may account for the absence of human remains.

Other types of inscriptions include tribal affiliations, eponymous deities of tribes, and personal descriptions such as "born of the raven."[21] Charles Graves (1812–1899), ogham scholar and professor of mathematics at Trinity College in Dublin, Ireland, noted that a few inscriptions referred to people who could be identified through genealogies in the *Book of Leinster*. Ogham inscriptions have also been found on small artifacts of ivory, bone, bronze, and silver. Although a few seventeenth and eighteenth-century manuscripts contain ogham inscriptions as margin notes, as an alphabet it is very cumbersome and was never used for long texts.

According to R. A. Stewart Macalister (1870–1950), professor of Celtic archaeology at University College in Dublin, the magical use of ogham may have been an important function. Although some of his theories are not supported by more recent scholarship, many agree that the ogham had some type of magical use. That said, while its use as a manual gesture alphabet of the Druids is still debated, it is generally accepted that the ogham served as a Bardic *aide memoire*. As such, it is not difficult to see that associations for memorization can also function as magical correspondences, which is how the ogham is widely used today. Also, some of the elaborate ogham variations from the *Book of Ballymote* seem to strongly suggest an esoteric or magical purpose.

The Ogham Alphabet

The ogham originally consisted of twenty characters with five added at a later time. There is a marked difference between the first twenty and the later five. The former are simple straight lines suitable for carving into wood or stone, while the latter are more complex and don't easily lend themselves to carving. The original twenty are referred

21. Lehmann, "Ogham: The Ancient Script of the Celts," 48.

to as *feda* and the additional five, *forfeda*, which means "supplementary letters."[22] The ogham characters are divided into groups of five. The original four groups are called *aicmi* (plural for *aicme* meaning "family" or "class").[23] Each aicme is named for the first character in the group, for example, aicme Beith, aicme Huath, and so forth.

Ogham symbols are written along a stem line called a *druim*, which means "ridge" and refers to the edge of a stone along which inscriptions were often written.[24] When written on stones, the vowels were often represented as dots or simple indentations along the stem line rather than a line that crossed it.

A unique feature of the ogham is that it can be written horizontally or vertically. When written horizontally (figure 6-2), it is read from left to right. When written vertically (figure 6-1), it is read from bottom to top.

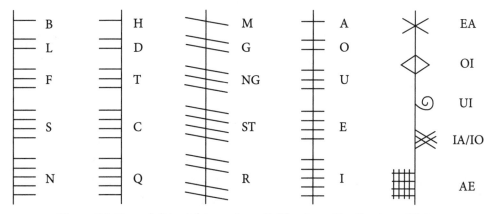

Figure 6-1. From left to right are aicme Beith, aicme Huath, aicme Muin, aicme Ailm, and the forfeda written vertically.

22. Peter T. Daniels and William Bright, eds., *The World's Writing Systems* (New York: Oxford University Press, 1996), 340.

23. Danver, *Popular Controversies in World History*, 56.

24. Ibid.

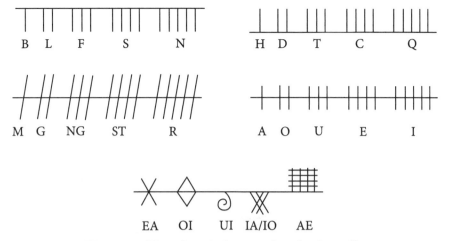

EA   OI   UI   IA/IO   AE

Figure 6-2. The ogham is shown written horizontally.

In later times, when written in manuscripts, the starting point of the stem line was often distinguished with a "V" or curlicue shape. When inscribed on a stone, the inscription usually began at the bottom left and followed the edge up, over, and down to the bottom right.

Table 6.1 The Ogham Symbols, Letters/Sounds, and Trees			
Name / Alternate Names	Character	Letters/Sounds	Trees
Ailm / Ailim		a	Elm, Fir, Pine
Amhancholl / Eamancholl / Mór		ae	Beech, Pine
Beith / Beithe / Beth		b	Birch
Coll / Call		c	Hazel
Duir / Dair		d	Oak
Ebad/ Éabhadh; also called Koad / Grove		ea, ch	Aspen

Table 6.1 The Ogham Symbols, Letters/Sounds, and Trees			
Name / Alternate Names	Character	Letters/Sounds	Trees
Edad / Eadha / Eadhadh		e	Aspen, Poplar (white)
Fearn / Fern		f	Alder
Gort		g	Ivy
Huath / hÚath / Uath		h	Hawthorn
Ioho / Idho / Iodho		i	Yew
Ifin / Iphin		io	Beech, Pine
Luis		l	Rowan
Muin / Muinn		m	Vine/Bramble, Vine/Grape
Nion / Nuin / Nuinn		n	Ash
Ngetal / nGétal / nGéadal		ng	Reed
Onn / Ohn		o	Gorse, Pine
Oir / Or		oi	Ivy, Spindletree
Quert / Ceirt		q/kw	Apple, Crabapple
Ruis		r	Elder
Saille / Saile		s	Willow
Straif / Straith		st and z	Blackthorn

Table 6.1 The Ogham Symbols, Letters/Sounds, and Trees			
Name / Alternate Names	Character	Letters/Sounds	Trees
Tinne / Teine	‖‖	t	Holly
Ur / Uhr / Ura	╫	u	Heather
Uilleann / Uilen / Uilleand	ᚓ	ui	Beech, Ivy

The Ogham in Magic

While divination is a popular way to use the ogham, it is commonly used in magic and ritual too. For example, the ogham can serve as a magic cipher. Instead of a long inscription, use one or two keywords such as "love" or "guide me" to carve into a candle or write on a piece of paper or picture of a tree. Of course, inscribing ogham symbols on a twig or piece of wood can add more power to your ritual or magic work. Like many symbols, ogham characters can be used to draw energy into an object that you plan to use as a talisman or charm.

Ogham staves (small sticks), which are used for divination, can be placed on an altar to emphasize tree energy for magic, meditation, and spells. Creating your own set of staves allows you to make them uniquely personal.

How to Make Ogham Staves

While sets of ogham staves can be purchased, it is simple enough to make your own. As with other magical tools, making your own imbues them with your energy, which personalizes and makes them more powerful.

Collect twenty-five twigs or branches that have about the same thickness, but not too skinny because you are going to draw or inscribe the ogham characters on them. The length of the twigs doesn't matter because you can cut them to a uniform size. Begin by removing any small side twigs and leaves. The bark can be stripped off or left on. If you strip the bark off, you can leave the wood in its natural state or use a little lemon oil to bring out its beauty.

After cutting the twigs down to size, cut one end of each stave at a 45-degree angle. This slanted surface can be used to carve or paint an ogham character. Alternatively, cut both ends straight across and draw or carve the ogham character on the side of the twig.

Instead of twigs, square pegs can be used. Check your local hardware store for square dowels that you can cut into short lengths. When using these, the ogham characters can be written along the edge as they were on ancient stones. Ogham tiles can be made by cutting horizontal slices from a tree branch or large dowel. Purchased wood samples can be used for tiles or staves too. Wood samples are ideal when working with trees that are not in your area or not included in the ogham. Carve or paint the name of the tree on the wood sample using the ogham alphabet.

As with other ritual or magical tools, consecrate your staves before using them. Call on the Celtic deities Ogma, Danu, and/or the Dagda to bless your tools.

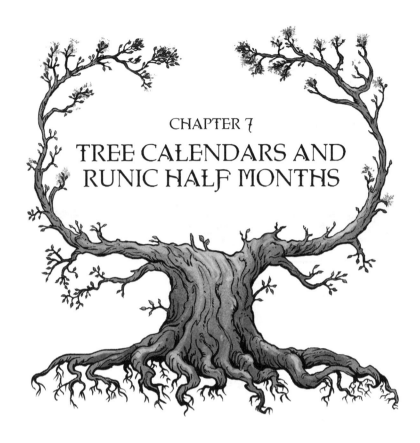

CHAPTER 7
TREE CALENDARS AND RUNIC HALF MONTHS

Through their connection with the Celtic ogham and Norse runes, some trees have become associated with periods of time. While these are discussed individually in the following sections, it is important to note that these calendars are modern constructs. However, their lack of ancient provenance does not make them less potent. These calendars have significance and meaning in current practices because of the concepts they embody.

The Celtic Tree Calendar

As mentioned in chapter 6, the ogham fell into obscurity until the nineteenth century Celtic Revival (also referred to as the Celtic Twilight) in literature and art. Aimed at reviving ancient Irish folklore and traditions, the movement also fueled interest in the ogham. The enthusiasm for all things Celtic spilled into the twentieth century and in the 1940s R. A. Stewart Macalister published a two-volume work on ogham inscriptions. While more recent studies do not support all of Macalister's work, he has been lauded for his meticulous drawings of ogham inscriptions.

Also published in the 1940s, *The White Goddess* by Robert Graves (1895–1985) has served as the basis for a great deal of popular information on the ogham. However, despite being the grandson of ogham scholar Charles Graves, Robert took liberties with the history of the script and added embellishments such as the thirteen-month ogham tree calendar. Nevertheless, the appeal and fascination of the mystical ogham continued. This alphabet and its related calendar have captured the imagination and curiosity of many of us who have incorporated it into our magical practices.

Table 7.1 The Celtic Tree Calendar		
Dates	**Ogham**	**Tree**
January 21 to February 17	Luis	Rowan
February 18 to March 17	Nion / Nuin / Nuinn	Ash
March 18 to April 14	Fearn / Fern	Alder
April 15 to May 12	Saille / Saile	Willow
May 13 to June 9	Huath / hÚath / Uath	Hawthorn
June 10 to July 7	Duir / Dair	Oak
July 8 to August 4	Tinne / Teine	Holly
August 5 to September 1	Coll / Call	Hazel
September 2 to September 29	Muin / Muinn	Vine/Bramble
September 30 to October 27	Gort	Ivy
October 28 to November 24	Ngetal / nGétal / nGéadal	Reed
November 25 to December 22	Ruis	Elder
December 23	The Nameless Day	Mistletoe
December 24 to January 20	Beith / Beithe / Beth	Birch

The Alternate Tree Calendar

Another type of tree calendar that has come into use has the misnomers of Druidic horoscope, Gallic horoscope, and Celtic tree horoscope. The dates are said to provide one's Celtic tree astrology sign. Although there are claims that this calendar is over two thousand years old, there is no evidence for this or its association with the Celts. Its only similarity to the Gaulish Coligny calendar, which is generally accepted as dating to the first or second century BCE, is the division of the months into segments. However, the Coligny calendar does not contain references to trees. As with Graves' Celtic tree calendar, relevance does not come from ancient provenance, but from the meaning and significance it holds in contemporary practice.

In this calendar, the periods of time for each month/tree are divided between spring and autumn and summer and winter. For example, the time periods for hazel are March 22 to 31 and September 24 to October 3. Exceptions are poplar and aspen, which occur in three seasons and the yew in one season. Four separate trees represent the equinoxes, the winter solstice, and midsummer.

Table 7.2 The Alternate Tree Calendar	
Dates	Trees
January 2 to 11	Fir, Spruce
January 12 to 24	Elm
January 25 to February 3	Cypress
February 4 to 8	Aspen, Poplar
February 9 to 18	Cedar, Hackberry, Larch
February 19 to 29	Pine
March 1 to 10	Willow
March 11 to 20	Linden
March 21 Spring equinox	Oak
March 22 to 31	Hazel
April 1 to 10	Rowan
April 11 to 20	Maple
April 21 to 30	Walnut

Table 7.2 The Alternate Tree Calendar	
Dates	Trees
May 1 to 14	Aspen, Poplar
May 15 to 24	Chestnut
May 25 to June 3	Ash
June 4 to 13	Hornbeam
June 14 to 23	Fig
June 24 Midsummer	Birch
June 25 to July 4	Apple
July 5 to 14	Fir, Spruce
July 15 to 25	Elm
July 26 to August 4	Cypress
August 5 to 13	Aspen, Poplar
August 14 to 23	Cedar, Hackberry, Larch
August 24 to September 2	Pine
September 3 to 12	Willow
September 13 to 22	Linden
September 23 Autumn equinox	Olive
September 24 to October 3	Hazel
October 4 to 13	Rowan
October 14 to 23	Maple
October 24 to November 2	Walnut
November 3 to 11	Yew
November 12 to 21	Chestnut
November 22 to December 1	Ash
December 2 to 11	Hornbeam
December 12 to 21	Fig
December 22 Winter solstice	Beech
December 22 to January 1	Apple

The Runic Half Months

Like the Celtic ogham, there are several theories for the origin of runic symbols as well as the name *rune*. According to Webster's Dictionary, the word *rune* comes from the Old Norse and Old English *rūn*, which had several meanings: "secret," "mystery," "a character of the runic alphabet," and "writing."[25] This word is also akin to the Old English *rūnian*, meaning "to whisper"; the Old High German words *rūna*, "secret discussion" and *rūnēn*, "to whisper"; the Old Norse *reyna*, "to whisper"; and the Latin *rumor*.[26] Although often written in stone, they were not a static set of symbols. Over time, the runes evolved with the changing linguistics of Europe. Once they were incorporated into folklore, the mystic quality of the runes emerged.

There are three runic alphabets; the oldest is the Elder Futhark. Due to linguistic developments over the centuries, the Younger Futhark emerged. It was more widely used in Denmark and Sweden and is sometimes known as the Viking runes. The Anglo-Saxons took the runes with them to England, where it developed independent characteristics. Information about the runic alphabets comes from the Anglo-Saxon rune poem written in the tenth century and the Norwegian and Icelandic rune poems written in the thirteenth and fourteenth centuries.[27]

While not every rune is directly associated with a tree, along the way in Pagan practices various attributes and qualities were matched up and entered common usage. I first read about the runic half months in *The Pagan Book of Days* by Nigel Pennick (1946–), an authority on ancient belief systems. The runic half months are associated with the energy and wisdom of their respective symbols. Table 7.3 includes the various spellings and permutations of rune names in the Elder, Younger, and Anglo-Saxon rune sets.

25. Editorial Staff, *Webster's Third New International Dictionary*, 1989.

26. Ibid.

27. Tineke Looijenga, *Texts and Contexts of the Oldest Runic Inscriptions* (Boston: Brill, 2003), 6.

Table 7.3 The Runic Half Months and Trees		
Dates	Rune	Trees
January 13 to 27	Perp / Peord / Perth	Apple, Aspen, Beech
January 28 to February 11	Algiz / Eolh / Elhaz	Reed, Rowan, Yew
February 12 to 26	Sowilo / Sol / Sigil	Juniper, Laurel, Mistletoe
February 27 to March 13	Tiwaz / Tyr / Tir	Oak
March 14 to 29	Berkanan / Bjarkan / Beorc	Birch, Fir
March 30 to April 13	Ehwaz / Eh	Ash, Aspen, Lilac, Oak
April 14 to 28	Mannaz/ Madhr / Mann	Alder, Ash, Elm, Holly, Maple
April 29 to May 13	Laguz / Logr / Lagu	Willow
May 14 to 28	Ingwaz / Ing / Inguz	Apple, Crabapple
May 29 to June 13	Opila / Ethel / Othala	Hawthorn
June 14 to 28	Dagaz / Daeg / Dag	Oak, Pine, Spruce
June 29 to July 13	Fehu / Fe / Feoh	Elder, Hornbeam
July 14 to 28	Uruz / Ur	Birch
July 29 to August 12	Thurisaz / Thurs / Thorn	Blackthorn, Hawthorn, Oak, Vine/Bramble
August 13 to 28	Ansuz / As / Os	Ash, Linden
August 29 to September 12	Raido / Reidh / Rad	Oak
September 13 to 27	Kenaz / Kaun / Cen	Pine
September 28 to October 12	Gebo / Gyfu	Ash, Elm

Table 7.3 The Runic Half Months and Trees		
Dates	Rune	Trees
October 13 to October 27	Wunjo / Wynn / Wyn	Ash, Blackthorn, Vine/ Bramble
October 28 to November 12	Hagalaz / Hagall / Haegl	Ash, Yew
November 13 to 27	Naudiz / Naudhr / Nyd	Beech, Rowan
November 28 to December 12	Isa/ Iss / Is	Alder
December 13 to 27	Jera / Ger / Jara	Elder, Oak
December 28 to January 12	Iwaz / Eoh / Eihwaz	Lilac, Yew

The Runic Alphabet

To aid you in working with the runes, table 7.4 provides a listing of the runic characters arranged by the letters/sounds they represent. This table also contains the Anglo Saxon and Younger Futhark runes that are used in the tree profiles of part two but are not included in the runic half months.

Table 7.4 The Rune Symbols, Letters/Sounds, and Trees			
Name / Alternate Names	Characters	Letters/Sounds	Trees
Ansuz / As / Os		a	Ash, Linden
Ac (Anglo Saxon)		a	Oak
Aesc (Anglo Saxon)		ae	Ash
Berkanan / Bjarkan / Beorc		b	Birch, Fir
Dagaz / Daeg / Dag		d	Oak, Pine, Spruce
Ehwaz / Eh		e	Ash, Aspen, Lilac, Oak
Iwaz / Eoh / Eihwaz		ei	Lilac, Yew
Fehu / Fe / Feoh		f	Elder, Hornbeam
Gebo / Gyfu		g	Ash, Elm
Hagalaz / Hagall / Haegl		h	Ash, Yew
Isa / Iss / Is		i	Alder
Jera / Ger / Jara		j / g	Elder, Oak

Table 7.4 The Rune Symbols, Letters/Sounds, and Trees			
Name / Alternate Names	Characters	Letters/Sounds	Trees
Kenaz / Kaun / Cen		k / c	Pine
Laguz / Logr / Lagu		l	Willow
Mannaz / Madhr / Mann		m	Alder, Ash, Elm, Holly, Maple
Naudiz / Naudhr / Nyd		n	Beech, Rowan
Ingwaz / Ing / Inguz		ng	Apple, Crabapple
Opila / Ethel / Othala		o	Hawthorn
Perp / Peord / Perth		p	Apple, Aspen, Beech
Raido / Reidh / Rad		r	Oak
Sowilo / Sol / Sigil		s	Juniper, Laurel, Mistletoe
Thurisaz / Thurs / Thorn		th	Blackthorn, Hawthorn, Oak, Vine/Bramble
Tiwaz / Tyr / Tir		t	Oak
Uruz / Ur		u	Birch

Table 7.4 The Rune Symbols, Letters/Sounds, and Trees			
Name / Alternate Names	Characters	Letters/Sounds	Trees
Wunjo / Wynn / Wyn	⊳	w	Ash, Blackthorn, Vine/Bramble
Yr (Younger Futhark)	⅄	y	Yew
Algiz / Eolh / Elhaz	Y	z	Reed, Rowan, Yew

In addition to the calendars in this chapter, some trees are associated with the sabbats and other dates. Refer to appendix C for a complete listing of tree/date associations.

PART TWO
THE TREE PROFILES

As mentioned, not all of the plants profiled in this book are trees and may not seem to measure up to their sylvan grandeur. In the past, many plants with woody stems such as ivy, heather, reeds, rushes, and others served valuable functions for everyday life. Reeds and rushes were used for thatching, heather and gorse for hearth fires, and ivy for tying things together. The ancient Brehon Laws of Ireland classified plants according to their importance, which included their practical uses, and placed penalties for their theft and wanton destruction. These plants have been included in this book to accommodate the Celtic ogham along with a few others with which to expand your magical work.

Each profile includes historical information and magical background, associated deities, items to purchase when the tree is not available, and suggestions for ritual and magical use. Seasonal details are provided for basic identification to help you get acquainted with each tree. Table A provides a few helpful terms used in the botanical descriptions.

Table A. Helpful Botanical Terms	
Axil	The area of a plant between a branch and a leaf stem.
Bract	A modified leaf that protects a young bud.
Catkin	A thick, usually drooping, cluster of tiny flowers.
Flower head	A dense, compact cluster of tiny flowers.
Lobed	A leaf with deeply indented edges, such as oak or maple tree leaves.
Toothed	A leaf with jagged edges; also called serrated.
Witches' broom	Knotted balls of twigs caused by mite and fungus infestations of leaf buds.

A book about trees and magic wouldn't be complete without mentioning dryads, Greek tree nymphs. Dryads were originally associated with the oak but came to represent woodland spirits of all trees. The name *dryad* comes from the Greek *drys* meaning "oak."[28] Classified as human-like nymphs in Greek mythology, dryads were believed to be born with, inhabit, and then die with a specific tree. Whereas the dryad came to be regarded as a more general spirit that dwelled among all the woodland trees, the hamadryad took on the role of a spirit who lived and died with a particular tree. The Greek word *hama* means "together with."[29]

Woodland spirits are not unique to Greek mythology and populate the forests of many cultures. They were often depicted as maidens clad in white or as huntresses. In Germany, the wood folk, also known as the moss people, were like the hamadryads living and dying with a particular tree. Woodland spirits associated with specific trees are included in the profiles.

28. Umberto Quattrocchi, *CRC World Dictionary of Plant Names: Common Names, Scientific Names, Eponyms, Synonyms, and Etymology: D-L*, vol. 2 (Boca Raton, FL: CRC Press, LLC, 2000), 848.
29. Jennifer Larson, *Greek Nymphs: Myth, Cult, Lore* (New York: Oxford University Press, 2001), 79.

ACACIA

Cat Claw Acacia (*Acacia greggii* syn. *Senegalia greggii*); also known as devil's claw, long flower cat claw.

Gum Arabic (*A. nilotica* syn. *A. arabica*, *Mimosa nilotica*); also known as babul acacia, Egyptian thorn, prickly acacia, prickly mimosa, scented thorn.

Red Acacia (*A. Seyal* syn. *Vachellia seyal*); also known as shittim, talh, whistling thorn, white-galled acacia, whitethorn.

The cat claw acacia is a shrubby, thicket-forming tree that reaches only five to twelve feet tall. It has creamy to yellowish-white flowers and small gray-green leaves that grow in clusters among thorns shaped like a cat's claws. This tree is native to the American Southwest and Mexico. Native to Africa, the Middle East, and India, the gum arabic tree reaches thirty to forty feet tall with globes of golden-yellow flowers and long thorns that grow in pairs. Reaching twenty to thirty feet tall, the red acacia has globes of bright yellow flowers and long thorns. It is native to Africa and the Middle East. These two acacias are evergreens with flattened, spreading crowns and fern-like feathery leaves. They are iconic landmarks of the African savannah. The name *acacia* is derived from the Greek *akis*, which means "a sharp point" in reference to the thorns.[30]

For thousands of years, people have relied on these trees for fuel, animal fodder, medicine, and more. From Africa to India, they were regarded as sacred. Surviving in the most arid conditions, these trees symbolized immortality and the afterlife to the ancient Egyptians. A large acacia branch was used as a funerary staff, also known as the staff of the dead, which was placed beside the deceased or depicted in a frieze on the tomb wall. The funerary staff was both an offering and an object to assist in the afterlife. Osiris was referred to as "the solitary one in the acacia" in some inscriptions and images of his mummy were shown protected by the tree.[31] To the Romans, the acacia symbolized immortality of the soul.

Throughout the ancient world, gum from the acacia was used to make sacred incense and in India the wood was used for ritual fires. The Hebrews called the tree *shittim*, meaning, "something sharp" and used the wood in their tabernacles. The red acacia may be the *talh* tree mentioned in the Quran.

Acacia wood was commonly used for boatbuilding in Egypt and other areas of Africa. According to myth, it was used for the sacred barge of Osiris. In other legends, it was the wood used for the first bull-roarer, which is a piece of wood with a hole bored through it. Attached to a rope, the device was whirled overhead to make roaring, booming sounds during certain ceremonies and initiation rituals. The sound also symbolized the voice of ancestors.

Greek physician Pedanius Dioscorides (c. 40–c. 90 CE) and Persian physician Ibn Sina (980–1037), who was also known as Avicenna, noted that acacia was used medicinally for a range of ailments. Flemish botanist and physician Rembert Dodoens (1517–1585) followed in their footsteps recommending various parts of the tree for healing. It is still used in Ayurvedic medicine.

A type of mistletoe (*Loranthus acacia*, syn. *Plicosepalus acaciae*) is specific to acacia trees and commonly found on them throughout the Middle East. With its bright flame-

---

30. Diana Wells, *Lives of the Trees: An Uncommon History* (Chapel Hill, NC: Algonquin Books of Chapel Hill, 2010), 9.

31. Marcel De Cleene and Marie Claire Lejeune, *Compendium of Symbolic and Ritual Plants in Europe, Vol. I: Trees and Shrubs* (Ghent, Belgium: Man & Culture Publishers, 2003), 67.

colored flowers, the combination of mistletoe and acacia is thought to be the burning bush mentioned in the Bible. Cat claw is frequently host to desert mistletoe (*Phorodendron californicum*).

Magical Connections

Element:	Air
Astrological influence:	Mars, Sun
Deities:	Astarte, Brahma, Diana, Ishtar, Isis, Neith, Osiris
Wildlife:	Bee, elephant
Powers/attributes:	Abundance, the afterlife, ancestors, awareness (enhance, heighten), balance/harmony, challenges/obstacles (overcome), consecrate/bless, death/funeral practices, divination, dream work, healing, inspiration, love, money/prosperity, negativity (remove, ward off), prophecy, protection, psychic abilities, purification, security, sex/sexuality, spirituality, wisdom
Other associations:	Samhain

Items to purchase when the tree is not available: Gum arabic, often from the red acacia and gum acacia (*A. senegal*) trees, is frequently used as a food additive and available in powdered form. Red acacia is available as gum nuggets, sometimes called *gum crystals*. Various parts of the gum arabic tree are used as an Ayurveda herb and usually called *babool*. Pieces of acacia bark and bark powder are also available.

Spellwork and Ritual

Burn a couple of gum nuggets on an incense charcoal to consecrate and cleanse ritual tools and space. Use acacia in spells to attract abundance and friendship. Moisten a pinch of gum arabic powder and use it to prepare candles for spiritual practices. For healing, use a photograph of an acacia tree on your altar inscribed with the name of the person to whom energy is being directed.

For protection spells, incorporate a picture of acacia thorns in your magic. For protective charms, place the picture where it is needed or carry it with you. Place a photo of the tree on your altar or burn gum nuggets when preparing for divination sessions or psychic work, especially clairvoyance. At Samhain, use acacia to honor your ancestors and loved ones who have recently passed.

ALDER

European Alder (*Alnus glutinosa*); also known as aller, black alder, common alder.

Red Alder (*A. rubra*); also known as Oregon alder.

Smooth Alder (*A. serrulata*); also known as hazel alder, tag alder.

Often sporting multiple trunks, the European alder reaches forty to seventy feet tall, the red alder sixty-five to one hundred feet, and the smooth alder ten to twenty. Slender, drooping male catkins and small pinecone-like female catkins appear before the leaves develop. Commonly called *cones* and *black knobs*, the female catkins stay on the tree and turn brown. Alders have rounded, glossy green leaves; the European alder leaves are notched at the tip. The European alder is native to Europe, northern Africa, and western Asia. Native to northwestern North America, the red alder is named for the distinctive color of its cut wood. Smooth alder is native to the eastern United States. Alders improve the soil around them because of the symbiotic relationship between their root nodules and nitrogen-fixing bacteria.

Since ancient times in Europe and North America, various parts of the alder have been used for brown, green, and red dyes. According to legend, fairies dyed their clothes green using the flowers/catkins. Through the centuries, the alder has been regarded as a highly magical tree and protected by fairies. Alder cones were frequently used to dress sacred wells for special occasions. The branches were commonly used as divining rods to find water, ores, and hidden treasure.

According to Norse mythology, the first man and woman were created from ash and alder trees, respectively. Highly regarded by Germanic peoples, alder was used for sacred fires when making offerings to deities. Branches and leaves that fell to the ground were believed to contain special healing power. A dense mass of branches called *witches' brooms* on an alder was considered especially potent for healing.

Despite its revered status, alder sometimes had a sinister connotation because of its brownish-red or orangish-red sap that, with some imagination, resembles blood. Flourishing in boggy marshes added to the alder's dark reputation and German author Johann Goethe (1749–1832) amplified this in his poem *Erlkönig*, "Alder King," in which a supernatural being snatched the life of a child. In similar tales, alder women were said to lure unsuspecting men to ruin. People in Somerset, England, avoided travel near an alder copse at night for fear they might disappear. Roman naturalist Gaius Plinius Secundus, better known as Pliny the Elder (23–79 CE), noted that the alder was a tree of misfortune because it did not provide fruit.

In his book, *The Complete Herbal*, English botanist and physician Nicholas Culpeper (1616–1654) recommended a number of uses for alder bark and noted where it could be gathered. Carrying a piece of alder in a waistcoat pocket was used as a charm against rheumatism. In Austria, drinking wine in which a piece of alder bark had been boiled was believed to counteract a love potion. Alder was also used to ward off misfortune.

According to German farming legends, passing seeds through a ring of braided alder branches before planting would keep sparrows from pecking them out of the soil. Placing alder branches at the four corners of a field was a charm to keep mice and moles away. A wreath of alder hung on the front door of a house would protect it from fire.

Young, green alder branches were used to make whistles by cutting both ends and pushing out the pith with a smaller stick. The hollow branches were cut to various lengths and tied together to create panpipes, named for the Greek forest deity Pan. Whistles made from this wood were said to have the ability to summon the four winds.

Magical Connections

Elements:	Air, fire, water
Astrological influence:	Mars, Venus; Aries, Cancer, Pisces.
Deities:	Cailleach Bheur, Freya, Manannan, Minerva, Pan, Venus
Magical beings, creatures, and woodland spirits:	Elves, fairies, unicorns
Wildlife:	Fox, hawk, raven, seagull (herring gull)
Ogham:	Fearn/Fern ᚃ Celtic tree calendar: March 18 to April 14
Rune:	Isa/Iss/Is ᛁ Runic half month: November 28 to December 12 Mannaz/ Madhr/Mann ᛗ Runic half month: April 14 to 28
Power/attributes:	Authority/leadership, banish, clarity (enhance, foster), death/funeral practices, divination, dream work, healing, intuition, knowledge (see, acquire), luck, negativity (remove, ward off), prophecy, protection, renewal, spirit guides/spirits, strength, transformation
Other associations:	Ostara

Items to purchase when the tree is not available: charcoal, wood chips, flower essences made from the red alder and the green alder (*A. crispa*).

Spellwork and Ritual

Because of its use in the past for making spinning wheels, alder is especially effective for any form of divination. Hold three leaves between your palms before a divination session to bring clarity. Use any part of the alder as a charm to strengthen intuition. Gather a handful of male catkins for magic work. Burn a few to aid in banishing rituals and spells, or crumble them onto your altar for water, wind, and general weather magic.

Burn a couple of wood chips before ritual, magic work, and divination to enhance your session.

Place a female catkin/cone in a decorative bag to take with you on travels or keep in your car as a protective charm. Because fairies are attracted to alders, leave an offering beneath one to signal that you would like to contact them. Holding a branch of alder helps to connect with spirit guides too. To invite prophetic dreams, place a leaf under your bed. Also use alder for meditation and healing energy.

ALMOND

Bitter Almond (*Prunus amygdalus* var. *amara*); also known as wild
    almond.
Sweet Almond (*P. dulcis* syn. *P. amygdalus* var. *dulcis*, *Amygdalus
    communis*)

The almond is indigenous from southwestern Asia to the eastern Mediterranean and
grows between thirteen to thirty feet tall. The lance-shaped leaves are medium green
and lighter underneath; they turn yellow in the autumn. The fragrant five-petaled flowers range from light pink to white. Taking seven to eight months to mature, the oblong
fruit resembles a peach. The almond is a seed contained within the fruit.

    Some botanists believe that the sweet almond may have been a hybrid of several bit-
ter almond species. Small amounts of bitter almonds were used medicinally in the past
even though they contain prussic acid (cyanide). With the prussic acid removed, bitter

almond oil is used in a range of cosmetic products and to make flavorings. Raw bitter almonds should never be eaten.

Evidence from Bronze Age sites in Greece and Cypress show that people enjoyed sweet almonds from a very early time. Able to grow in poor soil, by 1700 BCE this adaptable tree was being cultivated throughout the Middle East.[32]

The mythical Canaanite city of Lûz (the name means "almond" in Hebrew) was a center of worship for the goddess Astarte.[33] According to Rabbinic legend, the entrance to a city of paradise can be found through a hole in an almond tree. The almond was associated with the primal forces of creation by the Phrygians (c. 1200–700 BCE) who lived in what is now western Turkey.

The tree was regarded as a phallic symbol to the Greeks who used crushed almonds mixed with water to ceremonially represent the semen of Zeus.[34] According to myth, Attis the god of vegetation was born of the almond. Symbolizing fertility, almonds were scattered at weddings to wish the newlyweds many children. The tree's early flowering was representative of springtime renewal and to the Arabs it was a symbol of hope.

Although a pricey commodity, in the Middle Ages almonds became a popular part of European cuisine. Prepared in many ways for various dishes, marzipan is a treat that still delights taste buds. The word *dulcis* in the botanical name means "sweet."[35] Marzipan is a confection made with sugar, honey, and almond meal. It was used in love spells and as a maternity charm.

For medieval magicians, an almond branch was *the* rod of choice, and in Tuscany they were important as divining rods, especially when looking for treasure. Eating an almond in ritual was symbolic of partaking mystic knowledge. Almonds were used for protection against witchcraft and, because of their eye-like shape, protection against the evil eye. Sometimes found growing on almond trees, mistletoe added to its magical allure.

While the Greeks regarded it as phallic, Tantric Hindus related almonds to the yoni, female genital symbol. As a female symbol, the use of the almond-shaped symbol dates to

32. Frederic Rosengarten, Jr., *The Book of Edible Nuts* (Mineola, NY: Dover Publications, Inc., 2004), 4.

33. G. Johannes Botterweck, Helmer Ringgren, and Heinz-Josef Fabry, eds., *Theological Dictionary of the Old Testament*, vol. 7, trans. David E. Green (Grand Rapids, MI: William B. Eerdmans Publishing Company, 1995), 478; and Hageneder, *The Meaning of Trees: Botany, History, Healing, Lore*, 37.

34. De Cleene and Lejeune, *Compendium of Symbolic and Ritual Plants in Europe*, 82.

35. Lorraine Harrison, *Latin for Gardeners: Over 3,000 Plant Names Explained and Explored* (Chicago: University of Chicago Press, 2012), 145.

the Neolithic period and the worship of the Great Mother Goddess. In ancient texts, the symbol was often described as representing a gateway.

Magical Connections

Elements:	Air, fire
Astrological influence:	Jupiter, Mars, Mercury, Sun, Venus; Aquarius, Gemini, Virgo
Deities:	Astarte, Attis, Cybele, Hermes, Mercury, Thoth, Venus, Zeus
Magical beings and woodland spirits:	Fairies
Wildlife:	Honeybee
Powers/attributes:	Abundance, attraction, awareness (enhance, heighten), balance/harmony, changes/transitions, communication, consecrate/bless, creativity, divination, dream work, fertility, happiness, hope, intuition, knowledge (seek, acquire), love, luck, money/prosperity, peace, protection, psychic abilities, release (let go, move on), renewal, sex/sexuality, spirit guides/spirits, spirituality, wisdom
Other associations:	Ostara

Items to purchase when the tree is not available: almonds, almond milk, sweet almond oil, almond flour.

Spellwork and Ritual

Place a dab of almond oil over your third eye chakra to open your awareness for divination and connecting with spirits. Place several almonds on your bedside table to enhance dream work. Prepare a candle with almond oil for love spells. Pour a libation of almond milk to honor the God or include it in fertility spells. Use almonds in spells to attract abundance and prosperity.

Almond's association with cycles and renewal makes it a powerful oil to consecrate candles for your Ostara altar. Carry an almond in a silk pouch for luck. Follow tradition by using marzipan in love spells. Incorporate almonds into a handfasting ceremony to symbolize love and happiness as well as fertility. Eat three almonds before meditation when seeking knowledge and ancient wisdom. Hold an almond in each hand during meditation to bring peace.

Cultivated Apple (*Malus domestica* syn. *M. pumila*, *M. communis*); also known as silver bough.

The domestic or cultivated apple is believed to be a hybrid of several crabapple species. Today, there are hundreds of cultivars. Reaching between fifteen and forty feet tall, most apple trees have distinctive crooked trunks. The pointed, oval leaves range from yellowish green to dark green on top and lighter underneath. The white to pinkish-white, five-petaled flowers grow in clusters.

The genus name *Malus* is Latin meaning "bad," which harkens back to "that unfortunate incident in the Garden of Eden."[36] In Greek mythology, the golden apples that Gaia gave to Hera upon her marriage to Zeus were known as the fruit of immortality.

36. Jack Staub, *75 Remarkable Fruits for Your Garden* (Layton, UT: Gibbs Smith, Publisher, 2007), 55.

In Celtic lore, the apple is the fruit of knowledge, magic, and prophecy. In myth, a silver bough ladened with golden fruit and tinkling bells functioned as a key to the otherworld. Like its cousin the crabapple, the cultivated apple is associated with the legendary Avalon, Isle of Apples.

At Samhain, winning the game of bobbing for apples, or catching an apple suspended by a string, meant that the Goddess would bless you for a year. As a symbol of Avalon, capturing one from the water represented crossing to that holy isle. Winning in either game was also said to bestow the power of foresight.

In the weather lore of England, the sun shining through the branches of an apple tree on Christmas day meant a bumper crop at the next harvest. A tree blossoming out of season indicated misfortune or death. Forked branches from apple trees were frequently used as divining rods. The fruit was used in various forms of love divination. In Somerset, England, a spirit known as apple tree man was believed to inhabit the oldest tree in an apple orchard. The colt pixy, an orchard spirit that takes the form of a horse, was said to guard apple trees. In Cornwall, England, it was customary to leave a few apples on the trees after the harvest for pixies in the hope that they would help the trees produce a good crop in the following year.

Traditionally performed on January 6, wassailing was a ritual that marked the end of the Yuletide revels. The term *wassail* comes from the Old English *wæs hæl*, meaning "be healthy" or "be whole."[37] Wassailing was also intended to encourage a good harvest and keep animals healthy. A bowl of frothy wassail was taken into the orchard and the tips of tree branches were dipped into the liquid. Some of it was also sprinkled on the soil around the base of a tree to bless the ground. Wassail is traditionally a hard cider warmed over a fire with spices and a few whole apples, which burst producing frothy white foam.

The term *wæs hæl* was first used as a greeting, then a toast, and then for holiday door-to-door singing. Folklore has exploded with stories of singing, dancing, and a lot of drinking associated with wassailing. With as many wassail recipes as there are descriptions of old practices, consider keeping the ritual simple and heartfelt by wishing a Happy New Year to the woodland spirits who may inhabit your trees.

---

37. Niall Edworthy, *The Curious World of Christmas: Celebrating All That is Weird, Wonderful and Festive* (New York: Perigee Books, 2007), 23.

Throughout folklore, eating an apple opens the gateway into other realms, most often to fairyland. According to one version of Merlin's story noted by French philosopher and historian Jean Markale (1928–2008), as a shaman this legendary figure passed into another realm not in a crystal cave but in a magical apple tree where he waits and watches.[38] (Refer to the entry for pine on page 236 for another version of Merlin's story.)

Magical Connections

Elements:	Air, water
Astrological influence:	Venus; Aquarius, Cancer, Libra, Taurus
Deities:	Aphrodite, Apollo, Athena, Badb, Cailleach Bheur, Diana, Dionysus, Eros, Flora, Freya, Hera, Idunn, Lugh, Macha, Manannan, Rhiannon, Venus, Zeus
Magical beings and woodland spirits:	Apple tree man, elves, fairies, pixies and colt pixies, unicorns
Wildlife:	Butterfly, cedar waxwing, grosbeak, hedgehog, pig
Ogham:	Quert/Ceirt ⊥⊥⊥⊥⊥
Alternate tree calendar:	June 25 to July 4 and December 22 to January 1

Runes:	Ingwaz/Ing/Inguz ᛝ
	    Runic half month: May 14 to May 28
	Perp/Peord/Perth ᛈ
	    Runic half month: January 13 to 27

Powers/attributes:	Abundance, the afterlife, ancestors, attraction, balance/harmony, bind, consecrate/bless, creativity, death/funeral practices, divination, dream work, enchantment, fertility, happiness, healing, knowledge (seek, acquire), love, luck, money/prosperity, the otherworld, peace, renewal, security, sex/sexuality, shamanic work, spirit guides/spirits, strength, stress/anxiety (calm, release), success, wisdom
Other associations:	Beltane, Lughnasadh, Samhain, Yule

---

38. Jean Markale, *Merlin Priest of Nature*, trans. Belle N. Burke (Rochester, VT: Inner Traditions, 1995), 118.

Items to purchase when the tree is not available: fresh or dried fruit, apple juice or cider, flower essence.

Spellwork and Ritual

The apple pentagram, also called the *star of knowledge*, provides an easy way to incorporate the power of the apple into magic and ritual. Simply cut an apple horizontally to reveal the five-pointed star pattern within. Place both halves on your altar to represent the Lord and Lady. For an esbat ritual, leave the apple whole but carve the triple moon symbol (waxing, full, waning) into the skin. As a symbol of regeneration, use an apple in Samhain rituals as offerings to the dead to aid their progress to rebirth.

Eating an apple before any type of magical practice is an aid for accessing ancient wisdom and for enhancing work with the fairy realm. For a fertility spell, wash and clean some apple seeds, and then make a circle with them around the base of a candle on your altar. The flower essence can be used to consecrate candles for raising healing energy.

The color of an apple can provide a magical boost too. Use a red apple for love, passion, and desire; a yellow/golden apple for success; and a green apple for abundance and prosperity. Burn a small piece of apple wood to scent the home and attract abundance. An old form of love divination requires two apples. Carefully peel the skins off the apples in one long strip. Throw them over your shoulders, and then look for initials formed by the peels to indicate your true love.

ASH

Common Ash (*Fraxinus excelsior*); also known as English ash, European ash, Venus of the woods.

White Ash (*F. americana*); also known as Biltmore ash, cane ash.

Black Ash (*F. nigra*); also known as basket ash, brown ash, swamp ash.

The name *ash* refers to the color of the bark. Native throughout Europe, the common ash grows eighty to 130 feet tall. The white ash is native to eastern North America and reaches sixty to eighty feet. Up to ninety feet tall, the black ash is native to the northeastern United States and eastern Canada. Ash trees have lance-shaped leaves. Their small, greenish flowers produce clusters of seeds that remain on the tree through winter. Also called a *key* or *samara*, the flat seed has a straight wing, unlike the curved maple seed wing.

To the ancient Greeks, the ash tree represented stability. Ares, the Greek god of war and son of Zeus, was said to favor the ash because it produced excellent spear shafts. Greeks and Romans used the wood for lances; Germanic peoples favored it for bows, arrows, and shields. According to Greek physician Dioscorides and Roman naturalist Pliny the Elder, the ash tree repelled snakes. In later folklore, even the shadow cast by ash leaves was believed enough to frighten a snake away.

In Ireland and parts of Britain it was believed that where ash, oak, and hawthorn grow together the invisible world of the fairies could be seen. Three of the five great trees of Ireland were ash. Located in each of the five provinces, these trees symbolized guardians who protected the sovereignty of the land. In parts of England, ash was so highly regarded that it was believed extremely unlucky to use the wood for mundane purposes. Water that collected in the hollows between the branches of an ash was considered holy and especially potent.

In Norse mythology, the mighty ash Yggdrasil connected the realms of heaven and earth. Also known as the world tree, its leaves provided shade and shelter for the entire earth. It was from this ash tree that Odin was suspended in shamanic trance when he perceived the runes. During the Middle Ages, ash was reputedly the favored broom handle wood for witches' besoms.

Finding an ash leaf with an even number of leaflets was considered lucky and was often used in love charms. Because of its name *Venus of the woods*, placing an ash leaflet in the left shoe was believed to result in a person meeting their future partner. For love divination, the first man a single woman met after pulling an ash key from the tree would be her husband. The person on whose property an ash tree stood would be unlucky in love if seeds did not appear each year.

Ash keys were believed to attract luck and often carried like a four-leaf clover. A leaflet placed under the pillow at night was said to aid in dreamwork. In Ireland, the wood of an ash tree was burned to banish the devil. Ash trees were believed to protect against witches too. Twigs from an ash that had a horseshoe buried in its roots were regarded as particularly effective for warding off witches and evil in general. However, in Oldenburg, Germany, if an ash tree had few buds on it at Beltane, it was said that witches must have stopped to eat them on their way to Walpurgis. In Somerset, England, an ash gad (pointed stick) was used as protection from fairies and witches. In other parts of England, fairies and elves were said to protect the tree.

Magical Connections

Elements:	Air, earth, fire, water
Astrological Influence:	Mercury, Neptune, Sun, Uranus; Capricorn, Libra, Pisces, Taurus, Virgo
Deities:	Ares, Bel/Belenus, the Dagda, Eostre, Freyr, Frigg, Holle, Lir, Macha, Mars, Minerva, Nemesis, Neptune, Odin, Poseidon, Thor
Magical beings and woodland spirits:	Elves, fairies, Meliai (Greek tree nymph), Vila (Serbian mountain nymphs that frequent ash trees)
Wildlife:	Butterfly, snipe (common), goat, hedgehog, rooster
Ogham:	Nion/Nuin/Nuinn ᚅ Celtic tree calendar: February 18 to March 17
Alternate tree calendar:	May 25 to June 3 and November 22 to December 1
Runes:	Ansuz/As/Os ᚨ Runic half month: August 13 to August 28 Ehwaz/Eh ᛖ Runic half month: March 30 to April 13 Gebo/Gyfu ᚷ Runic half month: September 28 to October 12 Hagalaz/Hagall/Haegl ᚺ Runic half month: October 28 to November 12 Mannaz/ Madhr/Mann ᛗ Runic half month: April 14 to 28 Wunjo/Wynn/Wyn ᚹ Runic half month: October 13 to October 27 Aesc (Anglo-Saxon) ᚫ The rune name *Aesc* means ash.*
Powers/attributes:	Astral travel/journeying, awareness (enhance, heighten), balance/harmony, changes/transitions, communication, concentration/focus, creativity, divination, dream work, fertility, growth, healing, hexes (remove, ward off), inspiration, intuition, knowledge (seek, acquire), love, luck, money/prosperity, negativity (remove, ward off), peace, prophecy, protection, purification, renewal, shamanic work, spirit guides/spirits, strength, wisdom
Other associations:	Asgard, home of the Norse gods; Ostara, Walpurgis, Beltane

* Looijenga, *Texts and Contexts of the Oldest Runic Inscriptions*, 7.

Items to purchase when the tree is not available: flower essence made from the white ash, baskets made of ash twigs.

Spellwork and Ritual

To boost the energy of spells or divination, make a circle with ash keys around the base of a candle upon which you have carved the tree's associated runes and/or ogham. Burn a dried leaf for love spells. When seeking creative inspiration, light a candle inscribed with ash's ogham or any of the runes and place it on your desk or workspace. This is also helpful for raising healing energy.

Use ash keys or leaves in protection spells and as charms against any form of negativity. Burn a piece of ash wood for protection against or to break a hex. For dream work, place a leaf on your bedside table to stimulate psychic dreams. Because ash provides a connection with other realms whether dreaming or journeying, keep a small twig nearby to aid you. Ash is instrumental for developing intuition and communication skills. Before a divination session, rest for a few minutes with a leaf on your third eye chakra.

European Aspen (*Populus tremula*); also known as common aspen,
   Eurasian aspen, quaking aspen.
Quaking Aspen (*P. tremuloides*); also known as American aspen, aspen
   poplar, golden aspen, mountain aspen, quaking poplar, shivering
   tree, trembling aspen.

Aspens are a type of poplar. The quaking aspen has whitish-colored bark and grows
between twenty to eighty feet tall. Released from long green catkins, its tiny, cottony
seeds are dispersed on the wind. The rounded, nearly heart-shaped leaves are dark,
glossy green and flutter in the slightest breeze, giving the impression that they are trembling. They turn vibrant golden yellow in the autumn.

The quaking aspen is native to Canada, the northern United States, and further south in mountainous regions. The European aspen is very similar, but slightly taller with slightly darker bark. It is native to most of Europe and the British Isles.

Like its cousin the willow, aspen's slender branches bend with the wind. Aspens are one of the earliest trees to repopulate a forest after a fire or other disaster. Aspens stabilize a damaged ecosystem, and like alders, they are nurturers. Their shade provides a gentle nursery for other plants and trees to get established. Because of their vibrant root systems, aspens often survive fires and ice storms.

Although aspens can reproduce by seed, regeneration through sprouts from their long lateral roots is more common. Genetically identical trees are produced from these root sprouts. With a shared root system, these clones have identical characteristics such as leaf size, bark, and branching habits, which makes them distinguishable from neighboring clonal groups. A clonal grove in central Utah known as Pando is considered one of the largest living organisms on Earth. The Latin *pando* means, "I spread."[39] Consisting of over 47,000 trees, this grove covers 108 acres and while aspen tree trunks live only to 150 years, the root system of Pando is estimated to be about 80,000 years old.[40]

Mentioned by English botanist John Gerard (1545–1612), aspen bark was used medicinally for several ailments including arthritis and other joint issues. Like its willow cousin, aspen bark contains the anti-inflammatory agent salicin, which is similar in chemical makeup to aspirin.

Although the wood is light and soft, it was sometimes used for arrows in medieval England. The words *quaking* and *trembling* in its common names relate to the fluttering movement of the leaves. Because of their unusually flexible stems, both sides of the leaves can be exposed to sunlight, which boosts photosynthesis.

According to *Cormac's Glossary*, an Irish/Latin dictionary compiled around 900 CE, a rod or wand of aspen wood called a *fé* was used to measure a newly-dug grave to ensure its occupant would fit.[41] This gave rise to aspen's association with death. In

---

39. Peter Frances, ed., *Natural Wonders of the World* (New York: DK Publishing, 2017), 70.

40. Ibid.

41. Sanas Chormaic, *Cormac's Glossary*, trans. John O'Donovan, Whitley Stokes, ed. (Dublin, Ireland: The Irish Archaeological and Celtic Society, 1868), 75.

Russia, an aspen rod was laid upon the grave of a suspected witch or used to pierce the heart. Either way, the wood was believed to keep the witch in the grave.

Magical Connections

Elements:	Air, water
Astrological Influence:	Mercury, Saturn, Venus; Aquarius, Capricorn, Libra
Deities:	Apollo, Calypso, Danu, Frigg, Gaia, Hecate, Hercules, the Morrigan, Odin, Persephone, Tyr, Zeus
Wildlife:	Beaver, butterfly, dove (mourning), raven, swan
Ogham:	Edad/Eadha/Eadhadh ╫ Ebad/Éabhadh, also called Koad/Grove ✕
Alternate tree calendar:	May 1 to 14, August 5 to 13, and February 4 to 8

Runes:	Ehwaz/Eh ᛗ
	    Runic half month: March 30 to April 13
	Perp/Peord/Perth ᛈ
	    Runic half month: January 13 to 27

Powers/attributes:	Ancestors, astral travel/journeying, balance/harmony, communication, courage, death/funeral practices, determination/endurance, divination, enchantment, healing, hexes (remove, ward off), knowledge (seek, acquire), money/prosperity, negativity (remove, ward off), the otherworld, peace, protection, renewal, stress/anxiety (calm, release), success
Other associations:	Mabon

Items to purchase when the tree is not available: flower essence made from the European aspen, which is sometimes marketed as trembling poplar essence.

Spellwork and Ritual

Keep a wand or twig of aspen with you when journeying to aid in communication in other realms. For a protection spell, inscribe one of aspen's ogham or rune characters on a picture of an aspen tree to burn in your cauldron. Crumble and then burn a dried leaf to break a hex or ward off negative energy. Wear a pendant made of aspen wood to help confront your fears or when in the company of someone you believe has deceived you.

For support through difficult times, inscribe the word *aspen* on a white candle and burn it during meditation. Also do this when you just need a boost in a particular aspect of your life. Use a green candle for healing circles. Gaze at a picture of an aspen to instill a feeling of peace and harmony.

BAMBOO

Common Bamboo (*Bambusa vulgaris*); also known as golden
Hawaiian bamboo.

Giant Bamboo (*Dendrocalamus giganteus*); also known as dragon
bamboo.

Nuda Bamboo (*Phyllostachys nuda*); also known as nude sheath
bamboo.

While bamboo is a grass, its size and energy are every bit as impressive as a tree's. There are nearly 1,500 species worldwide. Common bamboo grows fifty to sixty feet tall. Its culms (stalks) can reach up to four inches in diameter and its yellowish-green leaves, three to four inches long. It is native to Indochina and southern China. Largest of them all, giant bamboo can reach eighty feet tall. Its green to bluish-green culms are twelve inches in diameter and leaves up to twenty inches long. It is native to Southeast Asia.

Most cold hardy of all the bamboos, nuda has culms that reach thirty feet tall with a two-inch diameter. Although bamboos are evergreens, nuda becomes deciduous in very cold climates. It is native to China, India, and Myanmar (Burma).

Native to all continents except Antarctica and Europe, bamboo evolved to coexist with trees in a forest environment. Some of these tree grasses produce flowers annually or intermittently, while others rarely bloom. Like other types of grasses, bamboo flowers look more like leaves, hang in clusters, and produce seeds. Gregarious flowering is an unusual behavior of some bamboo in which all the plants in a particular species, regardless of their location, bloom at the same time even if they haven't for many decades. Some species flower only once in a hundred years. The reason for this behavior is unknown. In the past, flowering bamboo was a bad omen that heralded a period of hunger. This is because the plethora of seeds that followed the flowering encouraged an increase in the rat population, which in turn decimated crop harvests.

The name *bamboo* comes from Dutch, which was adapted from the Malayan name for it, *mambu*.[42] Bamboo has been used medicinally and the young shoots for food. The wood has been put to a wide range of uses from baskets to furniture and from decorative fencing to industrial barriers for pouring concrete, and, of course, bamboo flutes and fishing rods. Its flexibility and durability have made it useful in sports such as kendo (Japanese fencing) and kyudo (Japanese archery). Bamboo's use in Japan dates to the middle or late Jōmon period (c. 2500–300 BCE) where archaeologists believe it was used for ritual objects as well as items for everyday use.

Even with a wide range of mundane uses, bamboo was considered sacred in many Asian cultures. Through the ages, this plant has been an important motif in Chinese art. In monasteries, painting a picture of bamboo while engaging one's intuition and perception was regarded as a spiritual exercise. The rustle of nearby bamboo leaves during meditation was considered a sign that enlightenment was about to occur. Temple priests used bamboo sticks made of culms and roots for divination. In later times, similar sticks were called *kau cim* or *chi chi* sticks and used for mundane fortune-telling.

A symbol of longevity in China and Japan, bamboo also represented endurance, courage, and gracefulness. Pieces of bamboo were burned to ward off evil and negative influences. Despite being regarded as one of the three good omen trees in Japan (the

42. Wells, *Lives of the Trees*, 39.

others are pine and plum), there was once a superstition that three years after planting bamboo a death would occur in the family.

My first encounter with bamboo was in a grove with twenty-five–foot culms at the Rutgers University gardens in New Jersey. While the energy can be incredibly uplifting and energizing, it is also calming and peaceful. The sound of wind through its leaves creates a beautiful, soothing symphony.

Magical Connections

Elements:	Air
Astrological Influence:	Sun
Deities:	Hina, Izanami, Thoth
Powers/attributes:	Adaptability, balance/harmony, courage, divination, dream work, happiness, hexes (remove, ward off), luck, negativity (remove, ward off), peace, protection, strength, wisdom, wishes

Items to purchase when the plant is not available: A wide range of products are made from bamboo including flutes, screens, rugs, and containers.

Spellwork and Ritual

To engender peace and congeniality in your household, place a piece of bamboo in a room where the family frequently gathers. Plant bamboo in front of your house or place a bamboo stick near the main entrance to your home to invite luck and harmony inside.

For luck, hold a bamboo stick or flute between your hands and make a wish. Alternatively, write what you are seeking on a picture of bamboo. Use bamboo to disperse negative energy or block spells that have been sent your way. It is especially effective for breaking hexes. Place a picture of bamboo on your altar to draw its energy into your rituals and meditations. Have a bamboo stick with you during divination sessions or keep your tools in a bamboo box.

BEECH

American Beech (*Fagus grandifolia*); also known as white beech.
European Beech (*F. sylvatica*); also known as common beech.
Copper Beech (*F. sylvatica* 'Purpurea'); also known as purple beech.

Often described as stately, the American beech averages fifty to seventy feet tall with gray bark. The pointed, oval leaves are dull green on top and lighter underneath. Clusters of flowers form yellow or reddish spiky balls in the early spring and develop into beechnuts. This tree is native to eastern North America. The European beech, native to southern England, Wales, and Europe, is slightly smaller at fifty to sixty feet tall. Its bark is a darker gray and its flowers are yellowish green. The leaves of both trees turn yellow bronze in the autumn. Copper beech is a cultivar of the European beech. Reaching up to one hundred feet, it has coppery-purple leaves that turn red in the autumn.

Beech leaves eventually turn brown as they dry and stay on the tree through winter. Beechnuts are encased in spiny, woody husks. These can be hard to open but give them a day or two indoors and they open on their own with the husk splitting into sections and looking like a spiny, four-petaled flower. The edible nut has a triangular shape. Like hazelnuts, beechnuts were believed to impart wisdom and used as amulets.

The Romans held the beech tree in high regard and used its wood for ritual libation bowls. Bacchus was said to drink from a beech goblet and beech wood jugs were used when making offerings to other deities. Both the Greeks and Romans regarded the beech as an auspicious tree. According to Greek poet Hesiod (lived c. 700 BCE), the sacred grove of Zeus at Dodona was comprised of oak and beech. He also noted that the oracle of the grove dwelled in the trunk of a great beech. Beech trees were part of the sacred grove of the goddess Diana too.

Because of its abundance of nuts, the beech was associated with fertility. As a tree of prophecy, an unusually high volume of beechnuts indicated that a higher number of illegitimate children would be born in a village. As a market index indicator, leaves appearing on the lower part of the tree first meant that grain prices would go up that year and vice versa if the leaves came out at the top of the tree first. Carrying a beech leaf inscribed with the letter *T* was believed to provide protection from witchcraft. The significance of this is unknown.

Germanic peoples dedicated the beech to Thor and believed it provided protection from his lightning. Statistically, beeches (and birches) appear to be struck less than many other trees, which may be because their smooth bark produces a continuous flow of rainwater down their trunks during a storm. As a result, when lightning strikes it is quickly conducted to the ground. Rough bark interrupts water flow and damage occurs to the tree because the lightning is not quickly grounded.

Boards of beech wood were frequently used for carving runes. Because the bark is excellent for carving, many people have inscribed their initials and other messages on beech trees. This practice is documented back to Roman times. In 1768, American pioneer Daniel Boone (1734–1820) noted that he had killed a bear beside the beech that bore the message, which could be clearly read for over a hundred years.[43]

According to seventeenth-century Swiss folklore, at a location where five brothers murdered each other, the leaves of the beech trees turned red from their blood. Legend

---

43. Wells, *Lives of the Trees*, 51.

has it in Somerset, England, if you are lost in the woods at night, sleeping under a beech will keep you safe. Forked beech branches have been popular for divining rods.

In England, the beech has been regarded as queen to the king oak. In the woods near where I used to live, I found a pair of trees that I called *the lovers*. It consisted of an oak with a beech growing on top of one of its roots. The limbs of the trees were intertwined in a beautiful embrace.

Magical Connections

Elements:	Fire, water
Astrological Influence:	Saturn; Gemini, Sagittarius, Virgo
Deities:	Apollo, Athena, Bacchus, Cerridwen, Diana, Dionysus, Freya, Frigg, Holle, Loki, Odin, Thor, Zeus
Wildlife:	Bluebird, deer, fox, turkey (wild)
Ogham:	Amhancholl/Eamancholl/Emancoll/Mór ᚙ Ifin/Iphin ᚘ Uilleann/Uilen/Uilleand ᚖ
Alternate tree calendar:	Winter solstice December 21/22

Runes:	Naudiz/Naudhr/Nyd ᚾ
	    Runic half month: November 13 to 27
	Perp/Peord/Perth ᛈ
	    Runic half month: January 13 to 27

Powers/attributes:	Abundance, ancestors, creativity, fertility, healing, knowledge (seek, acquire), luck, manifest (desires, dreams, will), money/prosperity, prophecy, protection, psychic abilities, renewal, transformation, wisdom, wishes
Other associations:	Litha, Midsummer's Eve, Samhain

Items to purchase when the tree is not available: beechnut oil and flower essence made from the European beech.

Spellwork and Ritual

Use beechnuts in spells to manifest what you seek. Keep a small twig in a prominent location in your home to promote stability in your life. Place a few husks on a shelf in the kitchen to attract abundance and prosperity to your home. Eat a few of the nuts to foster creativity and heighten second sight.

Write what you are wishing for on a picture of a beech tree. Meditate with it between your hands, and then burn it as you visualize your dreams coming to fruition. Place beech leaves on your Samhain altar to honor and enhance contact with ancestors. Burn a piece of wood to cleanse ritual space. Place a cluster of beechnuts in their husks on your altar as an offering to the Goddess.

BIRCH

American White Birch (*Betula papyrifera*); also known as canoe birch,
   silver birch, paper birch.

Silver Birch (*B. alba* syn. *B. pendula*); also known as common birch,
   European birch, European weeping birch, European white birch,
   lady of the woods, silver birch.

Growing fifty to seventy feet tall, the American white birch often has multiple slender trunks
with white bark that peels in strips. Its dull green leaves turn bright yellow in autumn.
This tree is indigenous to the cooler regions of North America. Native to northern Europe
and Asia Minor, the silver birch typically grows forty to fifty feet tall. It has long, drooping
branches and dark green leaves that turn yellowish in autumn. In early spring, both trees
produce drooping yellowish-brown male catkins and upright greenish female catkins.

   Because the birch is a tree of northern areas, the Greeks and Romans were not as
familiar with it. However, it was well known to Germanic and Scandinavian peoples,

who dedicated it to Thor. With its pale, almost silver bark, birch was also dedicated to the moon. Birch was associated with renewal because of its ability to take hold and grow more quickly than many other trees. As one of the earliest trees to come into leaf in the northern woods, it was traditionally included in Imbolc rituals. Integral to fertility rights and regarded as a tree of life, in Germany birch was one of the trees traditionally used for Beltane Maypoles. Midsummer garlands often included birch leaves.

Because the wood was often used for torches, birch was associated with light. In Wales, lovers' trysts were discretely held under birch bowers and a small wreath of twigs given as a token of love.

Although this tree is associated with birth, it also relates to rebirth after death. According to the *Book of Leinster*, bodies were transported to the grave in Ireland with bushy birch branches used as a covering called a *strophais* from *sēs rophuis* meaning "grave broom."[44] In Sweden, birch branches were sometimes used in burials to cover the deceased or placed underneath like bedding and a pillow. In parts of Finland, the deceased was covered or wrapped in birch bark as late as the eighteenth century.

Birch trees were believed to hold the spirits of ancestors, and in Siberia they were used in shamanic rituals of purification and initiation. Throughout northern Europe, birch had the power to protect people and their animals from vermin, disease, witches, and evil spirits. In Sweden, birch twigs were placed in front of homes and stables on Walpurgis to keep witches at bay. In England, birch branches wrapped with red and white ribbons were propped against stable doors for the same purpose on Walpurgis and at other times to keep the fairies from taking horses. Sapling branches were also placed in stables to promote animal fecundity. Birch wood's common use for broom handles linked it with witches. In western England, crossed birch twigs were hung over doorways for protection against enchantment. In other areas, it was believed that a birch tree that had been coppiced (drastically cut back to encourage new growth) could give rise to a dangerous spirit.

While the genus *Betula* is the Latin name for the tree, some sources indicate that it may have originated with the Celtic *betu* meaning, "tree."[45] The species name is from the Greek *papurus*, meaning "papyrus" or "paper," and *fero*, "to bear" or "to carry," making

---

44. Susan Leigh Fry, *Burial in Medieval Ireland 900–1500: A Review of the Written Sources* (Dublin, Ireland: Four Courts Press, 1999), 126.

45. Ernest Small, *North American Cornucopia: Top 100 Indigenous Food Plants* (Boca Raton, FL: CRC Press, 2014), 497.

this the paper-bearing tree.[46] The people of India had the same idea; the Sanskrit name for birch, *bhurg* means "a tree for writing upon."[47]

Magical Connections

Element:	Water
Astrological influence:	Jupiter, Moon, Sun, Venus; Capricorn, Sagittarius
Deities:	Angus Mac Og, Cerridwen, the Dagda, Freya, Frigg, Lugh, Thor
Magical beings and woodland spirits:	Fairies, Ghillie Dhu (a spirit that lives in the birch woods of Scotland), Lieschi (a Russian genii of the forest associated with birch trees)
Wildlife:	Cow (white), eagle, egret, pheasant, stag (white)
Ogham:	Beith/Beithe/Beth ⊤ Celtic calendar: December 24 to January 20
Alternate tree calendar:	June 24, Midsummer
Runes:	Berkanan/Bjarkan/Beorc ᛒ Runic half month: March 14 to 29 Uruz/Ur ᚢ Runic half month: July 14 to 28
Powers/attributes:	Abundance, astral travel/ journeying, awareness (enhance, heighten), banish, challenges/obstacles (overcome), changes/transitions, clarity (enhance, foster), concentration/focus, consecrate/bless, creativity, defense, determination/endurance, divination, fertility, growth, healing, inspiration, intuition, knowledge (seek, acquire), love, negativity (remove, ward off), protection, purification, release (let go, move on), renewal, security, shamanic work, spirit guides/spirits, stress/anxiety (calm, release), support (provide, receive), wisdom
Other associations:	Imbolc, Ostara, Walpurgis, Beltane, Litha, Midsummer's Eve, Yule

---

46. Ibid.

47. Wells, *Lives of the Trees*, 53.

Items to purchase when the tree is not available: essential oil made from the leaf buds of the silver birch; flower essence is also made from the silver birch.

Spellwork and Ritual

As a symbol of birth and renewal, birch helps to learn from the past, especially when making a fresh start. To aid in this, place a couple of small birch twigs on your altar during times of transition to aid in healing and personal growth. Larger twigs can be used like a broom to symbolically sweep and clear away negative energy before ritual or to provide protection during magic work. Birch is instrumental for focusing the mind and developing intuition.

To bring clarity and aid in receiving knowledge, hold a birch leaf between your palms to focus energy before a divination session. Use pieces of bark in a sachet for love spells and place a twig under your bed to aid in fertility. Crumble and sprinkle pieces of dried bark around your property to attract fairies. Burn a few small pieces of bark for purification and to bless the beginning of a project, relationship, new home, or when making any kind of fresh start. The bark of the American birch easily peals from the tree and has a smooth surface on its inner side, which can be used to write a spell.

BLACKTHORN

Blackthorn (*Prunus spinosa*); also known as black haw, blackthorn
plum, fairy tree, sloe plum, wild plum, wishing thorn.

Indigenous to Europe and western Asia, blackthorn is a shrubby tree with dense, spiny branches that grows about ten feet tall. Its white, five-petaled flowers bloom in early spring before the leaves appear and stand in stark contrast to the bark and thorns. The small, round blue-black fruit, called *sloes*, ripen in the autumn after the first frost.

Rich in vitamins, the sloes were used medicinally and as food by the Greeks, Romans, and Arabs. They are still used for jams, jellies, and for flavoring liqueurs, most notably gin. The Greeks used branches of blackthorn as drilling sticks to kindle sacred fires. They believed the tree could protect against witches and sorcery.

Blackthorn's dark, sturdy wood makes an attractive walking stick. In Ireland, it was the preferred stick because it could be used to ward off any form of evil encountered during an afternoon ramble in the countryside. It was also useful for dealing with ghosts. In England, blackthorn was occasionally used as a boundary tree.

Solitary blackthorns were never disturbed because fairies were believed to inhabit them. If one grew in the middle of a field, a farmer would plow around it rather than incur the wrath of the wee folk. Blackthorns were also believed to be a gateway to the fairy realm and otherworld.

This tree was traditionally used with hawthorn for hedges to keep animals out of orchards and gardens. They are still part of many hedgerows. Like other thorn trees, blackthorn was regarded as a guardian of sacred places. During my pilgrimage in Ireland, I saw blackthorns growing at most of the sacred sites I visited. Many of these places included holy wells. In the past, May 4th marked the veneration of the thorn; a day when devotees would circumambulate a sacred well or spring, and then make offerings to the thorn trees and any spirits that dwelled within.

As the earliest of the hedgerow trees to bloom in the spring, blackthorn's flowering is often followed by a cold spell, which is referred to as a blackthorn winter. According to weather lore in Somerset, England, a blackthorn winter meant a spoiled summer. In the autumn, a greater than usual abundance of sloes indicated a hard winter ahead. Like many white flowers, it was unlucky to take blackthorn blooms indoors. It was considered bad luck to wear one in a buttonhole and in some areas of England doing so meant someone in the family would die.

Although popular for walking sticks, a belief persisted that witches liked it, too, and often carved spells into the wood. Perhaps because of this, blackthorn branches were used to break hexes and after burning one, part of it was kept and hung in the house for further protection. Witches were also believed to use the thorns for black magic.

According to German legend, this tree sprang from the blood of a fallen Teutonic warrior. In Slavic folklore, carrying a piece of blackthorn or sewing it into clothing provided protection. Various parts of the tree were used as charms to cure a range of ailments from warts to coughs. As a wishing tree for divination, a small branch was thrown in water; if it floated, your wish would come true.

In Ireland, a tribe of fairies called the *Lunantishee* (moon fairies) was believed to serve as guardians of the blackthorn. Although the wood was popular for walking sticks and other uses, the Lunantishee would inflict bad luck on a person who cut anything from the tree on May 11th or November 11th. On the old Julian calendar, these dates would have been Beltane and Samhain. A change was made from the Julian to the Gregorian calendar to more accurately align the months with the seasons. This required ten days to be dropped during the year in which the switch was made.[48] In keeping with tradition, avoid taking anything from a blackthorn during these times of year and leave an offering at the base of the tree or in the branches.

Magical Connections

Elements:	Earth, fire
Astrological Influence:	Mars, Saturn; Aries, Scorpio
Deities:	Banba, Bel/Belenus, Bertha, Brigid, the Dagda, Holle, Loki, Macha, Ran
Magical beings and woodland spirits:	Fairies, Lunantishee
Wildlife:	Bee, butterfly, hedgehog, thrush
Ogham:	Straif/Straith ⵌ

Runes:	Thurisaz/Thurs/Thorn ᚦ
	    Runic half month: July 29 to August 12
	Wunjo/Wynn/Wyn ᚹ
	    Runic half month: October 13 to 27

Powers/attributes:	Authority/leadership, banish, challenges/obstacles (overcome), defense, hexes (remove, ward off), loyalty/fidelity, negativity (remove, ward off), protection, purification, strength
Other associations:	Imbolc, Walpurgis, Beltane, Samhain

Items to purchase when the tree is not available: flower essence, walking stick, dried sloes are often marketed as blackthorn berries, pieces of bark are often marketed as sloe tree bark.

Spellwork and Ritual

To prepare outdoor ritual space, strew crumbled dried blackthorn leaves around the area. This will also boost magical energy and may attract fairies. If the thorns are not

---

48. Esther Yu Sumner, "A Date is a Date is a Date," *Ancestry Magazine*, vol. 25, no. 2, March-April 2007 (Provo, UT: Ancestry, Inc.), 20.

available, draw the ogham Straif on small stones to use in their place. To honor and connect with the energy of this legendary fairy tree, sprinkle a little blackthorn flower essence on a stone marked with Straif and place it on your altar.

To strengthen the energy of a spell, crumble and burn a few leaves. Alternatively, draw its ogham on a piece of parchment paper to use in place of leaves. The sloes can also be used to strengthen spells. They can be dried and used as amulets for protection or to help gain control of a situation.

BOX

Boxwood (*Buxus sempervirens*); also known as American boxwood,
box, box tree, common box, European box.

Native to southern Europe, western Asia, and northern Africa, box is a multi-branched
hedge tree with dense, evergreen foliage that is often used for topiary. It usually grows
between fifteen to twenty feet tall and wide. It has small, oval leaves and rounded clusters of yellowish flowers. The seed capsules have three "horns" and turn brown when
they mature in late summer.

The Greeks and Romans found the dense wood of this tree perfect for making boxes
to hold small items and ointments. The Greeks called the tree *pyxides* and the Romans
buxus; both mean "a box."[49] Dedicated to gods of the underworld, Hades and Pluto, this

49. Wells, *The Lives of Trees*, 56.

tree represented the cycle of life encompassing love, fertility, and death. In Gaul, box represented eternal life and was regarded as sacred.

In Tuscany, boxwood flutes were used in sacred rituals. During the Baroque and Renaissance periods, box was popular for making flutes and recorders because of the beauty of the wood and the sweet sound it produced. Germanic peoples mounted a box branch on the roof of a new house as a symbol of joy for the household and to provide protection against natural and supernatural calamities. A box twig was often placed under the threshold of a barn or near a beehive to protect them. It was customary in the Netherlands to toss a few box leaves into the fireplace during a thunderstorm to shield a house from lightning.

Believed to have exceptional magical power, this tree was regarded as a protector of fields. Because of its vitality, farmers planted box trees near fields, in orchards, and in vineyards to foster growth and good harvests. In England, it was occasionally used as a boundary tree. Like ivy, box functioned as a forerunner of tavern signs. A handful of box branches tied to the end of a pole indicated that wine was sold on the premises. Box was also used to advertise alehouses.

In sixteenth-century Europe, box was used as an amulet against witchcraft and to make a potion for someone who had been hexed. A box tree was planted near the front door of a home to keep witches from entering because for some reason, they were believed to stop and count the leaves. In Bavaria, a piece of boxwood was placed in a baby's cradle to prevent fairies from substituting a changeling.

Wood from box tree roots was often used to make dagger handles because of its strength and because it was believed to repel evil. Wood from the trunk was used to make engravings. Box was also used for prophecy. On New Year's Eve, leaves were marked to represent each family member. If a leaf were green in the morning, that person would stay healthy all year. For love divination, after assigning a leaf to each potential suitor, they were placed in front of a fire. The leaf that wafted forward away from the fire would indicate the one to marry.

In seventeenth-century England, hedges of box were planted along the perimeters of villages in the belief that they would keep the plague from entering the town. Box hedges became popular for mazes in formal gardens in England and the United States. Box trees were planted near beehives to give the honeycomb exceptional healing properties. Box branches were used for well dressings on May Day and New Year's Eve.

This tree was commonly planted in European cemeteries. In England, sprigs of box were provided to mourners to carry in procession to the churchyard, and then toss into the grave. Box was sometimes combined with lavender and rosemary for this purpose. Box sprigs have been found in Romano-British burials too. Leafy branches were sometimes laid upon the grave for decoration. In Lancashire, England, the tree became known as burying box. As with a number of other plants, it was believed that taking a flowering branch into a house would be followed by a death in the family. Box is not related to the box elder tree (*Acer negundo*).

Magical Connections

Element:	Earth
Astrological influence:	Mars
Deities:	Apollo, Aphrodite, Circe, Cybele, Hades, Pluto, Venus
Magical beings and woodland spirits:	Fairies
Wildlife:	Honeybee
Powers/attributes:	Ancestors, death/funeral practices, defense, divination, fertility, happiness, hexes (remove, ward off), love, luck, money/prosperity, prophecy, protection, renewal
Other associations:	Ostara, Beltane, Samhain

Items to purchase when the tree is not available: candle rings and door wreaths made from leafy branches; the wood is widely used for figurines.

Spellwork and Ritual

Place a small box branch on your altar at Samhain to honor loved ones who have passed. As an alternative, use a picture of the tree and write the names of those you want to remember in ritual. To break a hex, use a box branch to "comb" your aura with downward strokes as you visualize any negativity being swept away from you. Do this, three nights in a row, and then bury the branch in the ground.

Grow a box tree on your property to invite prosperity and happiness to your family. Store a small branch with your divination tools to support and strengthen their energy. Place several leaves or a piece of bark in a small pouch to use as a love charm.

CEDAR

Atlantic Cedar (*Cedrus atlantica*); also known as African cedar, Atlas cedar, blue Atlas cedar.

Cedar of Lebanon (*C. libani*); also known as arbor vitae.

Eastern Red Cedar (*Juniperus virginiana*); also known as American red cedar, red juniper, Virginia juniper.

Western Red Cedar (*Thuja plicata*); also known as giant cedar, giant arborvitae, Pacific red cedar.

Although there are a number of trees called *cedar*, only those of the genus *Cedrus* are true cedars and come from the Mediterranean region. Although the New World trees come from different genera in the cypress (*Cupressaceae*) botanical family, their aromatic wood has a fragrance very similar to cedar. Like true cedars, many of them have been regarded as sacred.

Both of the true cedars included here have cylindrical cones that sit upright on the branches. The Atlantic cedar's short needles curve toward the tips of branches. Native to the Atlas Mountains of northern Africa, this tree usually grows forty to sixty feet tall. From the mountains of Lebanon, Syria, and Turkey, cedars of Lebanon can reach up to 130 feet with massive trunks. Its needles grow in widely spaced clusters that spiral around the branches. This tree can live up to a thousand years. Native to eastern North America, the eastern red cedar is a type of juniper. It has fans of scale-like foliage and blue berries. Growing thirty to sixty-five feet tall, it has a dense conical shape. Reaching over 200 feet tall, the western red cedar has fans of scale-like foliage and reddish-brown bark. It is native to the Pacific Northwest.

Cedars are called *arbor vitae*, "the tree of life," not only because of their majestic stature, but because for thousands of years they provided many essentials for daily life. In the Middle East, wood from the famed cedars of Lebanon was reputedly used for aesthetic purposes in the Temple of Solomon. The wood of the eastern red cedar tree is popular for storage chests and essential oil.

Cedars were associated with the Divine because it was considered a miracle that they could flourish in rocky areas seemingly without the need for soil or water. Throughout the Middle East, the wood was burned as sacred offerings. In Tibet, cedar was important temple incense. The genus name comes from the Greek word *kedros*, which was derived from the Indo-European root *ked* meaning, "to smoke."[50] In Egypt, cedar resin was used as incense for offerings to gods and goddesses. It was also used in the embalming process to purify the body of the deceased and to prepare the soul for the afterlife. The sun god Ra was sometimes noted as "he who dwelt among the cedars."[51]

For more mundane purposes, the Egyptians used cedarwood for ships, coffins, and sculptures. The Romans considered the wood sacred and produced statues of deities and ancestors with it. Because it was so resinous, the wood was commonly used for torches. During the Middles Ages and Renaissance, it was used for furniture, chest linings, and musical instruments. The mythical unicorn was said to keep his treasure in a cedarwood chest.

50. Wells, *Lives of the Trees*, 71.

51. E. A. Wallis Budge, *The Gods of the Egyptians: Studies in Egyptian Mythology*, vol. 1 (New York: Dover Publications, Inc., 1969), 361.

Native Americans used cedar bark fibers to make ropes, baskets, and mats. Wood from large logs was used for totem poles and canoes. The wood was also burned for purification rites. According to folklore, the legendary thunderbird was believed to nest in a cedar tree high in the mountains.

Magical Connections

Elements:	Air, earth, fire, water
Astrological Influence:	Jupiter, Mercury, Sun; Aries, Sagittarius, Taurus
Deities:	Arianrhod, Artemis, Astarte, Ba'al, Brigid, Ea, Odin, Osiris, Persephone, Ra.
Magical beings, creatures, and woodland spirits:	Elves, fairies, phoenix, thunderbird, unicorn
Wildlife:	Dove, goldfinch, robin
Alternate tree calendar:	August 14 to 23 and February 9 to 18
Powers/attributes:	Abundance, the afterlife, authority/leadership, balance/harmony, banish, challenges/obstacles (overcome), clarity (enhance, foster), communication, concentration/focus, confidence, consecrate/bless, courage, determination/endurance, divination, dream work, emotions (deal with, support), family and home, fertility, growth, healing, hexes (remove, ward off), inspiration, justice/legal matters, love, loyalty/fidelity, luck, money/prosperity, negativity (remove, ward off), peace, protection, psychic abilities, purification, release (let go, move on), renewal, security, spirit guides/spirits, spirituality, strength, success, wisdom
Other associations:	Imbolc, Beltane, Mabon, Yule

Items to purchase when the tree is not available: incense, cedarwood boxes, figurines and other objects made from the wood, essential oils made from the wood of the Atlantic cedar and the eastern red cedar, which is marketed as Virginia cedarwood.

Spellwork and Ritual

Cedar is especially effective for purification. Use a cedar bough to symbolically sweep ritual areas or store a small sprig with your magic tools to have them ready for use. Burn a small piece of cedarwood or incense to support focus and clarity for clairvoyance or any type of divination. The aroma also enhances psychic protection for these practices. Use cedar to remove negativity, break hexes, or to remove anything unwanted from your life.

The scent of cedarwood stimulates dream work and strengthens psychic abilities. It aids in finding peace of mind and fostering tranquility in the home. Use the foliage in spells to attract love or to encourage a lover to be faithful. Any part of the cedar can be used to facilitate communication with spirits. Use cedar at Imbolc to represent coming into the light from darkness. Cedar also aids healing and personal growth. Carry an amulet made of cedarwood when seeking justice, especially in legal matters.

CHERRY

Black Cherry (*Prunus serotina*); also known as rum cherry, wild cherry.

Sweet Cherry (*P. avium*); also known as bird cherry, mazzard, merry-tree, wild cherry.

European Bird Cherry (*P. padus*); also known as hackberry, witches' tree.

Largest of the cherry trees, the black cherry grows between fifty and eighty feet tall. The bark and glossy oblong leaves have a distinctive cherry-like odor when crushed. It has white flowers and purplish-black fruit. This tree is native to eastern North America, Mexico, and Central America. Only reaching thirty feet tall, the sweet cherry has white flowers and dark oval leaves. Its fruit is, well, cherry red. The European bird cherry grows twenty to forty feet tall with pointed leaves and showy white flowers. Its fruit is red but turns black as it ripens. Both of these trees are native to Europe, the British Isles, and Asia.

Cherries are a tasty treat that has been enjoyed for millennia; cherrystones found in European cave dwellings date to between 4000 and 5000 BCE.[52] Cultivation of the cherry tree began in Greece around 300 BCE and by the first century CE, Pliny the Elder recorded eight different species being grown.[53]

The cherry's reddish wood, which darkens with age, has been widely popular for carvings, furniture, cabinetwork, and paneling. During the Middle Ages and Renaissance, it was favored for musical instruments. Although bitter when eaten straight from the tree, black cherries make excellent jams and pies. They are also used to flavor liquors. Birds love the fruit of the sweet cherry; its species name *avium* is Latin for "bird."[54] Sweet cherry was known as merry-tree because of its festive clouds of flowers.

During medieval times, the acrid odor of European bird cherry bark was believed to ward off the plague. Pieces of bark were hung over doorways and sometimes placed inside the home. In Germany, the tree was called *hexenbaum*, "witches' tree."[55] Similarly, in parts of Scotland the tree was associated with witchcraft and the wood avoided for use in household items. The Scots called the fruit *hags-berry* and *fowl-cherry*, and the Swedes, *häggebär*.[56]

The cherry tree appears in Danish and Lithuanian folktales in connection with a spirit or guardian of the forest. In Serbian lore, beautiful fairy or elf-like beings known as Vila lived in the forests and loved to play near cherry trees.

Since the Middle Ages, the cherry has been associated with virginity and beauty as well as seduction. Cherrystones have been used as talismans to attract a lover and for divination to see if a wish may come true. Similar to divination with daisy petals, the process was to take a handful of cherrystones without counting them. With the wish in mind, the phrase "this year" was said when the first stone was set down; "next year" was said with the second; "sometime" with the third; "never" with the fourth. This was repeated until the last cherrystone was set down revealing the answer.

---

52. Jules Janick and James N. Moore, eds., *Fruit Breeding: Tree and Tropical Fruits*, vol. 1 (New York: John Wiley & Sons, Inc., 1996), 215.

53. Staub, *75 Remarkable Fruits for Your Garden*, 40.

54. Ernest Small, *Top 100 Food Plants: The World's Most Important Crops* (Ottawa, Canada: NRC Press, 1999), 149.

55. Hilderic Friend, *Flowers and Flower Lore*, vol. 2 (London: W. Swan Sonnenschein and Company, 1884), 538.

56. Ibid.

Magical Connections

Elements:	Fire, water
Astrological influence:	Mercury, Venus; Aquarius, Aries, Libra, Taurus
Deities:	Artemis, Flora, Mars, the Morrigan, Pan, Persephone, Thor
Magical beings, creatures, and woodland spirits:	Elves, phoenix, unicorn, Tuometar (a Finish tree fairy associated with the European bird cherry), Vila
Wildlife:	Cuckoo, fox (red), hawk (red-tailed)
Powers/attributes:	Abundance, attraction, balance/harmony, challenges/obstacles (overcome), creativity, divination, fertility, happiness, knowledge (seek, acquire), love, luck, manifest (desires, dreams, will), peace, renewal, spirituality, transformation, wisdom

Items to purchase when the tree is not available: fresh or dried cherries, cherry juice, pieces of dried bark from the black cherry, flower essence made from the Japanese flowering cherry (P. *serrulate*).

Spellwork and Ritual

In addition to functioning as a symbol of abundance, the cherry tree also attracts good luck. Place a few blossoms, or a picture of cherry flowers, on your altar for spells to stimulate and attract love. In a bridal bouquet, the flowers foster a long, happy marriage and increase fertility. Just as the flowers are associated with love, so too are the cherries. Use cherry juice to consecrate a red candle for love spells. To attract love, wash two cherrystones, let them dry, and then sew them into a small pouch to carry with you.

To heighten awareness during divination sessions, burn a small piece of cherry bark as incense. For help in overcoming an obstacle, press a cherry blossom in a book, and then keep it in your wallet. When the obstacle or situation is resolved, burn the flower as you affirm your gratitude for this tree's help. To help manifest dreams, take three cherries, and pull the stems off one at a time as you visualize what you want to achieve. After eating the three cherries, bury the stones in your garden or a wooded area.

CHESTNUT

European Chestnut (*Castanea sativa* syn. *C. vulgarus*); also known as
    Spanish chestnut, sweet chestnut.
American Chestnut (*C. dentata* syn. *C. americana*)
Horse Chestnut (*Aesculus hippocastanum*); also known as candle tree.

Native to southern Europe and western Asia, the European chestnut can reach up to one
hundred feet tall. Its oblong leaves are dark green and upright flowers yellow to greenish.
The American chestnut is native to eastern North America and grows up to seventy-five
feet tall. Its leaves are similar but dull yellowish green. Both of these trees have deeply
grooved trunks and widely spreading branches. Encased in pairs by a spiny round husk,
the nuts are flat on one side and rounded on the other.

    The horse chestnut reaches fifty to seventy-five feet tall. Its white flowers have a red
or yellow tint at the base and grow in showy upright clusters. It has dark green leaflets
arranged in a fan shape. The nuts grow in spiny, round husks. This tree is in a different

botanical family from the other chestnuts, and its nuts, commonly called *conkers*, are not edible. The horse chestnut is native to the Balkan Peninsula.

Medieval herbalist John Gerard recommended parts of both the sweet and horse chestnut trees for remedies. Greek physician Dioscorides first recorded the chestnut's medicinal uses. Worn in a bag around the neck or carried in the pocket, a chestnut was used to draw off disease or act as a charm against it.

During the Middle Ages and Renaissance, chestnut wood was valued for furniture and musical instruments. Because of its durability, it was sometimes used as a substitute for oak. The chestnut was a dominant woodland tree in North America until the early twentieth century when a fungus almost completely eliminated it. The tree is on the cusp of making a comeback.

The Romans ground chestnuts into meal and combined it with wheat flour to make bread. This practice continued into medieval times, especially during periods of famine. Meal made from the horse chestnut was used as starch to whiten linen cloth. Sweet chestnuts were sometimes used as tithes. For centuries, roasted chestnuts have been a popular winter snack. In the mid-nineteenth century, a specially designed grilling pan was *de rigueur* in French kitchens.

Highly prized by the Celts of Wales, chestnuts sometimes took the place of the revered hazelnut. In some parts of Ireland, if hawthorn wasn't available, chestnut branches were used to decorate cattle barns on May Day.

Well known for lining the beautiful boulevards of Paris, the horse chestnut was adopted as an ornamental tree throughout Europe. In Victorian England, *Chestnut Sunday* was a special day for middle class Londoners to visit Kew Gardens to enjoy the trees in bloom.

While the horse chestnut's upright flower stalks may have inspired the nickname *candle tree*, according to some legends, the flowers were burned by fairies to light their way home after a night of dancing. Carrying a sweet chestnut in the pocket was believed to improve a man's romantic chances. A horse chestnut was carried in the pocket for general good luck.

There are several theories to explain the word *horse* in horse chestnut. One is that it simply meant "coarse" because it is not a particularly elegant tree. Another theory is that the curved markings left on young branches by leaves that have fallen off resemble horse hooves. It is also thought to refer to the medicinal use for coughs and hoarseness of voice.

Magical Connections

Elements:	Air, fire, water
Astrological influence:	Jupiter, Sun; Cancer, Gemini, Sagittarius, Virgo
Deities:	Artemis, Boann, Diana
Magical beings and woodland spirits:	Elves, fairies
Wildlife:	Blue jay, grouse, swan
Alternate tree calendar:	May 15 to 24 and November 12 to 21
Powers/attributes all chestnuts:	Abundance, consecrate/bless, family/home, healing, hexes (remove, ward off), justice/legal matters, love, luck, money/prosperity, peace, protection, strength, wishes
Powers/attributes horse chestnuts:	Banish, divination
Other associations:	Beltane, Yule

Items to purchase when the tree is not available: flower essence made from the horse chestnut and marketed as white chestnut, edible chestnuts are often available peeled and roasted, horse chestnuts are also available.

Spellwork and Ritual

For banishing spells, write a few keywords about what you want to remove from your life on a picture of a horse chestnut tree in bloom. To finish your spell, burn the picture in your cauldron and scatter the ashes to the wind. Chestnut is instrumental when seeking justice, especially in legal matters. Carry a picture of the tree with you when meeting with your attorney.

To build protective energy against a potential hex, paint your initials on the flat side of a chestnut, and then hold it between your hands as you sit in front of your altar. Visualize energy from the chestnut surrounding you. When it is clear in your mind, end the session. Keep the chestnut with you until you feel that the threat is gone.

Use oil infused with chestnut flowers to prepare candles for spells to attract abundance and prosperity. Steep a few flowers in a couple of tablespoons of olive oil for a week. Strain the plant material out and store the oil in a dark glass bottle. Also use it to prepare candles for meditation, especially when seeking peace of mind.

CRABAPPLE

American Crabapple (*Malus coronaria* syn. *Pyrus coronaria*);
   also known as sweet crabapple.
European Crabapple (*M. sylvestris*); also known as appelthorn,
   scrog, wild crabapple.

With a short, crooked trunk, the crabapple usually reaches between fifteen to twenty-five feet tall. What this tree may lack in height, it makes up for with a showy display of fragrant flowers that can range from white to pink to almost rosy. It has oval leaves and its small branches have short thorns. By August, the little green crabapples become noticeable, and in the autumn, they turn dark red as they ripen. Less than two inches in diameter, the fruit is edible but bitter or sour. When cooked and sweetened, crabapples make excellent jams and jellies. Crabapples gathered after the first hard frost are not as tart.

As their names imply, one tree is native to North America and the other to Europe. The species name of the European crabapple, *sylvestris*, means "of the woods."[57]

Like other types of apples, crabapples were regarded as a fruit of knowledge, magic, and prophecy. The tree held an important place in Celtic mythology; one reason may be because it was often host to the mysterious mistletoe. The legendary Avalon, Isle of Apples, and the place where King Arthur was taken to recover from his wounds, was populated with wild crabapple trees. Encountering the tree in England, eighth-century Vikings called it *scrabba* or *scrab*, which eventually evolved into or was mistaken for the word *crab*.[58] According to folklore, the name refers to the sour taste, which was said to be as bad as the bite of a crab. In England, the fruit was known as *sur appel*, "sour apple."[59]

With the lack of clean drinking water during medieval times, crabapple cider was a safer alternative, assuming it wasn't as strong as the potent Celtic fermentation. Tea was made with crabapples by boiling and sweetening them. During the Middle Ages, a special beverage called *lamasool* or *lamb's wool* made with ale, sugar, spices, and roasted crabapples was reserved for the evenings of October 31 and November 1.[60] Highly astringent, crabapples were used medicinally to treat sore throats, inflammation, and skin ailments.

It was customary for young women to gather crabapples to use for love divination on Michaelmas (September 29), a Christian quarter day dedicated to the archangel Michael. When eaten with cucumber and cheese before going to bed, crabapples were said to inspire erotic dreams. In weather lore, a heavy crop of fruit in the autumn indicated a hard winter to follow. Occasionally used as a boundary marker in England, the crabapple tree was sometimes referred to as appelthorn.

57. Allen Coombes, *Dictionary of Plant Names* (Portland, OR: Timber Press, Inc., 1985), 202.

58. Staub, *75 Remarkable Fruits for Your Garden*, 55.

59. Hooke, *Trees in Anglo-Saxon England*, 249.

60. D. C. Watts, *Elsevier's Dictionary of Plant Lore* (Burlington, MA: Academic Press, 2007), 90; and Richard Folkard, *Plant Lore, Legends, and Lyrics: Embracing the Myths, Traditions, Superstitions, and Folklore of the Plant Kingdom*, 2nd ed. (London: Sampson, Low, Marston, & Company, 1892), 202.

Magical Connections

Elements:	Air, water
Astrological influence:	Venus; Aquarius, Cancer, Libra, Taurus
Deities:	Aphrodite, Apollo, Athena, Badb, Cailleach Bheur, Diana, Dionysus, Eros, Flora, Freya, Hera, Lugh, Macha, Manannan, Rhiannon, Venus, Zeus
Magical beings and woodland spirits:	Elves, fairies
Wildlife:	Butterfly, cedar waxwing, grosbeak, hedgehog, pig
Ogham:	Quert/Ceirt ⏇
Alternate tree calendar:	June 25 to July 4 and December 22 to January 1
Runes:	Ingwaz/Ing/Inguz ᛜ Runic half month: May 14 to May 28
Powers/attributes:	Abundance, ancestors, death/funeral practices, divination, enchantment, fertility, happiness, healing, love, money/prosperity, the otherworld, protection, spirit guides/spirits, wisdom
Other associations:	The otherworld; Beltane, Lughnasadh, Samhain, Yule

Items to purchase when the tree is not available: fresh or dried crabapples; flower essence made from the European crabapple.

Spellwork and Ritual

Use crabapple blossoms in spells to invite abundance and prosperity into your home. Before performing a spell to attract a lover, prepare yourself with a bath by sprinkling a handful of crabapple flower petals in the water. When you are finished bathing, collect the petals and place them in a bowl on your altar.

When interacting with fairies, carry a crabapple branch or wand to help open the way to their realm. It also provides magical protection. Hold a branch or wand while doing spells for protection or hang it over your altar. When seeking knowledge for making an important decision, light a candle and meditate as you sit in front of your altar holding a crabapple leaf in each hand. To raise energy for healing, prepare a candle with the flower essence.

Associated with Beltane, crabapple blossoms are a traditional and symbolic flower to place on the altar. If your tree blooms too early for the sabbat, place a few flowers in a container in the freezer, and then bring them out just before your ritual. For Samhain, place a circle of crabapples on your altar to acknowledge the dead and honor your ancestors.

CYPRESS

Italian Cypress (*Cupressus sempervirens*); also known as common
    cypress, graveyard cypress, Mediterranean cypress, tree of death,
    Tuscan cypress.
Arizona Cypress (*C. arizonica*); also known as silver cypress.

Reaching forty to sixty feet and sometimes eighty, the Italian cypress is an evergreen that grows in narrow, columnar form. Its dense, gray-green, scale-like foliage is strongly aromatic when crushed. Its round, knobby cones grow in clusters. After opening in early autumn to shed seeds, the cones stay on the tree for several years. The Italian cypress is native to southern Europe and western Asia. The evergreen Arizona cypress has scale-like foliage that ranges from gray-green to blue-green and has a silvery-gray shimmer. Its cones are small and reddish brown. Unlike its Italian cousin, it has the quintessential Christmas-tree shape. Native to the American southwest, Arizona cypress can grow forty to fifty feet tall and is often a host for mistletoe.

The genus *Cupressus* is the Latin name for this tree. Throughout the ancient world, the Italian cypress was highly valued for medicinal and religious purposes. A sacred grove of cypress once grew at the Nemea sanctuary of Zeus located on the Peloponnese peninsula of southern Greece.

Although there are a number of versions for the Greek myth concerning a young man named *Cyparissus*, the gist of them is that he was heartbroken after accidentally killing a beloved stag that belonged to Apollo. His grief was so great that he was transformed into a cypress tree, which at that time already represented sorrow. In keeping with the symbolism, Venus wore a cypress wreath while mourning for Adonis. Despite its association with death, planting two cypress trees near a home was said to bring peace and prosperity to the household.

Upper class Romans grew these trees around their villas and had them trimmed into exotic shapes. The cypress was an important part of Renaissance gardens and its use for topiary re-emerged in seventeenth-century France and England. Also popular for gardens in the Middle East, the cypress was frequently used as a motif in Persian carpets.

Valued by the Greeks for use in temples, cypress wood is hard and close-grained with a reddish hue. During the Middle Ages and Renaissance, the wood was commonly used for musical instruments, including church organ pipes. Imported from Italy, cypress chests were popular in England throughout the fifteenth and sixteenth centuries for storing linens and valuables.

As an evergreen with durable wood, Italian cypress is a tree of mixed messages. In ancient Egypt, the wood was used for coffins, which may have been the beginning of its association as a tree of death. On the other hand, because the tree can live up to a thousand years, it was also associated with immortality. However, once a cypress is cut down, it does not sprout back, which is why it symbolized the finality of death to the Romans.

In addition to using the wood for coffins during the Middles Ages in southern Europe, garlands of cypress branches were draped on funeral biers and sometimes placed in the coffins. In Turkey, these aromatic trees were planted in and around graveyards for the symbolism and to neutralize unpleasant odors. Perhaps inheriting the association with death from its European counterpart, the Arizona cypress is frequently found in Texan cemeteries.

Magical Connections

Elements:	Earth, water
Astrological influence:	Pluto, Saturn; Aquarius, Capricorn, Pisces, Taurus, Virgo
Deities:	Adonis, Aphrodite, Apollo, Artemis, Astarte, Cupid, Diana, the Fates, the Furies, Hades, Hecate, Jupiter, Mithra, Pluto, Saturn
Magical beings and woodland spirits:	Elves
Wildlife:	Owl
Alternate tree calendar:	July 26 to August 4 and January 25 to February 3
Powers/attributes:	The afterlife, ancestors, awareness (enhance, heighten), banish, bind, changes/transitions, clarity (enhance, foster), concentration/focus, confidence, consecrate/bless, death/funeral practices, defense, divination, emotions (deal with, support), growth, healing, justice/legal matters, knowledge (seek, acquire), loss/sorrow (ease, recover from), the otherworld, past-life work, peace, protection, release (let go, move on), renewal, security, strength, stress/anxiety (calm, release), transformation, wisdom
Other associations:	Samhain

Items to purchase when the tree is not available: essential oil made from the needles and twigs of the Italian cypress, boxes and other small items made from cypress wood.

Spellwork and Ritual

Cypress is a powerful ally to provide comfort and healing, especially when dealing with death and loss. Use cypress essential oil to prepare a candle or place it in a diffuser to scent a meditation space. At Samhain, place a sprig on your altar to remember and honor ancestors and other loved ones who have passed beyond the veil. Cypress is instrumental for past-life work.

Burning a piece of cypress wood is effective for centering and grounding energy before and after ritual. It is also an aid for focusing the mind. Burn a little piece of foliage or use the essential oil to consecrate and bless ritual objects or in spells for defensive magic. Hold a branch during ritual or meditation when seeking truth and knowledge and to stimulate growth and renewal. Holding a couple of cypress cones fosters awareness and clarity for divination and channeling. Place a branch of cypress on your altar for strength and wisdom when seeking justice. Hang one over your front door for protection.

DOGWOOD

Cornelian Cherry Dogwood (*Cornus mas*); also known as cornelian
  tree, European cornel.
Flowering Dogwood (*C. florida* syn. *Cynoxylon floridum*); also known
  as American boxwood, false box, Florida dogwood, pegwood.
Mountain Dogwood (*C. nuttallii*); also known as Pacific dogwood,
  Pacific flowering dogwood.

Reaching fifteen to twenty-five feet tall, the cornelian cherry dogwood is one of the earliest
trees to bloom in the spring. Its yellow, star-shaped flowers grow in tight, rounded clusters.
The edible fruit is bright red and closely resembles a cherry. This tree is native to central
and southern Europe and western Asia. The other two dogwoods are showy attention-
getters when they come into bloom. However, what appear to be large, notched white petals
are actually bracts (modified leaves) that protect the tiny cluster of greenish-white flowers

in the center. Native to eastern North America, the flowering dogwood reaches fifteen to thirty-five feet tall. This tree has white or pink flowers and dark-green leaves that turn scarlet in the autumn. Its bright red fruit is not edible for humans. The mountain dogwood is the western equivalent to the flowering dogwood. Reaching fifteen to forty feet tall, its white flowers are sometimes tinged with pink. The fruit is orange to red and its leaves turn yellow or orange in the fall.

The genus name of these trees comes from the Latin *cornu*, meaning "horn" because of the hardness of their wood.[61] Its common name has nothing to do with canines; in fact, in earlier times the tree was called *dagwood*. In Germany, the dense wood was used to make skewers and other pointed tools as well as sturdy prods for farm animals. The prods were called *dags*; pronounced with an "a" sound as in father.[62] In America, the name was misunderstood and evolved into dogwood.

Colonial settlers used the wood of the flowering dogwood to make weaving shuttles, pegs, spools, and pulleys. The bark, twigs, and fruit of these trees were used medicinally on both sides of the Atlantic. The roots of the flowering dogwood and the bark of the cornelian cherry have been used to make red dye. Cultivated since ancient times, the fruit of the cornelian cherry has been used for jams, desserts, liquors, and a wine called *vin de corneulle*. This tree was also used as a hedge plant in Europe. Cool weather that occurred after the dogwood bloomed was known as a dogwood winter.

In the Balkans, pieces of dogwood were worn as amulets for protection and placed in the cradles of newborns to ward off witches. There was also a belief that cutting down a young dogwood would bring death to a family. In the Basque area of northern Spain, branches were used as divining rods. In Germany, a handkerchief dabbed in the sap of a dogwood and carried on Midsummer's Day, was believed to make a wish come true.

In ancient Greece, the wood of the cornelian cherry was used for spear shafts, bows, javelins, and other weapons. According to Roman folklore, a dogwood tree sprung up on the spot where a javelin thrown by Romulus (the mythological founder of the city) hit the ground on the Palatine Hill. The tree became a protective talisman for the city. In later centuries, a spear of dogwood with a hardened tip was commonly used to challenge and declare war against enemies.

---

61. Barbara G. Hallowell, *Mountain Year: A Southern Appalachian Nature Notebook* (Winston-Salem, NC: John F. Blair, Publisher, 1998), 89.

62. Ibid.

Magical Connections

Elements:	Air, earth
Astrological influence:	Jupiter (cornelian cherry dogwood), Mars, Moon
Magical beings and woodland spirits:	Kraneia (Greek tree nymph that inhabits the cornelian cherry dogwood)
Powers/attributes:	Banish, creativity, defense, healing, inspiration, loyalty/fidelity, manifest (desires, dreams, will), protection, wishes
Other associations:	Ostara, Beltane, Midsummer's Eve

Items to purchase when the tree is not available: flower essence is made from the mountain dogwood and usually marketed as Pacific dogwood.

Spellwork and Ritual

The energy of the dogwood helps to foster and maintain loyalty and fidelity. Carry a small piece of twig to engender this in the people around you but only if you are deserving of it. Sitting under a dogwood is said to inspire new ideas and to help gain a new perspective on a situation or problem. The energy of the dogwood also provides emotional support.

To call on the protective power of this tree, place a few leaves under your welcome mat to serve as guardians of your home. Because we now call it dogwood, think of the leaves as guard dogs. A small piece of wood can be used as a protective talisman. Burn a few dried leaves to banish what you do not want in your life. While dogwood is associated with wishes and has been used in charms for getting one's own way, this purpose should be used judiciously. Ask for what you want without being manipulative in any way.

The yellow flowers of the cornelian cherry can be used on your Ostara altar to welcome the sun and change of season. Blooming in time for Beltane, use the flowers of the other dogwoods on your altar to boost energy. For esbat rituals, make a circle with a few white bracts on your altar to draw down lunar energy.

ELDER

American Elderberry (*Sambucus canadensis*); also known as American
 black elderberry, Canada elderberry, common elderberry.
European Elder (*S. nigra*); also known as black elder, elderberry, ellhorn, fairy tree, lady elder, pipe tree.

Growing five to twelve feet tall and wide, the American elderberry is native to eastern
North America. The European elder reaches between eight to twenty feet tall and wide.
It is native to Europe, northern Africa, and southwestern Asia. The leaves of both elders
are oval, and their small, white flowers grow in large umbel clusters that can reach up
to ten inches wide. An umbel is a type of flower head that resembles the structure of
an umbrella. The flowers give way to large pendulous clusters of bluish-black berries.
The flowers of the American elderberry have a lemon-like scent; the European elder are
musky.

Although the roots, stems, and leaves are toxic, they have been used for medicinal purposes in the past. The fruit is tart but edible and often used for jam and wine. Ripe elderberries appear light blue because of a waxy coating. Elderberries have an extremely long history of use and have been found in excavations of Stone Age sites. Also edible, elderflowers are used to make tea and wine.

In Denmark, it was believed that standing under an elder on Midsummer's Eve allowed a person to see the fairy king and his entourage. Likewise, in England, adding elderflowers to the Midsummer's Eve bonfire allowed people to see fairies and nature spirits. Growing this shrub in the garden served as an invitation to fairies and other nature spirits who were said to like swinging and playing amongst the branches. On the Isle of Man, most houses had at least one elder tree to please the *fae*.

Elder branches have been used to make flutes and pipes, which is the source of its name *pipe tree*. Music played on a flute of elder wood was said to have the same power as a wand. At Beltane, an elder branch was used to consecrate the circle and a woven crown of twigs was worn to foster second sight. At other times, the flowers and leaves were used for consecration and blessings. In Sweden, pregnant women would kiss an elder tree for good luck in childbirth.

Elder is a tree of the Crone. According to the folklore of several countries, an old female spirit lived in the elder tree. In Germany, this spirit was known as Frau Ellhorn; in Denmark she was Hyldemoer, "elder mother."[63] In England, cutting down an elder without asking for the Crone's permission was considered very unwise due to potentially negative consequences. This is why elders growing in hedgerows were often left untrimmed.

In tenth-century England, it was believed that the spirit of an elder tree could turn into a witch. In some parts of England, the tree itself was regarded as a witch. This belief was also held in Europe where elders were cut on Midsummer Eve "to make them bleed" and "deprive them of their powers."[64] Although it was thought that witches liked to gather under elders, the wood was believed to have the power to ward off evil and it was used as a charm against witchcraft. However, in Oxfordshire, England, burning elder wood could cause a person to become bewitched. In Germany, fingernail clippings were buried under an elder to keep witches from using them to cast spells and hexes. Also in

---

63. Porteous, *The Forest in Folklore and Mythology*, 90.

64. Watts, *Elsevier's Dictionary of Plant Lore*, 130.

Germany, the elder was associated with spirits because it often grew in boggy areas, the habitat of the will-o-the-wisp. While elder was believed to provide protection from fairies, it was also said to protect good fairies from bad ones.

Making a baby's cradle with elder wood was regarded unlucky because it was believed to bring problems later in life for the child. Because of their heavy, musty odor, the smell of European elder flowers was thought to cause illness or even death. Nevertheless, an elder tree growing on one's property indicated prosperity. According to weather lore in Belgium, a cut branch of elder was placed in a jug of water on December 30. If it developed buds, the summer would be fruitful; if not, the harvest would not be good.

Magical Connections

Elements:	Air, earth, fire, water
Astrological influence:	Mercury, Venus
Deities:	Bertha, Boann, Cailleach Bheur, the Dagda, Danu, Freya, Freyr, Gaia, Holle, Hulda, Rhea, Venus, Vulcan
Magical beings and woodland spirits:	Elves, fairies, will-o-the-wisp (a sprite carried by or existing as a wisp of light)
Wildlife:	Horse (European elder), pheasant, raven, rook
Ogham:	Ruis ⊪
Celtic calendar:	November 25–December 22

Runes:	Fehu/Fe/Feoh ᚠ
	    Runic half month: June 29 to July 1
	Jera/Ger/Jara ᛃ
	    Runic half month: December 13 to 27

Powers/attributes:	Abundance, banish, challenges/obstacles (overcome), changes/transitions, consecrate/bless, creativity, death/funeral practices, defense, dream work, healing, hexes (remove, ward off), knowledge (seek, acquire), love, loyalty/fidelity, money/prosperity, protection, purification, release (let go, move on), renewal, security, spirituality, success, wisdom
Other associations:	The Crone; Walpurgis, Beltane, Litha, Midsummer's Eve

Items to use when the tree is not available: elderberry juice, dried elderberries, elderberry seed oil made from the European elder, flower essences made from the European elder and the red elderberry (*S. racemose*).

Spellwork and Ritual

Use elderflowers to add power to spells. If you are concerned about hexes or dark magic, hang elderflowers over your altar and call on the power of Lady Elder for protection. Elderflowers can be used as an offering in ritual. Sprinkle flower water or flower essence to cleanse an area before ritual or magic work. As an alternative, burn dried elder leaves to smudge an area. Associated with death and funerals, burying elderflowers with the deceased or strewing them on the grave aids a loved one's passage into the otherworld.

Elderberries add potent energy to love charms and in spells to foster fidelity. For healing circles, place a handful of berries on your altar to support and boost the energy. The flower essence or a little elderberry juice can be used to consecrate candles. Use crumbled, dried berries in a sachet to enhance sleep and to encourage dreams. Place a picture of an elder tree on your altar during November and December to celebrate the power of the Crone.

ELM

American Elm (*Ulmus Americana* syn. *U. americana* var. *floridana*, *U. floridana*); also known as soft elm, water elm, white elm.

English Elm (*U. procera* syn. *U. campestris*, *U. surculosa*); also known as common elm, ellum, elven.

Wych Elm (*U. glabra* syn. *U. campestre*); also known as horn birch, hornbeam, quicken, Scots elm, witch elm, witchwood.

Indigenous to eastern North America, the American elm reaches sixty to eighty feet tall. Hanging clusters of tiny reddish-green flowers appear in the early spring before the dark green, slightly oval leaves emerge. The English elm is larger, reaching up to 130 feet tall. Appearing before the leaves, its small flowers hang in tassel-like clusters. This elm is native to southern and western Europe. The leaves of both these trees turn yellow in the autumn. Elm seeds are encased in an oval, papery wing. As large as the English elm, the wych elm can be difficult to distinguish from its cousin. However, its flowers and seeds are larger, and its leaves turn dull yellow in the autumn. The wych elm is native to northern and central Europe and Asia Minor.

Elm is an iconic shade tree that has been vividly described as "Gothic-arched sylvan splendor."[65] In the nineteenth century, the elm was the most popular city tree in America, and by the twentieth century this graceful tree shaded many urban streets.

Like the chestnut, the elm has fallen victim to disease. First noted in the Netherlands, Dutch elm disease is caused by a fungus that is spread by a bark beetle. Hybrids are being developed to withstand the disease. For now, it is difficult to find large elms because the disease kills young trees before their trunks can reach a foot in diameter.

Like witch hazel, the word *wych*, from Old English meaning "to bend," was applied to this tree because of its pliant branches.[66] Although today only one species is called *wych elm*, in the past all elms were known by this name in England.

The Greeks and Romans dedicated the elm to their goddesses Demeter and Ceres; the sacred grove of Juno contained elms. The Greeks also associated this tree with Morpheus, the god of dreams. In addition to this association, Roman poet Virgil noted that the elm was a tree of prophecy.

The tree was called *elven* because elves and fairies were said to be fond of it. Elms were believed to have the power to ward off evil spirits, witches, and devils. In many parts of England, twigs of wych elm were attached to the bridles of horses for protection while traveling. In Oxfordshire, this tree was used as a charm against witches and magic. Well into the early twentieth century in Germany, all types of elms served as rag and nail trees; petitioned for healing by nailing a piece of cloth or tying a hank of hair to the tree.

Regarded as a tree of justice and judgment, the Normans used elms as execution trees. For these purposes during the Middle Ages, elms were often planted in front of castles. They were also used as border markers between estates. The great elm of Gisors, France, located near Château de Gisors castle was a traditional meeting place for the Dukes of Normandy and the king of France. After discussions went awry with the Normans, King Phillip II (1165–1223) had the tree destroyed in 1188.[67]

---

65. William Cullina, *Native Trees, Shrubs and Vines* (New York City: Houghton Mifflin, 2002), 248.

66. Laura C. Martin, *The Folklore of Trees & Shrubs* (Chester, CT: The Globe Pequot Press, 1992), 207.

67. Daniel Power, *The Norman Frontier in the Twelfth and Early Thirteenth Centuries* (New York: Cambridge University Press, 2004), 16.

Magical Connections

Elements:	Air, earth, water
Astrological influence:	Mercury, Saturn; Capricorn
Deities:	Ceres, Cerridwen, Danu, Demeter, Dionysus, Gaia, Holle, Juno, Loki, Morpheus, Odin, Ran
Magical beings and woodland spirits:	Elves, fairies, Ptelea (Greek tree nymph)
Wildlife:	Deer, lapwing, rabbit, grouse (ruffed)
Ogham:	Ailm/Ailim ᚛
Alternate tree calendar:	July 15 to 25 and January 12 to 24

Runes:	Gebo/Gyfu X
	        Runic half month: September 28 to October 12
	Mannaz/Madhr/Mann ᛗ
	        Runic half month: April 14 to 28

Powers/attributes:	Attraction, changes/transitions, determination/endurance, divination, dream work, healing, intuition, justice/legal matters, love/loyalty/fidelity, manifest (desires, dreams, will), negativity (remove, ward off), prophecy, protection, psychic abilities, renewal, wisdom, wishes
Other associations:	Yule

Items to purchase when the tree is not available: flower essence is made from the English elm.

Spellwork and Ritual

Dedicated to the god of dreams, the elm is a good ally for dream work. Before bedtime, hold a picture of an elm tree between your hands, ground and center your energy, and clear your mind. Afterwards, place the picture on your bedside table. When you wake up in the morning, write down everything you can remember from your dreams. When seeking justice, write your goal on a picture of an elm. Safely burn it as you visualize the energy manifesting into reality. When the ashes are cool, scatter them outside.

Use an elm leaf for a love charm to invite romance into your life. To boost protective energy, place a twig near your front door or in the attic and visualize the energy of the elm surrounding your home. To enhance divination and psychic work, prepare a white candle by carving the word *elm* on it. Also use the candle during dark moon rituals. To raise healing energy, use a green candle.

EUCALYPTUS

Blue Gum Eucalyptus (*Eucalyptus globulus*); also known as eucalypt,
    fever tree, gum tree, southern blue gum, and Tasmanian blue gum.
Lemon-Scented Gum (*E. citriodora* syn. *E. maculata* var. *citriodora*,
    Corymbia citriodora); also known as eucalypt, lemon eucalyptus,
    lemon gum tree, spotted gum.

The blue gum eucalyptus is a massive tree that can reach 300 feet tall in its native habitat
of Australia. However, in areas where it was introduced, it reaches only about half that
size. The tree's smooth blue-gray bark peels off in large pieces exposing a creamy color
underneath. The blue gum has narrow blue-green to yellowish-green leaves, feathery

creamy-white flowers, and top-shaped seedpods. The lemon eucalyptus grows to about one hundred feet tall and has narrow tapering leaves. Its pale bark sheds in curling flakes giving the trunk a mottled or spotted appearance. When crushed, its pale green leaves have a lemony scent. It also has feathery creamy-white flowers but its seedpods are urn-shaped.

Known worldwide as a powerful antiseptic and a soothing cold remedy, eucalyptus oil was used medicinally for centuries by the Aboriginal people of Australia. They used eucalyptus wood and bark for items in and around the home and for canoes, spears, and boomerangs. Aboriginal artists used panels of bark as canvases for their paintings. Still used for making didgeridoos (a traditional ceremonial and ritual musical instrument), large, hollow eucalyptus branches are highly prized. This tree is integral to Aboriginal stories of the Dreamtime, the period when ancestral spirits created the world. Eucalyptus is regarded as particularly sacred to a number of Aboriginal tribes.

The genus and common names for these trees come from the Greek *eu*, meaning "well," and *kalypto*, meaning "covered", which describes how the dangling seedpods almost cover the young flower buds.[68] Eucalyptus is called *gum tree* in reference to the sticky gum-like substance it secretes. Although eucalyptus trees have been planted as ornamentals outside of their native Australia, they have escaped the garden and made themselves at home in the wild. In some areas of California, the blue gum is now regarded as an invasive species.

Landing in Australia in 1688, botanist and navigator William Dampier (1651/1652–1715) was the first Englishman to explore Australia and document the eucalyptus tree.[69] According to some sources, his voyage around the world wasn't completely above-board scientific exploration because he was a bit of a privateer and pirate, too, lifting bounty from other ships when the opportunity arose. Nevertheless, his botanical work piqued interest in these exotic trees back home in England and on the Continent. During the nineteenth century, eucalyptus was introduced into California, southern Europe, Egypt, South Africa, and India.

---

68. Martin, *The Folklore of Trees & Shrubs*, 79.

69. Wells, *Lives of the Trees*, 127.

Magical Connections

Elements:	Air, earth, water
Astrological influence:	Mercury, Moon, Saturn, Sun; Cancer, Pisces
Deities:	Luna, Mercury, Selene, Venus
Wildlife:	Koala, kookaburra
Powers/attributes all eucalyptus:	Ancestors, banish, communication, concentration/focus, consecrate/bless, determination/endurance, dream work, emotions (deal with, support), family and home, happiness, healing, knowledge (seek, acquire), loss/sorrow (ease, recover from), negativity (remove, ward off), past-life work, protection, psychic abilities, purification, release (let go, move on), security, spirit guides/spirits, spirituality, strength, wisdom
Powers/attributes lemon eucalyptus:	Balance/harmony, growth

Items to purchase when the tree is not available: leaves, seedpods, essential oils made from the leaves of both the blue gum and lemon-scented trees.

Spellwork and Ritual

Eucalyptus is best known for its powers of purification. Burn dried leaves to dispel negative energy and to consecrate your ritual space. Use a little of the essential oil to prepare a candle for meditation or magic work. Wear a sprig of leaves or flowers as an amulet for protection against emotional upsets. Diffuse a little essential oil for emotional healing after a quarrel. The scent is also effective for releasing sorrow and developing a sense of well-being and security. Use eucalyptus essential oil in the home to raise the spiritual vibration. When sending healing energy to someone, write the person's name on a piece of paper and dab it with the oil.

Eucalyptus provides strength and determination for carrying out a purpose. Use a strip of peeled bark to write a few keywords about your purpose, and then burn it in your cauldron as you visualize it manifesting into reality. Dried leaves and/or flowers facilitate dream and psychic work as well as communication with spirits. Keep a few with you in a small organza bag while you engage in these practices. Diffuse a little eucalyptus oil before spell work; the scent increases concentration. Eucalyptus attracts happiness when used in candle magic.

This tree is instrumental for protection and for banishing anything unwanted from your life. Any part of the tree can be used to support past-life work. Use seedpods to make a circle on your altar for esbat rituals to amplify lunar energy.

FIG

Bodhi Tree (*Ficus religiosa*); also known as bo tree, pipal, banyan fig, sacred fig.

Common Fig (*F. carica*); also known as Adriatic fig, cultivated fig, edible fig, true fig.

Sycamore Fig (*F. sycomorus*); also known as Egyptian sycamore, mulberry fig.

Figs are spreading trees that are usually as wide as they are tall. The fig is not a fruit per se, but a receptacle filled with tiny flowers that develop into ripened seeds. The Bodhi tree is an evergreen that stands between sixty and one hundred feet tall. It is native to India, Southeast Asia, and southwest China. Its purple fruit grows singly or in pairs. Indigenous to northwest India and southwest Asia, the common fig usually reaches ten to twenty feet tall. Growing singly, the slightly pear-shaped fruit ripens to a maroon-brown color. The sycamore fig is native to the Middle East and parts of Africa. It reaches forty to fifty feet tall. Growing in clusters, the fruit is smaller than the common fig.

People have enjoyed figs for thousands of years as evidenced by the seeds found in excavations of Neolithic sites in the Jordan Valley dating to around 11,000 BCE and in Egypt 5400–5600 BCE.[70] The Babylonians and the people of the Indus Valley revered the fig tree. The Arabs considered the fruit a gift from heaven. In symbol and fact, it was a tree of life. The fruit was an important food in the ancient world and the leaves were used to wrap fish and other food for cooking.

Revered as sacred, the Greeks and Romans dedicated the common fig tree to a number of gods and goddesses. Greek athletes consumed the fruit before competitions to enhance strength and speed. The Romans used figs as offerings in temples at the beginning of the new year. Statues of Saturn were crowned with fig leaves. Also dedicated to Juno, women left offerings to her underneath fig trees. Pliny the Elder noted that there were about twenty-nine types of figs under cultivation.

In addition to grape vines, Dionysus was often depicted with a crown of fig leaves. During Bacchanalian festivals, women wore necklaces of figs to symbolize fecundity. The tree was regarded as phallic and its milky sap represented the semen of the god Mars. The fruit was an important item on the menu at Roman wedding feasts. Many centuries later, figs remained a symbol of fertility and Bulgarian brides were given baskets of figs to represent future children. In Dutch folk medicine, eating figs during pregnancy was said to result in an easy birth.

While the Greeks revered this tree, they also mistrusted it and considered it unsafe to sleep under. In parts of Italy, there was a belief that an evil spirit lived in the leaves. On the other hand, a legend from India told of a wild fig tree that only flowered at night; to see it would endow a person with the ability to see departed friends and protect living ones from evil. The tree was also generally regarded as protective and a fig branch placed in front of the door before leaving home would ensure a person's return.

Although the Egyptians cultivated the common fig and used it for offerings, the sycamore fig was more highly revered. The name is often spelled *sycomore* to avoid confusion with the sycamore/plane tree of the *Platanus* genus. Osiris is associated with the fig tree, sky goddess Nut offered figs to the souls of the departed, and Hathor was known

70. Daniel Zohary, Maria Hopf, and Ehud Weiss, *Domestication of Plants in the Old World*, 4th ed. (New York: Oxford University Press, 2012), 129.

as the Lady of the Sycamore, referring to the fig tree. Considered a suitable food for the afterlife, figs were placed among the funerary objects in graves. The wood was used for mummy portraits and the fruit was depicted in paintings on the walls of tombs.

Siddhartha Gautama (c. 563/566–486 BCE), found a suitable place for meditation under a fig tree in Bodh Gaya, a small town in northern India, where he achieved enlightenment and became the Buddha. Over time, Bodhi trees were regarded as a symbol of the Buddha's presence and worshipped. Before the original tree in Bodh Gaya was destroyed, a young Buddhist nun took a cutting of it with her back to Sri Lanka in the third century BCE. Known as the Sri Maha Bodhi tree, it is still growing today. These trees have been planted at many Buddhist temples throughout the world. The Bodhi tree is also regarded as sacred in Hinduism and Jainism.

Magical Connections

Elements:	Air, water
Astrological influence:	Jupiter, Venus
Deities:	Bacchus, Buddha, Ceres, Demeter, Dionysus, Hathor, Hermes, Iris, Juno, Mars, Mercury, Nut, Persephone, Ra, Osiris, Saturn, Toth, Vishnu
Magical beings and woodland spirits:	Syke (Greek tree nymph)
Wildlife:	Baboon, wasp
Alternate tree calendar:	June 14 to 23 and December 12 to 21
Powers/attributes all figs:	Abundance, ancestors, balance/harmony, creativity, death/funeral practices, fertility, love, money/prosperity, peace, protection, psychic abilities
Powers/attributes Bodhi fig:	Awareness (enhance, heighten), knowledge (seek, acquire), spirituality, transformation, wisdom
Other associations:	Samhain

Items to purchase when the tree is not available: fresh or dried figs, fig juice.

Spellwork and Ritual

Place a fig on your altar as an offering to your chosen deity or use fig juice as a libation. Include the fruit on your Samhain altar to symbolically feed your ancestors. Eat a fig as part of a fertility spell. Used dried figs to attract abundance and prosperity. Burn a small piece of wood to deepen spiritual meditation and foster a sense of peace. Place a twig in your workspace to enhance creativity. Place a picture of a Bodhi tree on your altar when seeking wisdom.

FIR

Balsam Fir (*Abies balsamea*); also known as blister fir, Canadian balsam, eastern fir.

European Silver Fir (*A. alba*); also known as common silver fir.

White Fir (*A. concolor*); also known as Rocky Mountain white fir.

Reaching up to eighty feet tall, the balsam fir has a narrow spire-like crown. The upper branches grow at right angles from the trunk; the lower branches droop. Its curved needles are dark green, and its cylindrical cones are grayish green with a slight purple tinge. The European silver fir has a pyramid shape, but with age its crown becomes flattened. This tree can reach heights of 130 to 165 feet. The grooved needles are dark green, and the cylindrical cones turn reddish brown as they mature. The white fir typically grows forty to seventy feet tall but sometimes reaches over one hundred. It has a narrow conical shape with a spire-like crown that becomes flattened with age. It has blue-green needles and barrel-shaped cones that turn brownish purple with age. Also see the section "Is That a Spruce, Pine, or Fir Tree?" in the profile for spruce.

The coniferous trees of the genus *Abies* are native only to the northern hemisphere. Silver fir is native to the uplands of central and southern Europe and Germany's Black Forest. White fir comes from the mountains of western North America. Balsam fir is native to the northern Untied States and Canada. It is usually found in uplands as well as swampy areas. The balsam is popular as a Christmas tree because of its shape and pungent fragrance.

The genus name for these trees comes from the Latin *abire* meaning "to rise," in reference to the sometimes soaring height of the European tree.[71] While the tree's common name comes from the Old Norse *fyri* and Old Danish *fyr*, which were names for the tree, in Old English *fyr* meant "fire."[72] According to English botanist John Gerard, the fir was also called *firre tree* because fir-wood was good firewood due its resin, which made it burn well.[73] Fir tree resin has had a wide range of medicinal uses in Europe and North America.

Throughout Europe, the fir tree was considered the king of the forest and home to many powerful woodland spirits. Because it was associated with Artemis and Diana, huntsmen hung the heads of wolves on fir trees as offerings and asked for protection during their dangerous endeavors. In Scandinavian folktales, fir was associated with the general spirit of the forest. The tree was also believed to have a strong connection with the person on whose land it grew and any catastrophe that befell the tree was a bad omen for the landowner.

Regarded as a birth tree, fir needles were burned during childbirth to protect mothers and babies. In addition to birth, the fir tree was a symbol of rebirth and immortality. In Romania, boughs of fir were carried at the front of funeral processions. As the year turned toward a new beginning, German Pagans took boughs into their homes to celebrate Yule and to provide comfort for visiting elves.

71. Wells, *Lives of the Trees*, 136.

72. Gordon Gordh, comp. *A Dictionary of Entomology*, 2nd ed. (Cambridge, MA: CABI Publishing, 2011), 573.

73. John Gerard, *The Herball or Generall Historie of Plantes* (London: John Norton, 1597), 1181.

Magical Connections

Elements:	Air, earth, fire
Astrological influence:	Jupiter, Mars, Saturn, Uranus; Aries
Deities:	Artemis, Athena, Bacchus, Cybele, Diana, Dionysus, Frigg, Inanna, Isis, Osiris, Pan, Persephone, Rhea
Magical beings and woodland spirits:	Boruta (Polish wood sprite), dwarves, elves, fairies
Wildlife:	Lapwing, porcupine, sparrow
Ogham:	Ailm/Ailim ⊢
Alternate tree calendar:	July 5 to 14 and January 2 to 11
Rune:	Berkanan/Bjarkan/Beorc ᛒ Runic half month: March 14 to 28
Powers/attributes:	Awareness (enhance, heighten), balance/harmony, changes/transitions, clarity (enhance, foster), communication, creativity, death/funeral practices, defense, divination, emotions (deal with, support), growth, happiness, healing, hexes (remove, ward off), hope, inspiration, loss/sorrow (ease, recover from), money/prosperity, the otherworld, peace, protection, psychic abilities, purification, renewal, security, spirit guides/spirits, spirituality, strength, support (provide, receive), transformation
Other associations:	Beltane, Yule

Items to purchase when the tree is not available: essential oil made from the needles of the European silver fir.

Spellwork and Ritual

Fir is a tree of beginnings, energy, growth, and healing. Burn a few dried needles to purify an area before ritual or magic work and afterwards to aid in grounding energy. Hold a cluster of needles or a cone during meditation to foster clear communication and creative expression. To kindle inspiration, place a few needles or a couple of cones in your workspace.

As an all-purpose purifier, fir provides protection and helps to overcome and remove hexes. The scent of fir heightens awareness for divination and spiritual work and is especially effective for connecting with forest spirits. Use a small branch or a couple of cones for prosperity spells and for support during channeling. The scent of fir also aids in focusing energy inward to restore memories.

Associated with the otherworld and death, fir is an instrument of change that eases the transition from life through death to renewal while comforting those left behind in this world. Use it in rituals to honor loved ones who have passed. Through the most trying circumstances, this tree helps to foster hope, happiness, and peace.

Frankincense (*Boswellia carteri* syn. *B. sacra*); also known as incense
    tree, olibanum.

This shrubby evergreen tree is native to northeastern Africa, the Arabian Peninsula, and parts of India and Pakistan. Reaching between six and twenty-five feet tall, it has papery, peeling bark and a dense tangle of branches. The oblong leaves grow in groups at the ends of short branches. Growing in clusters, the small star-shaped flowers are white with orange and yellow centers. The flowers grow on long spikes among the leaves. Resin is obtained by making incisions in the tree.

The name *frankincense* dates to the tenth-century French words *frank*, meaning "genuine," and *encens*, "incense" in reference to the resin being high-quality incense.[74]

---

74. Robert K. Barnhart, ed., *The Barnhart Concise Dictionary of Etymology* (New York: HarperCollins, 1995), 298.

The Latin name *olibanum* comes from the Arabic, *al-lubān*, meaning "milk," alluding to the appearance of the resin before it turns orange yellow and hardens after exposure to air.[75] When burned, the tear-shaped grains of resin have a sweet, balsam-like aroma.

Believed to deepen the spiritual experience, frankincense was commonly burned in temples throughout China and India. Being enveloped by the fragrance during meditation was thought to open the way to enlightenment. The Egyptians valued the resin as incense for religious offerings; the smoke was believed to open the channels of communication with the deity to whom it was presented. Because of its color, frankincense was regarded as sacred to the sun god Ra. It was also used as a special offering to honor Isis, Osiris, and Bast, the cat-headed solar goddess. The Babylonians used frankincense to honor their god Bel, the Assyrians to honor Astarte and Ba'al, and the Greeks, Apollo. The Romans used frankincense for both religious and secular ceremonies. Included as an ingredient in the Hebrew's sacred incense, frankincense was regarded as a symbol of divinity.

Roman Poet Publius Ovidius Naso (43–17 BCE), better known as Ovid, explained the origin of the frankincense tree in a story involving Apollo and Leucothea, not to be confused with the Greek sea goddess of the same name. This Leucothea was the daughter of a Persian king who was enraged about his family's disgrace when he learned of her liaison with Apollo. As punishment, he had her buried alive. While in mourning, Apollo watered her grave with ambrosia and the frankincense tree sprouted into existence.

The tree was so highly prized that Queen Hatshepsut (reigned in her own right c. 1473–1460 BCE) had several transported to her gardens in Egypt. In addition to honoring deities, the Egyptians used frankincense in the embalming process, in medicinal remedies, perfumes, and cosmetics. Influenced by the Egyptians, Greek physicians also incorporated frankincense into their medicinal remedies.

Greek philosopher and student of Aristotle, Theophrastus (c. 371–287 BCE) who is regarded as the father of botany, noted that the best frankincense came from the southern coast of Arabia. Pliny the Elder, Dioscorides, and Greek physician Hippocrates (c. 460–375 BCE) touted its medicinal properties as did sixteenth-century English herbalist John Gerard. According to German herbalist Konrad von Megenberg (1309–1374), frankincense's protective powers could disperse evil spirits. During the Middle Ages, it

75. Tony Rodd and Jennifer Stackhouse, *Trees: A Visual Guide* (Berkeley, CA: University of California Press, 2008), 134.

was used in magical practices to fumigate divinatory mirrors and demarcate ritual circles. Frankincense was also used in charms to bring good luck.

Magical Connections

Elements:	Air, fire, water
Astrological influence:	Moon, Sun; Aquarius, Aries, Leo, Sagittarius
Deities:	Aphrodite, Apollo, Astarte, Ba'al, Bast, Bel, Helios, Ra, Venus
Powers/attributes:	Astral travel/journeying, attraction, authority/leadership, awareness (enhance, heighten), balance/harmony, banish, clarity (enhance, foster), concentration/focus, consecrate/bless, courage, death/funeral practices, defense, divination, dream work, emotions (deal with, support), growth, happiness, healing, inspiration, justice/legal matters, knowledge (seek, acquire), love, negativity (remove, ward off), past-life work, protection, psychic abilities, purification, release (let go, move on), renewal, spirit guides/spirits, spirituality, strength, stress/anxiety (calm, release), success, transformation
Other associations:	Yule

Items to purchase when the tree is not available: dried resin in crystal or powdered form, essential oil made from the resin.

Spellwork and Ritual

Prepare a candle with frankincense essential oil to foster happiness and invite love into your life. Burn grains of frankincense on a charcoal to enhance divination sessions. Use the smoke to create sacred space and to consecrate altar goods before ritual. Also use it as incense to honor and communicate with deities. The scent is especially effective for focusing energy and enhancing concentration for magic work.

Frankincense is instrumental for astral travel, dream work, and developing psychic abilities. Burn a few resin crystals before engaging in these practices to support and amplify your energy. Frankincense helps to reach higher levels of awareness.

As an aid for past-life work, the aroma of frankincense can break connections with things that inhibit personal or spiritual growth. The scent is instrumental for clairvoyance and for communicating with spirits. Frankincense is especially effective for banishing negativity, providing psychic protection, and adds power to any form of defense. It also aids in raising healing energy.

When seeking justice, frankincense brings clarity, courage, release, and success. Place a few drops of frankincense oil in the melted wax of a pillar candle for meditation and spiritual support. It is known to deepen the breath, which calms the emotions and focuses energy. Use frankincense to activate any chakra individually or to bring them all into alignment.

GORSE

Common Gorse (*Ulex europaeus*); also known as broom, fray, furze,
golden gorse, prickly bloom, whin.

Gorse is a scruffy evergreen shrub that reaches five to six feet tall and wide. Its branches
are densely packed with prickly, half-inch long spines that grow amongst the leaves.
The gray-green leaves resemble spruce needles. Although gorse produces a profusion
of bright yellow flowers in the spring and early summer, it often blooms throughout the
year. The flowers grow singly or in pairs and have a fragrance that is faintly reminiscent
of coconut. The black seedpods make a cracking noise when they pop open and catapult
their contents away from the bush.

Native to the British Isles and central and western Europe, gorse was introduced into
North America as an ornamental hedge plant, but its invasive nature caused it to fall out

of favor. The genus *Ulex* is the Latin name for spiny shrubs.[76] The common name for this plant evolved from the Middle English *gorst*, which came from the Old English *gors*.[77] This plant is sometimes called *broom* because it looks similar to and is often confused with the shrub more commonly known as broom (*Cytisus scoparius*).

Pliny the Elder noted that burnt gorse branches were used in sluices to filter and capture small pieces of gold in Roman mining operations. A holdover from the days of Pagan Samhain, fires of gorse were lit on the nights of November 1 and 2 (All Saints' and All Souls' nights) well into the eighteenth century throughout England to guide departed souls to their former homes.[78] In Ireland where gorse blooms year-round, a sprig in a bridal bouquet alluded to the saying that kissing was out of fashion only when the whin was out of bloom. In Ireland and Anglesey, England, a sprig of gorse was worn to bring luck. However, in some areas of England giving someone a sprig of gorse with flowers was considered unlucky because it would make people quarrel. In parts of Britain, children were afraid to pick the flowers or go near the bushes because of stories that small dragons lived in or were born in gorse thickets. Folklore from other countries indicates that gorse was an effective plant to use against fairy mischief.

Gorse was important to the rural economy throughout the British Isles and used as winter fodder for livestock. Commonly called *fuzz moots*, gorse roots were dried and burned as fuel. Well into the nineteenth century, they were used to fuel brick bread ovens, which were often called *furze ovens*. When the chimney became blocked, a branch of gorse was used to clear it.

Gardeners used gorse as a hedge plant because its dense, spiny branches were effective at keeping animals out of vegetables. For pest control, small pieces of gorse were sown along with peas. Gorse leaves have been used as an ingredient in beer, especially during the Middle Ages when the standard grains used today were not available. Gorse flowers have been used to make tea, wine, and dye for cloth. In some areas of the British Isles, gorse bushes were used as boundary markers.

Because of its bright yellow flowers, gorse has been associated with the sun. At the spring equinox, its yellow flowers seem to welcome and amplify the increasing sunlight. The ritual of sweeping away the remnants of winter with gorse branches was equated

---

76. Coombes, *Dictionary of Plant Names*, 197.

77. Barnhardt, *The Barnhart Concise Dictionary of Etymology*, 325.

78. Julia Jones and Barbara Deer, *The Country Diary of Garden Lore* (London: Dorling Kindersley Ltd., 1989), 103.

with sweeping away evil influences. It is customary to throw some gorse onto a Beltane fire. On Lughnasadh it is used to honor Lugh. The use of bright gorse flowers on Walpurgis gave it the reputation of warding off evil and dark influences.

Magical Connections

Element:	Fire
Astrological influence:	Mars, Sun; Aries
Deities:	Aine, Arianrhod, Bel/Belenus, the Dagda, Freyr, Lugh, Jupiter, Thor
Magical beings and woodland spirits:	Fairies
Wildlife:	Bee, cormorant, hare, hawk (harrier), horse
Ogham:	Onn/Ohn ╫
Powers/attributes:	Abundance, defense, determination/endurance, divination, family and home, fertility, hexes (remove, ward off), hope, love, money/prosperity, negativity (remove, ward off), protection, purification, renewal
Other associations:	Ostara, Walpurgis, Beltane, Lughnasadh, Samhain

Items to purchase when the tree is not available: flower essence.

Spellwork and Ritual

For protection spells, carve gorse's ogham character on a yellow candle and place a circle of spines (thorns) around the base of it. To protect a home, bury a sprig of gorse in front of it and visualize a shield of protective energy rising and surrounding the house. To remove hexes or for defense against dark magic, place gorse spines at each corner of your altar during a banishing spell.

Use the flowers in love sachets or scatter a few in your bathwater to increase personal power for magic. Burn a few leaves and/or spines for help in getting out of a rut. Place a sprig or two in any area of your home where energy has stagnated to get it moving.

Before Yule, use gorse branches to symbolically sweep your altar and ritual area to clear the energy for the sun's return. Also do this at Ostara to welcome spring and sweep away the staleness of winter.

HACKBERRY

Common Hackberry (*Celtis occidentalis*); also known as American hackberry, bastard elm, hoop ash, nettle tree, sugarberry.

European Hackberry (*C. australis*); al-mais, European nettle tree, hagberry, hag brier, honey berry, mays, Mediterranean hackberry, sugarberry.

Native to central and northeast North America, the common hackberry usually grows forty to sixty feet tall but occasionally reaches one hundred. This tree has bluish-gray bark with long ridges that can take on a corky appearance as the tree matures. The dull green leaves resemble those of the stinging nettle plant and turn yellow in autumn. Small greenish-white flowers blend in with the leaves. The small, cherry-like fruit is reddish orange and turns dark purple or blue black when ripe. The European hackberry is native to Europe, northern Africa, and Asia Minor. It reaches forty to seventy feet tall. Like its

American cousin, its leaves resemble the nettle plant; they are dark green and turn dull yellow in autumn. It also has small greenish flowers and cherry-like fruit.

Hackberry has grown in popularity as a shade tree because it has worked well as a substitute for elm after Dutch elm disease diminished their numbers. Although hackberry prefers moist areas, it is a rugged tree that has the ability to withstand drought, heat, and high wind, making it suitable for a wide range of locations.

Hackberry wood is heavy but soft and has commercial value for practical, utilitarian items such as barrel staves, fence posts, crates, and kitchen cabinets. Native Americans used the fruit to flavor food and the leaves and branches to make brown dye. Like cherries, the sweet hackberry fruit has been eaten for millennia as shown by archaeological evidence in Neolithic settlements of the Near East. Traces of hackberry wine have also been discovered at some of these sites.

The genus *Celtis* is the name the ancient Greeks used for trees bearing sweet fruit.[79] Because of the appearance of its fruit, the common name *hackberry* is thought to be a corruption of the Scottish *hagberry*, a folk name used for the European bird cherry (*Prunus padus*).[80] Hackberry is believed to be the tree noted as "unknown" by English settlers in the Mid-Atlantic colonies and *bois inconnu* "unknown wood" by French settlers in Louisiana.[81] The reason for the confusion may be hackberry's likeness to other trees. It resembles the elm but produces purple berries, which the elm does not. And while hackberry leaves somewhat resemble the linden, they are more like the nettle plant.

Throughout the Middle East, hackberry was known by its Arabic name *al-mais*, which was derived from the verb *mayasa* meaning "liberation of the moon."[82] According to folklore, the tree's round fruit was believed to grow only in the moonlight. Revered for protection, small pieces of hackberry wood were used as amulets. There was also a belief that anyone who slept under this tree would be protected from evil spirits.

The Arabic name was carried over to medieval Europe where the tree became known as mays. Hackberry was used as a boundary tree on estates in England and in gardens

---

79. David Gledhill, *The Names of Plants*, 4th ed. (New York: Cambridge University Press, 2008), 97.

80. Donald Culross Peattie, *A Natural History of Trees of Eastern and Central North America* (New York: Houghton Mifflin, 1966), 256.

81. Ibid.

82. Alan Dundes, ed., *The Evil Eye: A Casebook* (Madison. WI: The University of Wisconsin Press, 1992), 97.

for its shade. Its flexible wood was used for various crafts and the fruit was considered an aphrodisiac.

Frequently a host to mistletoe, hackberry commonly sports witches' brooms too. The hackberry emperor (*Asterocampa celtis*) is one of several species of butterflies that rely on this tree as a host for its caterpillars.

Magical Connections

Elements:	Fire, water
Astrological influence:	Moon
Wildlife:	Bee, butterfly, cedar waxwing, mockingbird, quail, robin, squirrel, woodpecker
Alternate tree calendar:	August 14 to 23 and February 9 to 18
Powers/attributes:	Abundance, adaptability, changes/transitions, creativity, healing, inspiration, loss/sorrow (ease, recover from), manifest (desires, dreams, will), negativity (remove, ward off), protection
Other associations:	Mabon

Spellwork and Ritual

With its historical lunar association, incorporate hackberry into your esbat rituals for a boost in energy. Make a circle in the middle of your altar with its berries or leaves or carve its name on a white candle to burn during ritual. Use a piece of hackberry wood as a protective amulet or burn it in a spell to raise protective energy around you or your home. Use a hackberry branch when casting a circle to remove any form of negativity.

When dealing with unsettling issues in your life, carry a picture of the tree with you to aid in creating stability. When seeking change, write your goal on a picture of the tree and burn it as you visualize the desired outcome. Hold a branch or leaf between your hands for an emotionally healing ritual to aid in allowing grief to run its course. Keep a picture of this tree in your workspace to boost the energy of creative projects.

HAWTHORN

Common Hawthorn (*Crataegus monogyna*); also known as one-seeded
   hawthorn, single-seeded hawthorn.
English Hawthorn (*C. laevigata* syn. *C. oxyacantha*); also known as
   haeg, hagthorn, Midland hawthorn.
Both trees are known as haw bush, May, Mayblossom, Maythorn,
   quickthorn, whitethorn, wishing tree.

Both of these hawthorn trees grow up to twenty feet tall. They have shiny leaves with
rounded lobes, and small thorns that grow along the branches. Their five-petaled flowers grow in clusters. The flowers of the common hawthorn are white, often with a blush
of pink; the English hawthorn has a slight purplish tint. Usually called *haws*, its oval red
fruit is also known as hoggins. The common hawthorn is native to Europe, northern

Africa, and western Asia; the English hawthorn to the British Isles, western and central Europe.

Hawthorn was commonly called *May* for the month in which it blooms, and whitethorn, because of its grayish-colored bark. The name *hawthorn* evolved from the Old English word, *haegthorn*, "hedge thorn."[83] The genus name *Crataegus* was derived from the Greek *kratos*, meaning "strength," which underlines its popularity for broomsticks and other sturdy utilitarian items including furniture.[84]

Regarded as a symbol of marriage, both Roman and Greek brides often wore crowns of hawthorn flowers. It was customary for Romans to attach a sprig of hawthorn to cradles to protect infants.

For centuries, hawthorn has been an important component of Britain's hedgerows. Garlands of hawthorn flowers were hung around doorways of homes and barns to celebrate Beltane. Collecting dew from the flowers and sprinkling it on the face on Beltane morning was said to ensure lasting beauty. As expected, may blossom wine is made from hawthorn flowers.

In Ireland, hawthorn trees are often found near sacred wells and will usually have offerings left around them on the ground as well as ribbons tied to their branches. This tree is also commonly found at crossroads, which is appropriate for its association with Brigid, the Celtic goddess who presides over holy wells and crossroads. Known as a wishing tree, it is not unusual to see strips of cloth or other small items hanging on a hawthorn regardless of its location.

Believed to mark a threshold to the otherworld, hawthorn is part of the triad of powerful fairy trees along with oak and ash. Like blackthorn, instead of removing a hawthorn that stands in the middle of a field a farmer usually plows around it rather than disturb the wee folk. The haws are sometimes called *pixie paws*.

In addition to fairies, witches were said to meet under solitary hawthorns. For this reason, this tree was often avoided on May Eve. Witches were said to use the thorns for spells and to be able to turn themselves into hawthorn trees. Despite this, hawthorns were also believed to protect against witches and witchcraft.

Like many plants, there is differing folklore about taking the flowers indoors. However, in Ireland on May Day, blossoms were placed indoors to protect a house from evil.

---

83. Wells, *Lives of the Trees*, 155.

84. Coombes, *Dictionary of Plant Names*, 98.

In England, the flowers were kept outside the house because they were associated with lust. Another belief was that a broomstick made of hawthorn should not be taken into the home because this action would be followed by a death in the family.

Used medicinally by the Greeks, hawthorn berries fell out of favor in later centuries. John Gerard, Nicolas Culpeper, and other herbalists of their day mentioned hawthorn but gave few recommendations. Today, haws are finding wider use in herbal remedies and as a culinary treat for making tea, jelly, and jam.

Magical Connections

Elements:	Air, fire
Astrological influence:	Mars; Aquarius, Aries, Gemini, Taurus
Deities:	Bel/Belenus, Brigid, Danu, the Dagda, Flora, Frigg, Thor, Zeus
Magical beings and woodland spirits:	Fairies, pixies
Wildlife:	Blackbird, cuckoo, night-raven/night-crow (black-crowned night heron), owl, purple martin, hedgehog, wolf
Ogham:	Huath/hÚath/Uath ⊥ Celtic tree calendar: May 13 to June 9
Runes:	Opila/Ethel/Othala ⋉ Runic half month: May 29 to June 13 Thurisaz/Thurs/Thorn þ Runic half month: July 29 to August 12
Powers/attributes:	Ancestors, astral travel/journeying, challenges/obstacles (overcome), changes/transitions, consecrate/bless, creativity, defense, emotions (deal with, support), enchantment, family and home, fertility, growth, happiness, hope, love, luck, money/prosperity, negativity (remove, ward off), the otherworld, peace, protection, purification, security, sex/sexuality, success, wisdom, wishes
Other associations:	Walpurgis, Beltane

Items to purchase when the tree is not available: dried berries from the common hawthorn are available whole or powdered, dried leaves and flowers from the English hawthorn.

Spellwork and Ritual

Use hawthorn leaves or flowers for protection spells. Also carry one in your pocket or purse. Dry a few haws, and then string them together to make an amulet. Sprinkle a handful of petals or a pinch of powdered haws on the ground just before a ritual to cleanse and sanctify the area. The flowers are effective in charms for attracting love. Include a few flowers in a bridal bouquet to strengthen the relationship.

Wear a sprig of hawthorn flowers or leaves to contact fairies and other nature spirits. Plant a hawthorn in your garden to attract them. Place a few haws on your outdoor altar along with a little food for fairies and pixies.

Consecrate a branch in the smoke of mugwort and lavender, and then place it in your home, workplace, or anywhere you need to repel negative energy. Burn a couple of dried leaves to prepare space for magic work. To boost a fertility spell, place a green candle on your altar and surround the base of it with a ring of haws. Line a kitchen windowsill with haws to attract prosperity. Lay out a group of haws in the pattern of the Huath ogham or Opila rune to call on the energy of the hawthorn in rituals. This tree is also instrumental for personal growth.

HAZEL

American Hazelnut (*Corylus americana*); also known as American
   filbert.
Common Hazel (*C. avellana*); also known as cobnut, common filbert,
   English hazel.

Both of these hazels are shrubby, multi-trunked trees that produce prominent yellow-brown male catkins and less obvious reddish female catkins in late winter/early spring. The common hazel reaches fifteen to twenty feet tall; the American hazelnut about fifteen feet tall. Both trees have rounded, heavily veined leaves. The nut is encased in a husk. Small, round nuts are called *cobs* or *hazelnuts*, and the larger ones are called *filberts*. That said, the names are often used interchangeably. The common hazel is native to Europe, the British Isles, and western Asia; the American to eastern and central North America.

Referring to the shape of the husk, the genus name comes from the Greek *korys*, meaning "hood" and the name *hazel*, from the Anglo Saxon *haesel*, meaning "bonnet."[85] Derived from the name of hazel's ogham Coll, *calltuin* is the Gaelic term for a hazel grove.[86]

Hazelnuts were associated with the mystic rites of Mercury and Apollo. Young catkin-bearing hazel branches were commonly called *wands*, and according to legend, Mercury's winged wand was made of hazel wood. According to myth, the staffs of Demeter and Hermes were also made of hazel.

The hazel was sacred to Germanic peoples and dedicated to Thor. Because of its association with this storm god, the tree was regarded as the embodiment of lightning. There was also a belief that the tree protected those who took shelter under it. While in German folklore a white snake was said to live under the hazel, in Sweden snakes were believed to lose their venom if touched by a hazel stick.

Hazel's importance in Ireland began with the pre-Celtic people who arrived during the Mesolithic Period (8,000–4,000 BCE). The nuts were one of the most import non-meat food sources of protein. In Celtic mythology, hazelnuts were closely associated with salmon and water. According to legend, nine hazel trees grew around the well of wisdom, which in some accounts was referred to as Connla's well. Nine is an important magical number as the triple of the sacred number three. The hazelnuts that fell from the trees fed the fish known as the salmon of knowledge. Although the details of this legend differ from one version to another, the hazelnut was considered a repository of wisdom. This wisdom was passed along to the salmon that ate the nuts as well as anyone who ate the salmon.

In parts of medieval England, brides were given small bags of hazelnuts. Like rice at weddings today, they symbolized fertility and abundance. As dowsing rods, hazel branches were believed to be particularly potent if cut from the tree on Midsummer's Eve. According to British folklore, a hazel gad (a sharp, pointed stick) had the power to fight off the legendary spectral black dog. Finding two conjoined hazelnuts was considered a good omen and carried as a charm against witchcraft. When hazel grows with apple and hawthorn, it is said to mark the boundary of a very magical place.

85. Rosengarten, *The Book of Edible Nuts*, 95.
86. Watts, *Elsevier's Dictionary of Plant Lore*, 183.

Known as Nutting Day, September 14 was the traditional day in England to go to the woods and gather nuts. While the reason for this date is unknown, taboos about gathering nuts on other dates may have related to their economic value and intended to level the playing field for everyone to get a fair share. At any rate, hazelnuts were regarded as especially magical when obtained on Nutting Day. The divination power of hazelnuts was believed to be at its peak on Samhain. When tossed into a fire, the resulting colors and noises provided answers to questions.

Magical Connections

Elements:	Air, fire, water
Astrological influence:	Mercury, Sun; Gemini, Leo, Libra, Virgo
Deities:	Aphrodite, Apollo, Arianrhod, Artemis, Boann, Danu, Demeter, Diana, Hermes, Manannan, Mercury, Odin, Ogma, Thor, Venus
Magical beings and woodland spirits:	Elves, fairies, Karya (Greek tree nymph), pixies
Wildlife:	Crane, owl, salmon
Ogham:	Coll/Call ⊥⊥⊥⊥ Celtic tree calendar: August 5 to September 1
Alternate tree calendar:	March 22 to 31 and September 24 to October 3
Powers/attributes:	Abundance, awareness (enhance, heighten), balance/harmony, banish, challenges/obstacles (overcome), changes/transitions, communication, creativity, defense, divination, fertility, healing, inspiration, intuition, knowledge (seek, acquire), loss/sorrow (ease, recover from), luck, manifest (desires, dreams, will), money/prosperity, the otherworld, past-life work, protection, psychic abilities, release (let go, move on), secrets, security, shamanic work, strength, support (provide, receive), wisdom, wishes
Other associations:	Beltane, Midsummer's Eve, Mabon, Samhain

Items to purchase when the tree is not available: hazelnuts, hazelnut oil made from the common hazel, flower essence made from the common hazel.

Spellwork and Ritual

Place a circle of hazel leaves or a small wreath made with a pliable branch on your altar for aid in all forms of magic, especially banishing spells. During divination sessions, place a forked hazel branch on your altar or table for guidance. Hang a hazel stick above your altar or over a doorway to foster protection and raise defensive energy. Use a hazel stick to draw a magic circle for extra protection. In place of a stick, use a brown candle prepared with hazelnut oil and carved with the ogham character Coll.

Place a handful of dried leaves or a few hazelnuts on your desk or in your workspace to stimulate inspiration and creativity. The leaves and nuts are an aid when initiating changes, plus they provide support for all forms of communication. Leaves or a small twig on your altar during meditation will help you connect with inner wisdom. Also use hazel to amplify the energy of dark moon rituals.

Eat a few hazelnuts before magic or psychic work, especially clairvoyance. Also eat hazelnuts before shamanic journeying to aid in acquiring knowledge. String nine hazelnuts together, consecrate them at Samhain, and then hang them in your home as a protective amulet and to bring luck.

HEATH AND HEATHER

Heather (*Calluna vulgaris*); also known as common hedder, heath, ling,
   Scots heather.
Heath (*Erica carnea* syn. *E. herbacea*); also known as alpine heath,
   spring heath, winter heath, winter flowering heather.

Although heath and heather are nearly identical and their names are often used interchangeably, there is a simple way to tell them apart. Heath has needle-like foliage like a
spruce tree while heather has scale-like foliage like a cedar tree.

   Heather grows in mounds from four to twenty inches tall. Depending on the variety, its
bell-shaped flowers can be white, pink, purple, or red. Heather usually flowers from summer to late autumn but can bloom into December. It is native to northern North America, northern Europe, and Asia. Native to the mountains of central and southern Europe,

heath also has bell-shaped flowers. It can begin blooming as early as November with some varieties lasting through May. It typically grows in mounds six to nine inches tall.

The genus name *Erica* was Pliny the Elder's translation of the Greek name that philosopher Theophrastus used for the plant.[87] Pliny noted that heath was used as a remedy to soothe snakebites. Heather's genus name comes from similar Latin and Greek words that have the same meaning of "brushing" or "sweeping."[88] This refers to the common practice of bundling heather plants together to use as a broom.

In the highlands of Scotland where trees are scarce, heather was used as fuel for hearth fires, mattress stuffing, and roof thatching. Various parts of the plant were used to produce yellow, indigo, and green dyes. On the Isle of Man, heather and heath were used to make rope to moor boats. According to Scottish legend, fairies used heather for food. Ale brewed from heather has been produced in Scotland since the time of the Picts (c. 325 BCE). While heather ale was known in other lands, only the Picts knew how to brew this particular drink. There are similar legends about the Danes making heather beer.

Because white heather was associated more closely with fairies, finding it was considered lucky. Giving someone a sprig of white heather was regarded as a declaration of love. It was also used as a good luck charm and tucked into bridal bouquets to ensure a happy marriage. According to legend, white heather was believed to bring luck and protection because it was not stained by the blood of the Picts in their battles against the Saxon invaders of Scotland. The word *heathen* comes from the Gothic *haithi*, meaning "dwelling on the heath" where Paganism lingered in Scotland long after Christianity was introduced.[89]

In the lore of Scotland, burning back the heather in early spring would bring rain. Both heath and heather were used for weather prophecy. When the flowers grew all the way to the tops of the stems, a severe winter was ahead. In Germany, Estonia, and Finland, the time to sow winter grains depended on the height of the blossoms on the stems: low on the plant meant sow early, slightly higher meant sow at the end of September.

---

87. Gledhill, *The Names of Plants*, 133.

88. Mario Molinari, *Divided by Words: A Case for a New Literacy* (Bury St. Edmonds, England: Arena Books, 2009), 32.

89. Barnhart, *The Barnhart Concise Dictionary of Etymology*, 346.

In Germany, heather flowers were placed in front of a shed door to ward off evil. On Walpurgis, heather was placed in barns to protect cattle from witches. In northern Italy, a heather broom was placed in front of a church door to reveal a suspected witch if she tried to enter. It was believed that a witch would turn away, but a non-witch would simply move the broom. As with other plants that were used to ward off witches, heather was also widely believed to have been employed by witches for besom brooms.

Magical Connections

Elements:	Water
Astrological influence:	Venus; Scorpio, Taurus
Deities:	Arianrhod, Isis, Venus
Magical beings and woodland spirits:	Fairies, pixies
Wildlife:	Bee, grouse (red), lark
Ogham:	Ur/Uhr/Ura ╫
Powers/attributes:	Adaptability, authority/leadership, awareness (enhance, heighten), changes/transitions, clarity (enhance, foster), confidence, defense, divination, dream work, family and home, growth, healing, knowledge (seek, acquire), love, luck, manifest (desires, dreams, will), peace, protection, psychic abilities, purification, spirit guides/spirits, spirituality
Other associations:	Walpurgis, Litha

Items to purchase when the plant is not available: flower essence made from common heather, dried heather flowers and plants.

Spellwork and Ritual

Make a sachet using white flowers for a good luck charm. Carry it with you or place it in a location where you will see it often. To strengthen love spells, place white and/or pink flowers on your altar for three days. To help foster a deeper connection with your spirit guides, use a sprig of purple flowers on your altar when you contact them. Alternatively, inscribe the ogham Ur on a purple candle.

Burn a few dried sprigs of heather or heath to bring clarity and awareness while developing psychic abilities. Burning the leaves also supports spiritual healing and personal growth. A sprig hung on a bedpost or placed on a nightstand enhances dream work and helps to interpret messages. Growing heather or heath in your garden provides protective energy around your home.

Keep a photograph of heather or heath in your pocket or purse during major transitions in your life to give you stability. Gazing at a picture of either plant before meditating instills a deep sense of peace.

HOLLY

American Holly (*Ilex opaca*); also known as Christmas holly, prickly
   holly, white holly.
English Holly (*I. aquifolium*); also known as common holly, European
   holly, hollin.

Native to Europe and the British Isles, English holly reaches thirty to fifty feet tall and
about half as wide. Its glossy, dark green leaves have wavy margins with sharp spines.
American holly is native to eastern and central United States. Reaching twenty-five to
fifty feet tall, its leaves are matte green. Both trees produce clusters of small white flowers. Holly produces male and female flowers on separate trees; berries occur only on the
female tree.

    In winter when most plants have faded or died off, holly is bright and vigorous with
the promise of ongoing life. Associated with the Great Mother Goddess, the red berries

were said to represent her life-giving blood and her power of transformation from death to rebirth.

Regarded as extremely powerful, holly was paired with oak to represent the two dominant forces of the natural world. While the year is divided by months and seasons, it is also split in two with a light half and dark half. The Holly King is the sovereign and guardian of the waning year and begins his reign just after the summer solstice as we head toward shorter days and darkness. At the winter solstice they switch. The old king dies and the young one, the Oak King personifying the New Year, takes over, symbolizing the succession of father to son and the passage from death to rebirth. The Christian church's juxtaposition of the birthdays of Jesus (winter solstice) and John the Baptist (summer solstice), echo the ancient Pagan myth of the holly and oak kings. The story also plays out in the Arthurian legend of Gawain (oak) and the Green Knight (holly).

In Roman legend, Saturn, the god of agriculture and time, possessed a deadly club made of holly. Sprigs of holly were used to decorate Roman homes during the festival of Saturnalia, which had its dual light and dark aspects. Because its wood burns extremely hot, metal smiths used holly for their fires when making weapons.

Celebrated on January 6, Twelfth Night/Epiphany marked the end of the Yuletide revels. In parts of northwest England, it was customary to carry a flaming branch of holly through the town accompanied by a loud band and fireworks. Even though Yule festival greens are traditionally burned at Imbolc to symbolically break the bonds of winter, a small sprig of holly was sometimes kept for luck throughout the year. This sprig was also used to protect against elf and fairy mischief. Holly has also been regarded as the male counterpart to the female ivy. Refer to the profile on Ivy for more on this relationship.

In some areas of England, it was thought unlucky to take holly indoors except at Yule and it was considered very unlucky to cut down a living holly tree. In other areas, holly was often used for the clavy, a piece of wood above or added onto a kitchen fireplace mantel to hold keys. At an inn in Somerset, England, the clavy was the preferred sitting spot for a hobgoblin known as Charlie. Throughout many European countries, holly trees were planted near homes for protection against witchcraft and lightning.

As with other trees in weather lore, holly berries were regarded as a gauge for the coming winter. A profusion of berries meant that it would be hard because the Goddess had provided for the birds with a good crop of berries. A small number of berries meant that the weather would be mild enough for birds to find food elsewhere. Where grass doesn't grow under a holly tree, it was said to be the spot where the Cailleach Bheur, the personified spirit of winter, threw her staff when spring arrived.

Magical Connections

Elements:	Air, earth, fire
Astrological influence:	Mars, Saturn; Aries, Cancer, Capricorn, Leo, Sagittarius
Deities:	Ares, Cailleach Bheur, Cernunnos, the Dagda, Danu, Freyr, Gaia, Holle, Lugh, Saturn
Magical beings and creatures and woodland spirits:	Elves, fairies, unicorns
Wildlife:	Cardinal, donkey, starling
Ogham:	Tinne/Teine ⵑⵑⵑ Celtic tree calendar: July 8 to August 4
Rune:	Mannaz/ Madhr/Mann ᛗ Runic half month: April 14 to 28
Powers/attributes:	Balance/harmony, banish, consecrate/bless, courage, death/funeral practices, defense, divination, dream work, enchantment, family and home, healing, hexes (remove, ward off), intuition, luck, protection, renewal, security, spirit guides/spirits, spirituality, strength, support (provide, receive), transformation, wishes
Other associations:	Litha, Midsummer's Eve, Saturnalia, Yule

Items to purchase when the tree is not available: flower essence made from English holly.

Spellwork and Ritual

With sharp spines, holly leaves are the epitome of protection. To enhance the defense of your home, place three leaves under the front door mat or in flowerpots on a porch. The leaves can also be used in spells for protection against hostile magic. Burn a holly leaf to consecrate ritual space. Tuck a leaf into your purse or wallet to carry for good luck.

Dry several clusters of flowers, and then sew them (or a picture of holly flowers) into a sachet. Place it under your pillow to enhance dream work, especially divination through dreams. Put holly flowers on your altar for spiritual guidance.

On January 6, have your own Twelfth Night/Epiphany celebration but on a quieter scale and more in keeping with the definition of *epiphany*. Usually associated with Christianity, the word *epiphany* has Pagan origins. Drawn from the Greek word *epiphaneia*, meaning "appearance," or "manifestation," in the Greco-Roman world it signified a deity visiting devotees in a sacred place as well as revealing him/herself in order to aid humans.[90] Since holly is associated with divinity, burn a few leaves to honor your special deity. Write the name of a goddess or god on a holly leaf or on a piece of paper cut in the shape of one. Use additional leaves or a sprig of holly to honor multiple deities. When the ashes cool, scatter them outside.

90. A. G. Martimort, I. H. Dalmais, and P. Jounel, eds., *The Liturgy and Time: The Church at Prayer: An Introduction to the Liturgy,* vol. 4 (Collegeville, MN: Liturgical Press, 1986), 80.

HORNBEAM

American Hornbeam (*Carpinus caroliniana*); also known as blue
    beech, water beech.
European Hornbeam (*C. betulas*); also known as common hornbeam,
    hard beam, horse beech, yoke elm.
Both trees are also known as ironwood, muscle wood.

Hornbeam trees have multiple trunks with smooth, gray bark and a dense growth of
branches. Large branches usually have a distinctive rippling texture that gives them a
muscle-like appearance. Hornbeams have yellowish male catkins and shorter greenish
female catkins on the same tree. Female catkins develop into clusters of winged nutlets enveloped in three-lobed bracts that look like woody petals. Native to eastern North
America, the American hornbeam grows twenty-five to thirty-five feet tall. Its leaves are
dark green and turn yellow, orange, and red in the autumn. Native to Europe and Asia

Minor, the European hornbeam reaches between forty to sixty feet tall. Its dark green leaves turn an undistinguished yellow or orange in the fall. Mistletoe occasionally grows on hornbeam trees.

The name *hornbeam* comes from its characteristic hardness, which has been likened to animal horn, and *beam*, the Old English word for "tree."[91] The name *yoke elm* comes from its use for making oxen yokes and its resemblance to the elm tree. The American hornbeam is sometimes known as water or blue beech because it is often mistaken for a beech tree because of its leaves.

Also known as ironwood, the hornbeam's hardness often makes it difficult to work with, especially for carving. Good for burning as fuel, Pliny the Elder noted that hornbeam was mostly used for torches. Archaeological evidence in southern England indicates that the occupying Romans used hornbeam charcoal for smelting iron ore. The inner bark of the hornbeam has been used to make yellow dye.

The species name of the European tree, *betulas*, means "beech-like."[92] As mentioned, hornbeams are most often mistaken for beeches but frequently elms too. Adding to the confusion, the wych elm was sometimes known as hornbeam in some areas. During the Middle Ages, herbalist John Gerard not only likened hornbeam to elm, but also witch hazel. In fact, for a time hornbeam was called *witch hasell*. Although Gerard noted that it was not used for medicinal purposes, it has had some limited applications for treating a few ailments.

From the fifteenth through seventeenth centuries, hornbeam was popular for knot gardens, hedges, and topiary. The famous maze at Hampton Court Palace in England was created for King William of Orange (1650–1702) in the late seventeenth century; however, many of the hornbeams have since been replaced with other types of trees. Originally installed in the early nineteenth century, a circular hornbeam maze was re-created in the gardens at Woburn Abby, the ancestral home of the Dukes of Bedford in Woburn, England.

German abbess, mystic, and herbalist Hildegard von Bingen (1098–1179) wrote that the hornbeam was effective for warding off demonic spirits, magic words, and curses. She suggested that if one were to sleep in a forest, it was best to do so underneath a

91. Gabriel Hemery and Sarah Simblet, *The New Sylva: A Discourse of Forest and Orchard Trees for the Twenty-First Century* (London: Bloomsbury Publishing Plc., 2014), 226.

92. Wells, *Lives of the Trees*, 169.

hornbeam for protection. Conversely, in Romania there was a belief that the devil lived in hornbeam trees. Because of this, use of the wood was usually avoided there.

In northern France, a hornbeam or birch twig was hung in front of a sweetheart's door on May Day morning as a symbol of devotion. Hornbeams were used in sympathetic magic for healing too. Driving a nail or two into a hornbeam was believed to draw vitality from the tree to the person suffering from an ailment.

Magical Connections

Elements:	Fire, water
Astrological influence:	Saturn; Taurus
Wildlife:	Deer, rabbit (cottontail)
Alternate tree calendar:	June 4 to 13 and December 2 to 11
Runes:	Fehu/Fe/Feoh ᚠ Runic half month: June 29 to July 1
Powers/attributes:	Banish, changes/transitions, determination/endurance, love, money/prosperity, negativity (remove, ward off), protection, release (let go, move on), strength

Items to purchase when the tree is not available: flower essence made from the European hornbeam.

Spellwork and Ritual

Use the flower essence to prepare a candle for banishing spells to remove anything unwanted from your life. Place a few leaves wherever you feel the need to dispel negative energy. Also burn a few leaves to prepare ritual space. Keep a small twig in a prominent location to remind you that you are strong. Wrap a twig in red ribbon to give to your sweetheart on Beltane as a symbol of your love. Include a picture of a hornbeam in rituals that mark important transitions in your life.

IVY

Common Ivy (*Hedera helix*); also known as bindwood, English ivy,
   ground ivy, true ivy.

Ivy is a familiar evergreen vine with woody stems and leaves with three to five lobes.
There are hundreds of cultivars based on leaf shape, size, and variegation. Ivy grows as a
climbing vine or a trailing ground cover. It has two stages: In the juvenile stage, it climbs
and spreads. In the adult stage, it becomes more shrub-like and produces clusters of
greenish-white flowers that develop into blue-black berries. Ivy is native to Europe, the
British Isles, and western Asia. The botanical name is a combination of the Latin name
for ivy and the Greek name for twining plants, meaning "winding."[93]

93. Gledhill, *The Names of Plants*, 193–194.

Ivy's association with renewal and rebirth dates to ancient Egypt. According to Greco-Roman philosopher and writer Plutarch (c. 46–120), ivy was dedicated to Osiris and called *chenosiris*, "the plant of Osiris."[94] The Romans believed that ivy could bestow the power of prophecy. They associated it with the god Saturn because his symbol, the gold crested wren (now known as the golden-crowned kinglet), made its nest in ivy vines. Along with holly, ivy was used as decoration for the mid-December Saturnalia festivals.

On December 26 in the British Isles, a custom called *the hunting of the wren*, which may have roots in the Bronze Age with some influence from Saturnalia, marked the transition from the old year to the new. According to legend, the wren represented the old year and took shelter in an ivy bush but was hunted down and killed by a robin, the spring bird that carried a birch twig in its claws.

Because of its association with Paganism, the use of ivy for decoration within church buildings was forbidden in England. However, its association with resurrection was too much to ignore and the plant's reputation was rehabilitated. Ivy became an important symbol of Yule, especially when paired with holly. Echoes of Paganism remained with the custom of ivy girls and holly boys symbolizing the struggle for balance between the light and dark times of the year. As part of the Yuletide revels, boys and girls competed against each other in games that culminated in the burning of ivy girl and holly boy plant effigies.

As stocks of fodder ran low around Imbolc, English farmers fed their cattle ivy left over from Yule. In Germany, when cows were taken out to pasture in early spring, a wreath of ivy was placed around their necks to ensure a good supply of milk all summer.

Just as circlets of laurel were used to crown athletes, ivy was used to honor Greek and Roman poets. The Greek muses of comedy and tragedy, Thalia and Melpomene, were depicted wearing ivy wreaths. According to lore, Bacchus/Dionysus was frequently crowned with ivy, as were his companions. Binding the brow with ivy reputedly prevented intoxication while enhancing the effects of fermented beverages. The medieval English ivy ale was an especially intoxicating drink. As a forerunner of pub signs, tavern owners advertised the brew's availability with an ivy-covered pole called a *tod* or *tavern bush*.[95] This custom continued in Normandy and Brittany, France, through the nineteenth century.

---

94. Gardner Wilkinson, *The Manners and Customs of the Ancient Egyptians*, vol. 5, 3rd ed. (London: John Murray, 1847), 265.

95. Watts, *Elsevier's Dictionary of Plant Lore*, 211.

In Scotland, strands of ivy were draped over barn doors to ward off witches. If ivy grew on the walls of a house, the occupants were safe from witches and misfortune. If the ivy died, the family was in for disaster. In England, wearing a crown of ivy on Beltane Eve was said to enable a person to see witches. In the Balkans, woody pieces of ivy stems were worn as charms. According to love divination, if a young woman put an ivy leaf in her pocket before leaving the house, the first man she encountered would become her husband. A sprig of ivy placed under a bed pillow would cause a person to dream of their true love.

Magical Connections

Elements:	Air, earth, water
Astrological influence:	Saturn, Venus; Gemini, Scorpio
Deities:	Arianrhod, Bacchus, Cernunnos, Danu, Dionysus, Freya, Hermes, Holle, Loki, the Muses Melpomene and Thalia, Ogma, Osiris, Pan, Persephone, Rhea, Saturn
Magical beings and woodland spirits:	Fairies, satyrs
Wildlife:	Butterfly, lark, swan (mute), swallow, wren
Ogham:	Gort ─╫─ Celtic tree calendar: September 30 to October 27 Oir/Or ◇ Uilleann/Uilen/Uilleand ⌐
Powers/attributes:	Attraction, balance/harmony, bind, challenges/obstacles (overcome), divination, fertility, growth, healing, inspiration, knowledge (seek, acquire), love, loyalty/fidelity, luck, negativity (remove, ward off), prophecy, protection, renewal, secrets, security, spirituality, transformation
Other associations:	Beltane, Mabon, Saturnalia, Yule

Items to purchase when the plant is not available: dried leaves, flower essence.

Spellwork and Ritual

Grow ivy on your property or place it as a houseplant in a front window to guard against negative energy and to attract luck. Wind a piece of ivy around the bottom of a candle as part of a binding spell. Place a couple of sprigs on your altar for spiritual journeys that take you inward as well as guide you back out into everyday life. Ivy is instrumental when seeking personal and spiritual growth. Incorporate white ivy leaves into your esbat ritual, as they are associated with the moon. To represent the balance of light and dark, place ivy on your Mabon altar.

Ivy is associated with the Goddess because it grows in a spiral, which is one of her symbols. Create a spiral on your altar with a strand of ivy or draw a spiral on a picture of ivy to symbolize your spiritual journey through the wheel of the year.

Common Juniper (*Juniperus communis*); also known as fairy circles,
gin berry, hackmatack, savin.

Native to northern parts of Europe, Asia, the United States and southern Canada, this is the most widespread species of juniper. Usually reaching four to six feet tall with multiple stems, it is a spreading evergreen with brown to reddish-brown bark. The foliage consists of needles in sets of three that grow in whorls, a circular or spiral pattern around the branches. While young plants have needle-like leaves, mature ones develop scale-like foliage. Like holly, juniper has male and female flowers on separate plants, and you need one of each type if you want berries. The round berries come from the female flowers and are technically cones. Taking about two years to mature, the berries turn from green to blue-black and usually have a dusting of white powder.

Dedicated to the Furies, the Greek goddesses of vengeance, juniper wood was used in the temple of Diana. The Greeks and Romans burned young roots as incense offerings to deities. The wood was used to fumigate houses where a death had occurred, and the berries were burned at funerals to keep away evil spirits. During the Middle Ages in Germany and Italy, juniper boughs were used to symbolically sweep illness from the home. Juniper was also burned to ward off dragons from the underworld and to call on Hecate for protection.

Juniper was sacred to Germanic peoples who referred to the berries as holy berries. It was regarded as equally important as the elder tree for magic. When walking by a juniper, it was customary to remove one's hat to show respect for the spirit of the juniper, Frau Wachholder. The name was derived from *wachen*, "to guard."[96] Providing help when called upon, fairy-like spirits called *Hollen* were also associated with the juniper. In England, old junipers were called *fairy circles* because as new stems sprout from outward-growing roots and the center stems die, a circle is formed by the living shrub.

In Scotland, branches were used to bless and fumigate the home on New Year's Day. Like holly, juniper was burned on Twelfth Night to mark the end of the Yuletide revels. It was also burned on Walpurgis and boughs hung on doors to ward off witches. The wood was used in counterspells to destroy charms and break hexes. In Estonia, juniper was used to seal up cracks in the walls of homes to prevent evil from entering. Planting a juniper in front of the house was believed to protect against witches, who were, for some inexplicable reason, expected to count all the needles on the tree before they could pass through the doorway. A sprig was worn for protection from accidents.

In England, the scent of juniper berries was believed to ward off bad luck, however, a person who cut down a juniper could expect to die within a year. Long, thin juniper sticks were used as whips by wagon drivers to keep demons and evil spirits from blocking the roadway. During the Middle Ages, juniper was burned as protection against the plague. It was also used during childbirth to prevent fairies from substituting a changeling for the baby.

Juniper berries are well known as a flavoring for stews and roasts, and especially gin. In Belgium and several Scandinavian countries, a juniper branch was used as a tavern

---

96. De Cleene and Lejeune, *Compendium of Symbolic and Ritual Plants in Europe*, 366.

sign indicating the sale of wines, beer, and other drinks. This practice was carried well into the nineteenth century. In many areas, juniper was regarded as a wishing tree.

Magical Connections

Elements:	Earth, fire, water
Astrological influence:	Mars, Mercury, Moon, Sun; Aries, Leo, Sagittarius
Deities:	Balder, Diana, the Furies, Hecate, Holle, Loki, the Morrigan, Ran
Magical beings and creatures and woodland spirits:	Dragons, dwarves, fairies, Frau Wachholder, Hollen, Katajatar (Scandinavian tree fairies)
Wildlife:	Cedar waxwing, deer (white tailed), goose
Runes:	Sowilo/Sol/Sigil ⚡ Runic half month: February 12 to 26
Powers/attributes:	Abundance, balance/harmony, banish, challenges/obstacles (overcome), defense, divination, dream work, emotions (deal with, support), family and home, fertility, growth, happiness, healing, hexes (remove, ward off), knowledge (seek, acquire), love, manifest (desires, dreams, will), money/prosperity, negativity (remove, ward off), protection, psychic abilities, purification, release (let go, move on), secrets, security, spirit guides/spirits, spirituality, strength, success, transformation, wishes
Other associations:	New Year's Day, Twelfth Night, Walpurgis

Items to purchase when the tree is not available: dried berries, essential oil is made from the berries.

Spellwork and Ritual

Burn dried juniper needles as incense to purify a large space. They can also be burned to ward off the energy of negative people or to release something you no longer want in your life. Burn a small twig for defense; juniper is especially effective against black magic, hexes, and dealing with unwanted spirits. Burning any part of a juniper provides psychic protection and keeps energy grounded in the physical world.

String berries together into a circlet, let them dry completely, and then use it as a charm to attract a lover. Use dried berries in a sachet to enhance divination and dream work. The berries also help increase psychic abilities. A juniper bush on your property is effective for manifesting abundance and prosperity. As an offering, tie three small, dark blue ribbons within the thick foliage of a juniper. This tree is also helpful in fostering happiness and emotional healing.

American Larch (*Larix laricina*); also known as eastern larch, hackmatack, tamarack.

European Larch (*L. decidua* syn. *L. europaea*); also known as common
larch, false manna, larick, white larch.

Larches grow high on rocky mountain slopes in conditions where other conifers can't
survive. They have tufts of gray-green needles that grow in tight spiraling clusters
around the branches. The larch is the only coniferous tree that is deciduous. The needles
turn golden yellow in the autumn before they drop. Native to northern North America,
the American larch usually grows between forty to sixty feet tall and sometimes reaches
eighty. Its small, round cones are brown. On young trees the bark is smooth and gray; on
mature trees it is reddish brown and scaly. The European larch is indigenous to central

and southern Europe. It grows to between sixty to one hundred feet tall with reddish-brown bark that becomes scaly on mature trees. The cones are also reddish brown.

According to Pliny the Elder, the largest known tree growing in Rome during the first century CE was a larch. Regarded as sacred in many areas of the Alps, the larch was especially revered in the Tyrol region of Austria where offerings to deities were placed underneath them. The larch was considered so sacred that quarreling and swearing were forbidden in their vicinity. Courts of law were held under these trees. A belief persisted that children were brought into the world from larch trees. It was also believed that anyone who damaged a larch would become sick until the tree healed.

Pliny noted that larch wood would not burn and could not be used to produce charcoal. A sacred larch in the southern Tyrol was said to have never burned despite several forest fires that had swept through the area. With its reddish bark, this tree was believed to protect against fire. Fourteenth-century German herbalist Konrad von Megenberg noted it as a guardian tree and that a few planks of larch added to a house would protect it from fire. Twigs were placed on houses for protection against lightning strikes too.

According to Tyrolean folklore, a spirit dressed in white called the *Salgfraulien* often sat underneath old larch trees singing. Salgfraulien were a type of forest spirit that aided humans. According to some legends, they were said to have made their homes under the rocks around the roots of larches. In other areas, they were known as the Seliges Fraulines and believed to be fairies who watched over certain plants.

Regarding groups of seven larches as particularly sacred, the Khanty people of central Russia left offerings in the niches formed by forked tree trunks. Siberian Tungus shaman used larch wood to make parts of their drums. The Slavs put amulets of larch on their children to protect them from the evil eye. In parts of Poland, larch twigs were used to seal doors and windows on Walpurgis for protection against witchcraft. Despite beliefs about larches not burning, the smoke from a larch was said to ward off spells. Like other trees employed against witches, the larch was believed to have been used by them. According to legend, the sap was an ingredient in witches' magical brews.

Larch needles and resin were used medicinally and for sympathetic magic. Pliny the Elder recommended a larch remedy for a toothache. During the Middle Ages, when a tooth was removed it was placed in a niche or driven into a larch to protect against further toothaches. In Yorkshire northern England, the afterbirth of a foal was hung on a larch to bring the horse good health and luck throughout its life. Larches were also believed to drive away snakes.

This tree has been called *false manna* because of the sweet, white substance that is occasionally secreted from its needles. In France, it was called *manna of Briançon* for the location where it was found and used medicinally.[97] The names *tamarack* and *hackmatack* for the American larch are corruptions of the Algonquian *akemantak*, meaning "wood for making snowshoes."[98]

Magical Connections

Elements:	Fire
Astrological influence:	Jupiter
Magical beings and woodland spirits:	Fairies, Salgfraulien
Alternate tree calendar:	August 14 to 23 and February 9 to 18
Powers/attributes:	Healing, intuition, justice/legal matters, knowledge (seek, acquire), luck, protection, shamanic work, spirituality, success
Other associations:	Walpurgis

Items to purchase when the tree is not available: flower essence is made from the European larch, essential oil is obtained from the American larch needles and sometimes marketed as tamarack oil, larch resin chewing gum is made from the Siberian larch (*L. sibirica*).[99]

Spellwork and Ritual

Place a few larch needles in a small pouch to keep with you for a boost in confidence. Use a small piece of wood or a twig as an amulet for good luck. Burn a small piece of resin on an incense charcoal to aromatically enhance shamanic work or spiritual meditation. Also use the incense as an offering to deities.

---

97. Folkard, *Plant Lore, Legends, & Lyrics*, 403.

98. Wayne Grady, *The Great Lakes: The Natural History of a Changing Region* (Vancouver, Canada: Greystone Books, 2007), 97.

99. I do not know how this product tastes or any safety issues that may be related to it. It is recommended for magical use rather than consumption.

Sprinkle a circle of larch needles in your garden as a gift for the fairies. For a success spell, prepare a candle with the essential oil or flower essence. Write the name of someone to whom you want to direct healing energy, and then wrap it around two pieces of resin gum. Hold it between your hands as you visualize sending healing energy. Bury the bundle outside.

LAUREL

Bay Laurel (*Laurus nobilis*); also known as Apollo's laurel, bay tree,
laurel, Roman laurel, sweet bay, true laurel.

Laurel is an evergreen that can grow up to fifty feet tall, but it is most often kept pruned
as a shrub. It may be most familiar as a small, potted tree cut into pom-poms or other
topiary shapes. Growing on short stems, the dark green leathery leaves are sharply
pointed. They are commonly known as bay leaves. Blooming in early spring, the small
flowers are greenish yellow and grow in clusters. The oval berries are small and turn bluish black when ripe.

Sacred to the Greeks and Romans, laurel was used in purification rituals where a
branch was dipped in water from a sacred well and sprinkled on participants. In addition to decorating shrines and other public spaces with laurel, they used the leaves for
culinary and medicinal purposes. The most famous story involving this tree is the Greek

legend about the wood nymph Daphne who avoided the unwanted attentions of Apollo by turning into a laurel. Undaunted, Apollo adopted the laurel as his sacred tree. Feasts to honor Apollo were kicked off with a procession to his temple lead by people bearing laurel branches. The tree was also dedicated to his sister Artemis.

It was customary for the Greeks and Romans to praise people of accomplishment with wreaths of laurel. Crowning with laurel was also symbolic of purification. The Greeks regarded the tree as a powerful aid for divination and prophecy; the priestesses of Delphi wore laurel leaves to support their work. In one form of divination that required burning the leaves, a crackling noise was a favorable sign when a question was posed.

The Romans regarded this tree as a symbol of wisdom and of victory. Triumphant Roman emperors returned from battle wearing laurel crowns. Laurel sprigs adorned soldier's weapons and battleships after a victory. Other countries adopted this practice and centuries later British mail coaches carrying news of Napoleon's defeat at Waterloo were festooned with laurel. This tree continues to be a symbol of truce, peace, and security.

Laurel sprigs and wreaths were standard accoutrements in burial practices. During the seventeenth century, it was customary in the Netherlands to place a laurel wreath on the head of the deceased. In nineteenth-century Wales, laurel leaves were strewn along the route to the graveyard.

Throughout Europe, laurel was used as a magic charm. Lovers would break a leaf in two and each carry half as a symbol that they would be reunited. Placing laurel under the bed pillow on Valentine's night was believed to foster dreams of love. A charm to win back a lover included burning a piece of laurel. Medieval magicians wrapped objects in laurel leaves to imbue them with magical energy.

English herbalist Nicolas Culpeper noted that the tree could be used to resist witchcraft. He also mentioned that wherever a laurel tree grew, witches and the devil could not harm people. This protective aspect echoes the belief in ancient Greece that a laurel by the front door of a house would keep the occupants safe from the plague and other epidemics. Pliny the Elder recommended laurel for a plethora of ailments. Healing charms were written on the leaves and placed under a sick person's pillow. During the Middles Ages, bay was used as a strewing herb for its fragrance and antiseptic properties.

Magical Connections

Elements:	Air, fire
Astrological influence:	Sun; Gemini, Leo, Pisces
Deities:	Adonis, Apollo, Artemis, Asclepius, Bacchus, Balder, Ceres, Cernunnos, Daphne, Diana, Dionysus, Gaia, Helios, Hermes, Mars, Mercury, Ra
Magical beings and woodland spirits:	Elves, fairies
Runes:	Sowilo/Sol/Sigil ᛋ Runic half month: February 12 to 26
Powers/attributes:	Abundance, awareness (enhance, heighten), banish, challenges/obstacles (overcome), clarity (enhance, foster), courage, creativity, defense, determination/endurance, divination, dream work, family and home, healing, hexes (remove, ward off), inspiration, intuition, justice/legal matters, loyalty/fidelity, manifest (desires, dreams, will), money/prosperity, negativity (remove, ward off), peace, prophecy, protection, psychic abilities, purification, release (let go, move on), spirituality, strength, success, wisdom, wishes
Other associations:	Litha, Saturnalia

Items to purchase when the tree is not available: dried bay leaves, available whole and powdered; essential oil is obtained from the leaves; hydrosol.

Spellwork and Ritual

Laurel aids in prophetic dreaming, divination, and clairvoyance. Burn a leaf before psychic work to boost skills. Its purification properties also provide protection during this work. Prepare a candle for divination sessions with the essential oil or make your own hydrosol with the leaves. Laurel also clears and protects the home from negativity; sprinkle powdered leaves around the exterior. It is instrumental in boosting healing energy. Hang a sprig of bay leaves in the kitchen to invite abundance.

Burn dried leaves to enhance defensive magic and remove hexes. To release something that you no longer want in your life, write a keyword on a bay leaf and burn it. Carry a leaf to ward off any type of negative energy, especially when dealing with legal issues. At Yule, hold a bay leaf as you visualize your wishes and desires for the coming year, and then throw it on the sabbat bonfire or burn it in your cauldron. The scent of bay complements the other aromas of the winter holiday season; add some leaves to a door wreath as well as your Yule altar.

Lemon (*Citrus limon* syn. *C. limonum*, *C. medica* var. *limonum*); also
known as true lemon.

The lemon tree reaches between ten and twenty feet tall. Starting as fragrant reddish
buds, the leaves are dark green on top and light green underneath. Sharp thorns line the
branches and discourage animals from dining on tender leaves. The white flowers are
tinged with pink and grow singly, in pairs, or in groups of three. The oval fruit is yellow
and dotted with oil glands.

The lemon's exact origin is unknown, but it is believed to have been a natural hybrid
that developed in the area of northeast India and Myanmar (Burma) where the cultivation of citrons (*C. medica*) and limes (*C. aurantifolia*) overlapped.[100] Although the
French word *citron* now refers to lemon, it was derived from Latin and used in reference

100. James F. Hancock, *Plant Evolution and the Origin of Crop Species*, 3rd ed. (Cambridge, MA: CABI,
2012), 229.

to all citrus fruit and trees. The Greek word *kitrion* is thought to have come from *kedris*, "cedar cone," referring to the appearance of the immature fruit.[101]

The lemon fruit that was known to the ancient Greeks and Romans was most likely the large, knobby citron. (*C. medica*). Both Theophrastus and Pliny the Elder described this fruit in their writings. However, it didn't take Arab traders long before they successfully introduced the true lemon into the Mediterranean region where it became valued for medicinal purposes. The lemon blossoms became widely treasured for their fragrance.

Westerners who traveled to the Middle East during the first crusade (1095–1099) brought the fruit back with them into central and northern Europe. By the thirteenth century, lemons were being grown in the warm regions of Italy, France, and Spain. Spanish and Portuguese explorers of the fifteenth century are responsible for spreading the tree around the world. By the late Middle Ages, lemon trees were grown as much for their beauty as for the practical use of their fruit. Used throughout Europe for a wide range of ailments, lemons were considered a potent cure-all and became standard cargo on British naval ships, especially for preventing scurvy.

During the Middle Ages, the lemon was a powerful symbol of life that was also believed to protect against poison, the plague, and bewitchment. In art, it became a symbol of faithful love (despite its sour taste) and fertility (for its abundant fruit). According to folklore, a slice of lemon placed under the chair of a visitor would gain his or her friendship. In India, lemons were used to remove the effects of the evil eye. In seventeenth-century Asia, a widow carried a lemon at her husband's funeral to represent the bitterness of life.

Magical Connections

Elements:	Air, earth, water
Astrological influence:	Mercury, Moon; Aquarius, Cancer, Gemini, Pisces
Deities:	Anubis, Durga, Hermes, Ma'at, Odin, Parvati, Thoth
Powers/attributes:	Abundance, awareness (enhance, heighten), banish, challenges/obstacles (overcome), clarity (enhance, foster), communication, concentration/focus, confidence, consecrate/bless, divination, emotions (deal with, support), happiness, knowledge (seek, acquire), love, manifest (desires, dreams, will), psychic abilities, purification, secrets, spirit guides/spirits, spirituality, strength, stress/anxiety (calm, release), success, support (provide, receive)

---

101. Toby Sonneman, *Lemon: A Global History* (London: Reaktion Books Ltd., 2012), 13.

Items to purchase when the tree is not available: fresh or dried fruit, lemon juice, flower essence, dried lemon peel, hydrosol, essential oil is obtained from the fruit.

Spellwork and Ritual

When preparing for divination or for dealing with everyday problems, spend a few minutes inhaling lemon essential oil fragrance to gain a clear perspective. By raising awareness, lemon increases psychic abilities and inspires movement to a higher spiritual plane. Place a drop or two of the essential oil in the melted wax of a candle for meditation or divination sessions. Known for its cleansing properties, spray a little lemon hydrosol to prepare an area for ritual.

Use three wheels of sliced lemon to create the triple goddess symbol of a full, waxing, and waning moon. Place this on your altar to amplify energy for moon magic and esbat rituals. Use lemon oil or juice to prepare candles and to purify magic or ritual objects when they come into your life. The scent of lemon is helpful for connecting and communicating with spirit guides. Use a piece of dried peel as an amulet when you want to renew a friendship.

To boost a spell, use lemon juice to write a few keywords about what you want to achieve on a small piece of paper. When the juice dries, it will be invisible. Fold the paper, and then hold it between your hands as you visualize the desired outcome. Just before releasing your energy, hold the paper close enough to a candle to warm it, but not burn it. When the writing becomes visible, allow the paper to catch fire, and then drop it into your cauldron. Also use lemon juice to write secrets.

LILAC

Common Lilac (*Syringa vulgaris*); also known as blue pipe, French
lilac.
Fairytale Series Cultivars:
Tinkerbelle Lilac (*S.* x 'bailbelle')
Fairy Dust (*S.* x 'baildust')
Sugar Plum Fairy (*S.* x 'bailsugar')

Native to southeastern Europe, lilac is a multi-stemmed shrub that reaches twelve to
fifteen feet tall and can spread eight to twelve feet wide. The lilac is beloved for the fragrance of its four-lobed, tubular flowers that hang in inverted pyramidal clusters. They
range from white, to lilac, to purple. The pointed heart-shaped leaves range from gray
green to blue green. Reaching only about six feet tall, the fairytale series cultivars are
a cross between the Korean lilac (*S. meyeri*) and the little leaf lilac (*S. pubescens* subsp.
microphylla). The flowers of the Tinkerbelle are deep pink, Fairy Dust flowers are pink

and very fragrant, and the Sugar Plum Fairy has rosy-lilac flowers. The compact size of the fairytale lilacs makes them just right for small gardens.

The delightful fragrance of lilacs is so popular that many arboretums have a special event called *Lilac Sunday* so people can enjoy them in full bloom. This plant's genus name comes from the Greek word *syrinx* meaning "tube" or "pipe."[102] It is also the name of the water nymph mentioned in the profile *Reeds, Rushes, and Cattails*. The lilac genus and folk name *blue pipe* refer to the custom of hollowing out the stems to make pipes for utilitarian and musical use.

The lilac has been wildly popular since the time of King Henry VIII (1491–1547). For seventeenth-century settlers in the New World, lilacs were a link to the homeland they left behind. The lilac was the second flowering shrub transported to North America from Europe; rose was the first. According to folklore in England, white lilacs were considered unlucky to wear except on May Day. If a lilac bush was cut down, it was believed that other lilacs in the area would mourn and not produce flowers the following year.

In Norfolk, England, lilacs were generally regarded as unlucky. In addition to purple being a mourning color, the flowers were often used to line coffins and graves to add beauty and offer solace as well as combat odors. According to legend, a vase of lilac flowers was never placed in a sick room because the strong scent would be too much for someone weakened by illness. When it came to love, a woman who inadvertently wore lilac flowers was destined to never marry, and when sent to a fiancée they were a signal that the marriage was off.

In the weather lore of Wales, lilac flowers were an indication for the summer season. If the buds formed late and then opened quickly, it would be rainy. If the flowers faded faster than normal, summer would be very warm. In Russia, it was believed that a baby placed under a lilac bush would receive the gift of wisdom.

Magical Connections

Elements:	Water
Astrological influence:	Mercury, Moon, Venus; Libra, Taurus
Magical beings and woodland spirits:	Fairies

---

102. Umberto Quattrocchi, *CRC World Dictionary of Plant Names: Common Names, Scientific Names, Eponyms, Synonyms, and Etymology: R-Z*, vol. 4 (Boca Raton, FL: CRC Press, LLC, 2016), 2617.

Wildlife:	Butterfly

Runes:	Ehwaz/Eh ᛗ
	    Runic half month: March 30 to April 13
	 Iwaz/Eoh/Eihwaz ᛇ
	    Runic half month: December 28 to January 12

Powers/attributes:	Banish, challenges/obstacles (overcome), concentration/focus, creativity, defense, divination, dream work, emotions (deal with, support), family and home, happiness, hexes (remove, ward off), inspiration, love, luck, negativity (remove, ward off), past-life work, peace, prophecy, protection, psychic abilities, purification, release (let go, move on), renewal, security, spirit guides/spirits, spirituality, wisdom
Other associations:	Beltane

Items to purchase when the tree is not available: flower essence made from the common lilac.

Spellwork and Ritual

Lilac supports divination and psychic work, especially clairvoyance, and is an aid when accessing past-life memories. Dry a few leaves and burn one before engaging in these practices. A vase of fresh-cut lilac flowers in the bedroom encourages prophetic dreams. The scent is especially helpful for focusing the mind. Place a twig on your desk or somewhere in your workspace to help foster inspiration and increase creativity.

Place white lilac flowers on your altar to enhance an esbat ritual or amplify lunar magic. Dry some lilac-colored flowers to use as a charm to attract love. Use the flower essence to prepare a candle for a love spell. Dried leaves or flowers can be burned for defensive magic and to break hexes. In addition to repelling negative energy, the smoke aids in banishing unwanted spirits. Burn a few dried leaves to clear ritual space. Carry a piece of bark or part of a twig as a good luck charm or protective amulet.

Although it was once customary to plant lilacs in front of a house, growing it anywhere on your property will invite nature spirits and fairies to take up residence. Lilac also fosters peace and happiness and deepens spirituality.

LINDEN

American Linden (*Tilia americana*); also known as basswood, bee tree, lime tree.

Common Linden (*T. x europaea* syn. *T. x vulgaris*); also known as European linden, lime tree.

Lindens are stately trees with ridged bark and heart-shaped leaves. They are most notable for their fragrant, creamy-white flowers that hang in clusters. These are followed by pea-sized nutlets. The American linden reaches fifty to eighty feet and sometimes taller. Its bark is gray brown and its leaves dark green. It is native to central and eastern North America. Native to Europe, the common linden is a hybrid of the small-leaved linden (*T. cordata*) and large-leaved linden (*T. platyphyllos*). It reaches fifty to ninety feet and sometimes taller. Its bark is pale gray and leaves dark green. The leaves of both trees turn dull yellow in the autumn.

This tree had a mystical importance to the Scythians (c. 900–200 BCE), the nomadic people of the Black Sea region. According to legend, their seers would stand underneath linden trees to make prophecies. The tree was sacred to the Greeks and Romans. At festivals honoring Ceres, her statues were adorned with linden. The Romans regarded a linden as a safe place to hold confidential discussions. Pliny the Elder noted that this tree was highly prized for its medicinal uses.

In eastern and central Europe, linden trees were an integral part of the culture and were usually planted to mark a place of importance such as a town center, a spring, a well, or a castle. In more recent times, lindens were used as shade trees to line city streets with Berlin's Unter Den Linden being the most famous. The term *under the linden* could refer to walking under the trees or to being protected since linden was the conventional wood used for battle shields by Germanic peoples. Also regarded as justice trees, courts of law were often conducted, and judgments passed under lindens. In later centuries, they were planted in front of courthouses in the Netherlands to serve as symbols of justice.

In the Middle Ages, the linden was a tree of love where couples made their marriage vows. Centuries later in Belgium, lindens were known as sacrament trees. Into the early twentieth century in France, it was customary for newlyweds to walk under lindens to ensure a happy marriage. In Estonia and Lithuania, libations were made at lindens for fertility in marriage, and in Germany a linden was traditionally planted when a girl was born.

Like other trees located beside wells and springs, lindens were regarded as sacred and protective. A linden located at a three-road junction was regarded as particularly powerful. Even touching a linden was believed to take away illness. These trees were also used to cast spells. A woman spurned or cheated on would hammer a nail into a linden while wishing the man illness or death. A nail was also driven into a linden to remove illness. Carrying a piece of bark was protection against magic and witches.

Although in parts of Germany witches were believed to live in these trees and to gather underneath them on Walpurgis, linden branches were placed in front of houses to keep witches away. Branches were attached to houses and stables at Whitsuntide, the seventh Sunday after Easter and the following week, for protection from witches. The reason witches were thought to attack at this time is unknown. In Austria, this was done on St. John's Day, June 24, when the trees were in bloom and fragrant. In addition to witches, fairies were believed to hide in the bark of lindens; in southern Germany, it was dwarves. Dragons were said to enjoy laying in the shade of a linden and elves favored them for dancing around on clear nights.

Magical Connections

Element:	Air
Astrological influence:	Jupiter, Mercury, Sun; Gemini, Sagittarius, Taurus
Deities:	Arianrhod, Ceres, Eostre, Freya, Frigg, Holda, Lada, Odin, Philyra, Tyr, Venus
Magical beings and creatures and woodland spirits:	Dragons, dwarves, fairies
Wildlife:	Bee, butterfly, dove (turtle)
Alternate tree calendar:	March 11 to 20 and September 13 to 22
Runes:	Ansuz/As/Os ᚨ Runic half month: August 13 to 28
Powers/attributes:	Attraction, changes/transitions, communication, defense, divination, dream work, happiness, justice/legal matters, love, loyalty/fidelity, luck, negativity (remove, ward off), peace, prophecy, protection, strength, stress/anxiety (calm, release), support (provide, receive), transformation
Other associations:	Ostara, Walpurgis, Beltane, Litha

Items to purchase when the tree is not available: dried leaves and flowers, flower essence is made from the American linden.

Spellwork and Ritual

Use linden flowers in a spell to attract love and romance. Incorporate a few leaves or a picture of a linden in your handfasting ritual to strengthen your vows. Use linden in charms to enhance fidelity in a relationship. The flowers foster a peaceful frame of mind and aid in sharpening communication skills.

Burn a dried leaf in your cauldron and waft the smoke in an area where you need to remove negative energy; also do this for a protection spell. Place a leaf or a picture of the tree in an organza bag on your bedside table to enhance dream work, especially prophetic dreaming. Use the flower essence to prepare candles for divination sessions.

When seeking justice, write a few keywords on a picture of the tree and carry it with you when going to court or meeting with your lawyer. Also carry a picture with you for general good luck. Linden is also an aid for initiating changes in your life and developing strength.

LOCUST

Black Locust (*Robinia pseudoacacia* syn. *Acacia americana*); also
  known as false acacia, honey locust, yellow locust.
Honey Locust (*Gleditsia triacanthos*); also known as honeyshuck, sweet
  bean, sweet locust, thorn tree, thorny locust.

Although these trees have different genera, they come from the pea (*Fabaceae/Legumino-sae*) botanical family and produce legume-like seedpods. Both trees grow between thirty-five to seventy-five feet tall and have feathery green leaves that turn yellow in the autumn. Native to central and eastern North America, the honey locust has dark reddish-brown bark and small greenish-white flowers. Long, twisted seedpods form in late summer and stay on the tree into winter. The honey locust trunk and branches sprout reddish thorns with three or more points. Up to six or more inches long, the thorns often grow in clusters.

Native to eastern North America, the black locust has fragrant white flowers in long drooping clusters that reach eight or more inches long. Its seedpods are straight rather than twisted. Unlike the impressive thorns of the honey locust, the black locust has small sharp spines that grow in pairs at the leaf axils. The word *black* in its name refers to the tree's dark-colored bark and seedpods.

The species name of the honey locust comes from Greek and means "three thorn" in reference to the number of points that often occur on the thorns.[103] Although the locust has been described as a sinister tree because of its large thorns, Native Americans put them to practical use for spear points and animal traps. The bark, seedpods, and leaves of the black locust are poisonous, which may have added to its dark reputation.

Honey is derived mainly from the flowers of the black locust; it is fragrant, fruity, and pale to lemon yellow in color. The more mono-floral the honey, the lighter the color to the point of being almost clear. Despite the tree's name, very little honey is produced from the honey locust. Instead, it refers to the sugary-sweet pulp contained in the seed-pods. Home brewers follow tradition and use the pulp for making beer. While the seeds of the honey locust can be eaten raw or cooked, the pods are usually used for animal feed.

The first written mention of the locust tree was by English writer and Jamestown resident William Strachey (1572–1621) in his *Historie of Travaile into Virginia Britannia* published in 1610.[104] Because of the resemblance, Strachey named it for the locust tree mentioned in the Bible, which is the carob tree (*Ceratonia siliqua*). According to Middle Eastern mythology, jinn, spirits that could take human or animal form as well as possess people, inhabited carob trees. This belief carried over, which resulted in the notion that locust trees were frequently haunted.

Both the honey and black locusts are susceptible to the formation of witches' brooms. The term comes from the German *hexenbesen* meaning "a bewitched bundle of twigs."[105] According to legend, some of the alleged witches of Salem, Massachusetts, were hanged on a locust tree. In the eighteenth century, locust trees were planted over the graves of several witch trial victims.

---

103. Raymond L. Taylor, *Plants of Colonial Days* (Mineola, NY: Dover Publications Inc., 1996), 49.

104. Donald Culross Peattie, *A Natural History of North American Trees* (San Antonio, TX: Trinity University Press, 2007), 332.

105. Paula Flynn, "Witches' Brooms on Trees," Iowa State University Extension and Outreach, last updated February 23, 2005, https://hortnews.extension.iastate.edu/2005/2-23-2005/witchesbroom.html.

In weather lore, when locust trees begin to bloom, it is time to plant cotton. If there is a profusion of flowers, the corn crop will be good. For reasons unknown, folklore states that a locust tree should only be cut down during the dark/new phase of the moon.

Magical Connections

Elements:	Earth, water
Astrological influence:	Aries
Deities:	Cerridwen, Hecate, the Morrigan
Wildlife:	Finch, rabbit, squirrel
Powers/attributes:	Balance/harmony, bind, challenges/obstacles (overcome), defense, determination/endurance, love, loyalty/fidelity, negativity (remove, ward off), protection, secrets, strength
Other associations:	Mabon, Samhain

Items to purchase when the tree is not available: black locust honey, flower essence made from the black locust.

Spellwork and Ritual

To stimulate protective energy, place a large thorn from a honey locust or several spines from a black locust on a windowsill pointing in the direction from which you feel a threat. Place three thorns under your front porch to prevent negative energy from entering your home. The thorns and spines can also be used in spells to strengthen determination when working to overcome obstacles.

Burn a few dried leaves to seal a pledge. Use locust honey in spells to attract love. Dried seedpods can be used as rattles for dark moon rituals. Any part of the tree, especially the thorns and spines, aids in connecting with dark goddesses. While the energy of the locust can be a challenge to work with, persistence and honesty go a long way with this tree.

MAPLE

Field Maple (*Acer campestre*); also known as European field maple,
   hedge maple, maplin tree, mazer.
Sugar Maple (*A. saccharum*); also known as bird's eye maple, hard
   maple.

These two types of maples have gray bark and their leaves have three to five lobes. In the spring, they produce clusters of small greenish-yellow flowers. Pairs of winged seeds called *samara* and *keys* mature in the autumn. Well known for its fiery autumn colors, the sugar maple grows to a height of sixty to seventy-five feet and sometimes one hundred. This tree is native to eastern North America. The field maple reaches only twenty-five to thirty-five feet tall. Its leaves turn yellow in autumn. It is native to Europe, western Asia, and Africa.

The genus name *Acer* is Latin meaning "sharp."[106] This may refer to the sharply pointed leaf tips or to the Greek and Roman use of the wood for spears and lances. The Greeks dedicated the tree to Phobos, the god of fear and the son of Ares, the god of war.

The name *bird's eye maple* refers to the eye-like patterns that are exposed when the wood is sliced. The Old English name for this tree, *mazer* or *maser*, was also applied to a drinking bowl made from a large burl, a large rounded outgrowth on a tree trunk.[107] The traditional wassail bowl was made from maple. From the Old English *malpulder*, the maple was also called *maplin* tree and sometimes *maypoling* tree in Gloucestershire, England.[108] Maples were sometimes used as boundary trees in England. Leaves of the field maple were often worn as a substitute for oak leaves on Oak Apple Day, May 29. (Refer to the entry for oak on page 214 for more on this.)

The sugar maple's species name *saccharum* refers to the tree's sweet sap.[109] Native Americans were tapping the trees long before Europeans arrived in North America. Colonial settlers used the unprocessed sap medicinally to treat several ailments. The most highly prized maple syrup is produced by sugar maples in New England. The chilly nights and warm days of late winter/early spring are necessary to make the sap run. The sugar season usually lasts five to six weeks. Here in Maine, where I live, the fourth Sunday in March is celebrated as Maple Sunday.

In weather lore, if the first sap from a tree is not sweet, it will be a long maple syrup season. If the first sap is sweet, the season for tapping will be short. The undersides of the leaves turning upwards were an indication that rain would arrive within twenty-four hours. Maple branches were sometimes used as divining rods.

According to a legend in the Alsace region of France, storks used branches from the field maple in their nests to frighten bats away. The reason that bats would fear maple branches is unknown. Another legend explained that the leaves became red in the autumn because the fairy living in the tree painted them. Fairies were also said to sit along maple branches to watch human activities. In Germany, a type of fairy referred to as the *wood folk* were believed to have skin like maple bark and clad themselves in moss from the root of the tree.

---

106. Wells, *The Lives of Trees*, 209.

107. Small, *North American Cornucopia*, 651.

108. Wells, *The Lives of Trees*, 210; Watts, *Elsevier's Dictionary of Plant Lore*, 150.

109. Coombes, *Dictionary of Plant Names*, 17.

In parts of England, it was believed that passing a child through the branches of a maple would ensure long life. When a particular maple was scheduled to be cut down in Sussex, England, the townspeople rallied together to prevent its destruction and ensure that future children would have long lives. Passing a child through the branches was also done to cure rickets and to avert the evil eye. According to other folklore, popping a maple key (breaking the two seeds apart) in front of someone's face would give him or her freckles.

Magical Connections

Elements:	Air, earth
Astrological influence:	Jupiter; Cancer, Libra, Virgo
Deities:	Ares, Athena, Phobos, Rhiannon, Venus
Magical beings and woodland spirits:	Fairies, wood folk
Wildlife:	Deer, hedgehog, owl (horned), moose, rabbit, stork
Alternate tree calendar:	April 11 to 20 and October 14 to 23
Runes:	Mannaz/ Madhr/Mann ᛗ Runic half month: April 14 to 28
Powers/attributes:	Abundance, astral travel/journeying, balance/harmony, communication, creativity, divination, dream work, loss/sorrow (ease, recover from), love, money/prosperity, prophecy, release (let go, move on), support (provide, receive), transformation, wisdom
Other associations:	Mabon, Ostara

Items to purchase when the tree is not available: maple syrup, flower essence made from the sugar maple.

Spellwork and Ritual

Place a green leaf under a green candle on your altar to attract prosperity. Scatter dried red leaves on your altar as part of a spell to attract or rekindle love. Place a few winged maple seeds and dried leaves in a sachet and hang it on a bedpost to foster prophetic dreams. Burn a couple of dried leaves to release whatever you no longer want in your life. Maple is also instrumental for divination sessions and when seeking wisdom. For esbat rituals, use seeds to make a circle on your altar with the seed ends touching each other and the wings pointing outward.

When grieving for a loved one, before lighting a remembrance candle, dab a little maple syrup on it to symbolically sweeten their transition to the otherworld. Use red leaves to work with the fairy realm. Press a variety of colored leaves in a book, and then place them on your desk or workspace to boost creativity. Maple is also helpful to hone communication skills. Place a few leaves or seeds in the kitchen to attract abundance. Look for fallen maple branches as they make excellent wands.

MISTLETOE

American Mistletoe (*Phoradendron leucarpum* syn. *P. flavescens*); also
  known as oak mistletoe.
European Mistletoe (*Viscum album*); also known as all heal, golden
  bough.

Mistletoe is a semiparasitic evergreen shrub that grows in clumps on tree limbs.
Although it is sometimes called *oak mistletoe*, it grows on a wide range of trees. In fact, it
is unusual for European mistletoe to grow on oaks. Mistletoe has thick, leathery leaves,
small white or greenish-white flowers, and white or yellowish berries.

   While its roots tap into the host tree's circulatory system for water and minerals,
these two species of mistletoe contain chlorophyll and produce their own food. They are
not considered serious pests. However, the plants that grow in the western United States,

known as dwarf mistletoe from the genus *Arceuthobium*, are parasitic and harmful to their hosts.

Growing in the heavenly realm, mistletoe was considered magically powerful, especially for fertility. At Yule, its plentiful white berries symbolized the sacred seed of the God who embodied the spirit of vegetation and the divine spark of life. Because it rarely grows on the sacred oak, when found there it was considered a precious commodity. There are numerous stories about how the Druids gathered mistletoe. However, Celtic scholar Peter Berresford Ellis believes that Pliny the Elder's description of the elaborate procedure may have been mistakenly attributed to Celtic Druids of the British Isles instead of the Germanic tribes on the Continent near Gaul.[110]

Growing atop trees, mistletoe seemed to suddenly appear out of nowhere. However, by the fifth or sixth century, people had figured out that birds dropped the seeds. The word *mistletoe* was derived from the Old English *mistiltān*, which may have meant "bird twig," referring to the thrush that fed on the berries.[111] However, most etymologists refer back to the Old High German *mist* meaning, "dung."[112] So basically, the plant may have been known as "bird dung twig."

According to Norse mythology, after the god Balder was slain with a branch of mistletoe, which was the only thing that could harm him, his mother Frigg was inconsolable. Taking pity on her, the other gods brought Balder back to life. Frigg declared that from that time forward mistletoe would be a plant for love, not death. Mistletoe's association with love remains to this day with our custom of kissing under it at Yule. In the past, it was believed that sweethearts who kissed under a sprig were destined to marry, but only if the mistletoe was burned on Twelfth Night/January 6. Mistletoe gathered at the summer solstice was used as a household amulet and hung above a doorway to ward off mischievous spirits.

In Greek mythology, mistletoe was a key for entering and returning from the underworld. Persephone used it to return to her mother for part of the year. However, although British anthropologist and folklorist James George Frazer (1854–1941) designated mistletoe as the golden bough carried by Trojan hero Aeneas to gain access to the underworld,

---

110. Peter Berresford Ellis, *A Brief History of the Druids* (New York: Carroll & Graf Publishers, 2002), 61.

111. Barnhart, *The Barnhart Concise Dictionary of Etymology*, 481.

112. Walter W. Skeat, *The Concise Dictionary of English Etymology* (New York: Cosimo, Inc., 2005), 288.

the yew has more recently become the candidate for this. Refer to the profile on yew for more about this.

In the folklore of Germany, Austria, and Flanders, mistletoe grew where an elf had sat in a tree. In other places, sprigs were hung in stables and homes to keep elves away and to avoid misfortune. Called *witches' broom* and *witches' nest* in Germany, it was called *devil's grass* in the Netherlands. According to legend, a person could see and talk to ghosts while holding a piece of mistletoe. In England, Wales, and France, it was regarded as a plant of good fortune. A sprig was hung in the home for a year and replaced with a fresh one at Yule.

Magical Connections

Elements :	Air
Astrological influence:	Mercury, Sun; Leo
Deities:	Apollo, Arianrhod, Asclepius, Balder, Demeter, Hades, Freya, Frigg, Jupiter, Odin, Persephone, Pluto, Venus, Zeus
Magical beings and woodland spirits:	Elves, fairies
Wildlife:	Thrush
Ogham:	Blank, the nameless day Celtic tree calendar: December 23
Runes:	Sowilo/Sol/Sigil ϟ Runic half month: February 12 to 26
Powers/attributes:	Banish, challenges/obstacles (overcome), changes/transitions, consecrate/bless, creativity, death/funeral practices, defense, divination, dream work, family and home, fertility, healing, love, luck, money/prosperity, negativity (remove, ward off), the otherworld, peace, protection, purification, renewal, secrets, security, sex/sexuality, spirit guides/spirits, success, transformation
Other associations:	Twelfth Night, Litha, Yule

Items to purchase when the plant is not available: dried, chopped European mistletoe is marketed as mistletoe herb.

Spellwork and Ritual

Make a ring of mistletoe berries around the base of a green candle for fertility spells and for dealing with any issue related to sex. Use mistletoe leaves for spells to attract love and romance. To provide protection, hang a large sprig in an area of your home where it will not be seen often. Allow it to dry and stay in place all year, and then burn it at Yule. Burn a few mistletoe leaves to remove negative energy or as part of a banishing spell. The smoke can be used to purify and consecrate ritual space.

As a plant of in-between places, hold a sprig before divination and dream work to enhance your experiences. Hang a small sprig over your altar when facing challenges or dealing with change. Use it in rituals, along with holly, to honor the God and Goddess.

MULBERRY

Black Mulberry (*Morus nigra*); also known as common mulberry, Persian mulberry, Spanish mulberry.

White Mulberry (*M. alba*); also known as Russian mulberry, silkworm mulberry.

Originating in the Middle East, the black mulberry tree grows approximately thirty feet tall. It has a short trunk and long spreading branches that usually need support as the tree ages. It has small green catkins and dark green, heart-shaped leaves that turn dull yellow in autumn. The green fruit turns red, and then black as it ripens. Mulberries resemble large blackberries. The white mulberry is native to China. It grows between thirty to fifty feet tall and develops a wide, spreading crown. It has yellowish-green catkins and glossy dark leaves that turn yellow or yellow brown in autumn. The fruit is white to pink and sometimes red or purplish black.

The genus name *Morus* may have been derived from the Greek *mora*, "delay," in reference to the tree not coming into bud until winter is well over and gone.[113] It is the reason Pliny the Elder called it *Sapientissima arborum*, "the wisest of all trees."[114] The Latin word *morum* was used for both mulberry and blackberry.[115]

The black mulberry is grown for its fruit, which is said to be tastier than other types of mulberries. The white mulberry is grown to feed silkworms, which thrive on its leaves. In medieval Europe, an image of mulberries on a sign above the entrance to a business indicated that it was in the silk trade.

The Chinese considered the mulberry a sacred tree that symbolized cosmic order. In the tale of Pyramus and Thisbe by Roman poet Ovid, which may have been the inspiration for Shakespeare's Romeo and Juliet, a mulberry tree was the meeting place for the star-crossed lovers. In the story, juice from the mulberries that dropped from the tree stained the ground blood red and set off a series of misunderstandings and tragic events.

Dedicating the tree to Minerva and Pan, the Romans sometimes used mulberry juice to color their faces for rituals and festivals. Like many plants, they transported the black mulberry into northern Europe and England. Both the Greeks and Romans were fond of the fruit and added it to wine to give it a darker color and enhance the flavor. The Romans also used it to make a wine called *moretum*. The Anglo-Saxon drink *morat* was made with honey and mulberry juice. The Danes adopted the drink.

In parts of Italy, the mulberry was regarded as a tree of good luck and a piece of twig was carried as an amulet. In Warwickshire, England, a mulberry had to be planted with a quince (*Cydonia oblonga*), otherwise, bad luck would befall the owner of the house. In other areas, this pair of trees was regarded as husband and wife and when planted together, the family would prosper. For reasons unknown, the mulberry had to be planted to the south and quince to the north. In China, a mulberry tree planted in front of a house was believed to bring sorrow. It was customary to carry a mulberry walking stick to indicate that a person was in mourning after the death of his or her mother.

In weather lore, it was said that there would be no more frost after the first green leaf appeared on a mulberry tree. An exceptionally large crop of mulberries meant famine or

113. Wells, *Lives of the Trees*, 218.

114. De Cleene and Lejeune, *Compendium of Symbolic and Ritual Plants in Europe*, 428.

115. Roy Vickery, ed. *Oxford Dictionary of Plant-Lore* (Oxford, England: Oxford University Press, 1997), 250.

generally hard times were coming. To keep children from overindulging in mulberries, they were told that the devil used them to blacken his boots.

From ancient times through the Middle Ages, the black mulberry was used for a wide range of ailments as noted by Pliny the Elder, Nicolas Culpeper, and John Gerard. The white mulberry had limited medicinal purposes.

Magical Connections

Elements:	Air
Astrological influence:	Mercury, Venus; Gemini, Virgo
Deities:	Athena, Diana, Hermes, Mercury, Minerva, Pan, Venus
Wildlife:	Dove, magpie, partridge
Powers/attributes:	Challenges/obstacles (overcome), consecrate/bless, creativity, divination, dream work, inspiration, luck, protection, psychic abilities, secrets, success, wisdom
Other associations:	Ostara

Items to purchase when the tree is not available: fresh or dried mulberries, dried leaves from the white mulberry, black mulberry juice.

Spellwork and Ritual

With a mulberry twig or wand, walk in a circle to consecrate a ritual space. Eat a few mulberries to heighten awareness before a divination session or any type of psychic work. Use mulberry juice as a libation for deities. Place a few leaves or a picture of a mulberry tree on your bedside table to aid in dream work. Keep a twig in your workspace to boost inspiration for creative work. For aid in keeping a secret, write a keyword or two on a picture of a mulberry tree, and then burn it in your cauldron as you think about the confidence you are keeping.

When dealing with challenges, this tree can help gain a successful outcome. Use mulberry juice to prepare a candle for protection spells. Place a circle of berries on your altar when seeking wisdom.

Common myrtle (*Myrtus communis*); also known as myrtle, Roman myrtle, sweet myrtle, true myrtle.

Native to the Mediterranean and southwestern Europe, myrtle is an evergreen shrub that reaches eight to twelve feet tall. Its glossy dark leaves are lance-shaped and pleasantly aromatic when crushed. In late spring or early summer, its showy white flowers sweetly scent the air. The fragrance of the bluish- to purple-black berries is reminiscent of eucalyptus or pine. The leaves, flowers, and fruit are used to flavor food.

Myrtle was sacred to Aphrodite, who was often depicted wearing a crown of flowers and leaves. The Greek Muses and the Roman Lares (household spirits) also wore crowns of myrtle. Adorning her temple in Rome, Venus is frequently depicted wearing myrtle, too, as were her attendants. Myrtle trees were planted in the grounds around her temples, and she was sometimes known as Myrtilla or Myrtea. By the Middle Ages, the tree was a symbol of love.

Chaplets of myrtle were worn by the participants in the Eleusinian Mysteries, the annual rituals in honor of Demeter and Persephone. In Egypt, the flowers and leaves were used for adornment at the feasts of the pharaohs. In addition to Venus, the Romans also dedicated this tree to Mars. While traveling, ordinary Romans wore a sprig of myrtle leaves as a talisman or carried a myrtle stick to keep them from growing weary and to ensure a successful journey. Myrtle was also regarded as a protective plant. The tree was sometimes used to indicate an inn for travelers.

Associated with death and immortality, the Greeks used myrtle to adorn graves, often pairing it with the herb helichrysum (*Helichrysum angustifolium*), which was also associated with immortality. With powers of purification, myrtle was believed to prepare the deceased for the afterlife. The Egyptians placed myrtle leaves in and on graves. Centuries later, it was customary in France to put a myrtle branch in someone's coffin if the tree grew on that person's property.

In some versions of the Greek story of Daphne and Apollo, it was a myrtle tree rather than a laurel into which Daphne transformed, which may be the basis for the belief that it protects against enchantments. Myrtle and olive sprigs bundled with roses were believed to be a powerful combination for black magic of a sexual nature.

To the Greeks and Romans, myrtle served as a symbol of authority; to the Hebrews, a symbol of peace and reconciliation. Until the early twentieth century in Wales, myrtle was planted on both sides of a house to symbolically hold love and peace within the home. However, these trees could never be disturbed, otherwise calamity would ensue. A sprig was placed on cradles to keep babies happy and protect them from witches. Myrtle was also used for protection against lightning.

With the Greek practice of steeping myrtle boughs in wine to enhance its taste, the tree became associated with festivity. As a symbol of love, it was customary in Palestine for both the bride and groom to wear myrtle and roses at the wedding celebration. The Romans used it at weddings too. Centuries later, it was customary in England for one of the bridesmaids to plant a sprig from the bridal bouquet. If it didn't grow, the bridesmaid would remain unmarried. In Victorian England, myrtle flowers were included in the bridal bouquet for good luck and fidelity in the marriage. According to tradition in Wales, the bride would give each of her bridesmaids a sprig of myrtle. It was believed that placing it under the pillow would produce dreams of their future husbands.

In Germany, the myrtle crown worn by a bride at her wedding would be used to make medicinal remedies. Both Dioscorides and Pliny the Elder recommended the berries to treat a number of ailments. In medieval Europe, myrtle continued to be revered for its healing properties.

Magical Connections

Element:	Water
Astrological influence:	Moon, Venus; Sagittarius, Taurus
Deities:	Aphrodite, Artemis, Astarte, Athena, Dionysus, Eros, Hathor, Ishtar, Mars, Venus
Powers/attributes:	Abundance, the afterlife, authority/leadership, communication, consecrate/bless, creativity, death/funeral practices, determination/endurance, dream work, emotions (deal with, support), family and home, fertility, growth, healing, loss/sorrow (ease, recover from), love, loyalty/fidelity, luck, money/prosperity, the otherworld, peace, protection, psychic abilities, purification, release (let go, move on), sex/sexuality, strength, success
Other associations:	Ostara, Litha, Lughnasadh, Mabon

Items to purchase when the tree is not available: dried leaves, essential oil is made from leaves and twigs.

Spellwork and Ritual

Prepare a red candle with myrtle essential oil to use for love spells. Write the word *love* on a picture of myrtle flowers and place it under your pillow to help you dream of romance. Wear a crown of myrtle at a handfasting ceremony. Make a circle with the berries on your altar for healing rituals and leave them in place for three days. Carry a picture of the tree for luck or place it in your luggage while traveling for a smooth journey.

Burn a dried leaf as part of a protection spell or to purify ritual space. The smoke is also instrumental for banishing spells or releasing unsettled emotions. Place a sprig of leaves on your altar for meditation to aid in recovering from grief after the death of a loved one. Also place a sprig on the grave, if appropriate.

OAK

Black Oak (*Quercus velutina*); also known as eastern black oak.

English Oak (*Q. robur*); also known as common oak, European oak, truffle oak.

White Oak (*Q. alba*); also known as fork-leaf oak, ridge oak.

The distinctive oak leaf shape has deep indentations with five to seven lobes that can have multiple points at the ends. The oak nut (acorn) is topped by a woody cap. Native to the eastern United States, the black and white oak trees are some of the most common in North America. Although the black oak usually reaches fifty to seventy feet tall, it can top one hundred. The bark is gray but turns almost black on mature trees. Its leaves have pointed lobes tipped with tiny bristles. The white oak reaches fifty to eighty feet tall. Its leaves are rounded and smooth. The English oak is native to Europe and southwestern

Asia. Growing between fifty to one hundred feet tall, its bark is dark gray to blackish brown. The leaves have rounded lobes with smaller ones at the base.

In almost every country where the oak grows, it has been regarded as sacred. The Greeks and Romans associated this tree with their most powerful gods. According to various texts, the oracle of Zeus was in a grove of mostly oak trees in Dodona, Greece, where answers were interpreted from the sounds of rustling leaves as well as doves sitting in the oaks. Roman emperors wore crowns of oak to associate their power with the gods. Statues of the most important gods and goddesses were adorned with oak leaves and wreaths were hung on the doors of highly respected people.

Associating the oak with their gods Bilé and the Dagda, the Celts held important ceremonies underneath oak trees. When seeking favor with the gods or a cure for illness, the Celts of Gaul hung offerings and gifts on an oak, and then circled it nine times while reciting an incantation or prayer of thanks. Regarding the oak as sacred, Germanic peoples worshipped Thor, and other gods, underneath these trees. Because they were believed to hold divine wisdom, oaks were also regarded as justice trees. Unfortunately, it was the opposite for Joan of Arc (1412–1431). Her visits to the fairy oak of Bourlemont aroused suspicion that she worshiped either the tree or its otherworldly spirit in exchange for strength in battle.

Along with ash and hawthorn, the oak was part of the Celtic triad of powerful fairy trees. Each Celtic tribe had its special oak tree that functioned as the community's talisman. In Germany, oak twigs were hung outside windows and in front of stable doors for protection on Walpurgis, however, they were never to be carried across the threshold. It was believed in Somerset, England, that angry spirits would haunt the trunk of an oak if the tree had been coppiced (severely cut back to encourage new growth and increase the amount of firewood that can be harvested). Such a tree was avoided after sundown. In other areas, fairies were said to inhabit some oaks. The holes created by branches that had fallen off were known as fairy doors. It was believed that touching a fairy door could heal disease. In India, a hole in an oak was believed to be a pathway for the spirit of the tree to pass in and out. Pilgrimages to sacred wells and springs during the month of May were common in Cornwall, England. Rags were tied to nearby oaks for protection against sorcery and to appease any fairies that frequented the well.

Oaks were regarded as trees of prophecy, especially those struck by lightning. Oddly enough, acorns were carried as protection against lightning; this practice continued into the twentieth century.

Yuletide is when the Oak King takes over from the Holly King to reign for half the year. Refer to the profile on holly for more on this. Oak is one of the traditional woods for the Yule log and a rare host for the mystical mistletoe.

Oak Apple Day was a celebration on May 29 to commemorate the restoration of the British monarchy in 1660. According to legend, King Charles II escaped capture by hiding in an oak tree. For several centuries, it was customary to wear oak leaves or oak apples (galls); field maple leaves were sometimes used as a substitute. Resembling a small, spongy apple, an oak apple is an abnormal growth that forms when an oak apple gall wasp lays eggs in the tree. Oak apples were used for divination. To tell if a child had been bewitched, three oak apples were placed in a pail of water under his or her bed. If they sank, the answer was affirmative.

Oak apples were also used in weather divination. If at the end of September a small worm was found inside an oak apple (after the wasps had evacuated it), the season would be pleasant. A fly meant the winter would be moderate and a spider meant scarcity and poverty ahead.

Magical Connections

Elements:	Air, earth, fire
Astrological influence:	Jupiter, Sun; Cancer, Gemini, Leo, Sagittarius, Virgo
Deities:	Artemis, Apollo, Ares, Balder, Bilé, Brigid, Ceres, Cernunnos, Cerridwen, Cybele, the Dagda, Demeter, Diana, Dôn, Donar, the Green Man, Hades, Helios, Hera, Juno, Jupiter, Mars, the Morrigan, Odin, Pan, Perkunas, Perun, Pluto, Rhea, Thor, Zeus
Magical beings and woodland spirits:	Balanos (Greek tree nymph), dryads, elves, fairies, hamadryads
Wildlife:	Bee, boar, chameleon, cicada, horse (white), oriole, wolf, woodpecker, wren
Ogham:	Duir/Dair ⊥⊥ Celtic tree calendar: June 10 to July 7
Alternate tree calendar:	March 21/spring equinox

Runes:	Dagaz/Daeg/Dag ᛞ
	    Runic half month: June 14 to 28
	Ehwaz/Eh ᛖ
	    Runic half month: March 30 to April 13
	Jera/Ger/Jara ᛃ
	    Runic half month: December 13 to 27
	Raido/Reidh/Rad ᚱ
	    Runic half month: August 29 to September 12
	Thurisaz/Thurs/Thorn ᚦ
	    Runic half month: July 29 to August 12
	Tiwaz/Tyr/Tir ᛏ
	    Runic half month: February 27 to March 13
	Ac (Anglo-Saxon) ᚪ

Powers/attributes:	Abundance, the afterlife, ancestors, authority/leadership, awareness (enhance, heighten), challenges/obstacles (overcome), confidence, consecrate/bless, courage, death/funeral practices, defense, determination/endurance, enchantment, family and home, fertility, growth, healing, inspiration, justice/legal matters, knowledge (see, acquire), loyalty/fidelity, luck, manifest (desires, dreams, will), money/prosperity, negativity (remove, ward off), the otherworld, prophecy, protection, purification, renewal, secrets, security, sex/sexuality, shamanic work, spirit guides/spirits, strength, success, wisdom
Other associations:	Walpurgis, Beltane, Litha, Midsummer's Eve, Lughnasadh, Mabon, Yule

Items to purchase when the tree is not available: dried bark from the white oak is available in pieces or powdered, flower essence is made from the English oak.

Spellwork and Ritual

Oak leaves in the home help clear away negative energy, and when used on the altar in ritual, they represent the potency of the God. For healing or when seeking wisdom, hold a piece of bark between your hands and visualize your desired outcome. Also use a piece of bark to help ground energy after ritual. Hang a small twig with leaves in your kitchen to invite abundance into your home. Leaves placed under the bed aid fertility and virility. To add power to spells, make a cross by tying two bare twigs together with black thread, which will create elemental balance and draw in the strength of the oak. The associated ogham or runes can be carved into a brown candle to represent the oak.

Use an acorn in spells to manifest what you need. Carry one for protection or place several on a windowsill to protect your home. An acorn on your altar during ritual or meditation aids in connecting with ancient wisdom. Place three acorn cups (the top of the nut) in a row on a kitchen windowsill and ask for abundance, blessings, and love for your home and family. Leave several acorn cups in your garden with food for the fairies.

Common Olive (*Olea europaea*); also known as European olive.

Native to the Mediterranean region, this evergreen tree reaches twenty to thirty feet tall. Olive trees have smooth gray bark that becomes gnarled with age. It has narrow waxy leaves and small white flowers. The oval green fruit ripens to black and contains a single pit. Its genus name comes from the Latin name for the tree.[116] The tree can live and bear fruit for more than a thousand years, with some sources indicating up to two thousand.

The olive tree is one of the oldest domesticated plants and was *the* fruit tree of classic ancient civilizations. It was regarded as a gift from the gods. Domesticated between 4000 and 3000 BCE in the Near East, it was a valuable source of food and oil.[117] Olive oil was a major commodity for trade as evidenced by the thousands of amphorae found in ancient shipwrecks.

116. Coombes, *Dictionary of Plant Names*, 140.

117. Joan P. Alcock, *Food in the Ancient World* (Westport, CT: Greenwood Press, 2006), 87.

According to one Greek myth, Athena struck the ground with her spear to bring forth the olive tree as a gift to humans. In another, it was Hermes who grew the first olive tree. Whatever its source, the tree played a part in other legends too. In *The Odyssey* by Greek poet Homer (c. 9th or 8th century BCE), the hero Ulysses' spear of olive wood brought down the fearsome Cyclops. Hercules' great club was also made of olive wood. Statues of Greek deities were crowned with olive wreaths. Winners of the early Olympic competitions were awarded jars of olive oil and crowned with the leaves. Twigs for wreaths to commemorate military victories were said to have been cut from the tree with a golden sickle.

The Romans allowed the wood to be used only for sacred purposes, such as lighting temple fires or when making offerings to deities. The ancient Arabs and Hebrews also venerated this tree. The Greeks considered olive oil an essential component of sacred rites so much so that those employed in its cultivation were exempt from military service. They also used olive oil in everyday life with functions for cooking, lighting, and personal body care. Likewise, Roman soldiers and athletes rubbed their bodies with olive oil for its healing and protective properties. The Romans often depicted deities holding olive branches and Germanic peoples anointed statues of deities with the oil. Emperors and high priests were anointed with olive oil, which was symbolic of conferring divine power on them. This practice has continued for centuries in the coronation of monarchs, including Britain's Queen Elizabeth II (1926–) who was anointed with olive oil and balm.

Not only was the olive tree significant in life, but also death. The Greeks and Romans buried loved ones with olive branches with the intention of helping them rest in peace. Wreaths were also laid on top of graves. The Egyptians placed crowns of olive leaves on mummies to aid them in the afterlife.

The olive tree's association with peace extended to the belief that pouring olive oil on a stormy sea could calm the waves. Olive branches were placed in the home to protect it from lightning and other evils. According to legend, witches stayed away from houses consecrated with olive oil. In Italy, a branch was hung over the doorway to a home to keep out wizards and devils.

Associated with divination, olive branches were carried by visitors to the oracle at Delphi. Olive leaves were used for marriage prophecy in nineteenth-century Italy. A young woman would spit on a leaf and toss it into the hearth fire. If it turned over or floated up, she would marry; if it burned, she would not.

Magical Connections

Elements:	Air, earth, fire, water
Astrological influence:	Jupiter, Mercury, Moon, Sun; Aquarius, Aries, Leo
Deities:	Amaterasu, Amun, Apollo, Athena, Brahma, Fides, Flora, Hermes, Horus, Indra, Jupiter, Minerva, Pele, Poseidon, Ra, Saturn, Zeus
Magical beings and creatures and woodland spirits:	Unicorn
Wildlife:	Dove
Alternate tree calendar:	September 23/autumn equinox
Powers/attributes:	Abundance, attraction, balance/harmony, consecrate/ bless, death/funeral practices, divination, family and home, fertility, healing, hope, love, loyalty/ fidelity, luck, manifest (desires, dreams, will), money/ prosperity, peace, protection, purification, renewal, security, sex/sexuality, spirit guides/spirits, spirituality, success

Items to purchase when the tree is not available: olives, olive oil, dried leaves

Spellwork and Ritual

A symbol of peace, hope, and prosperity, olive is a tree of the home and healing. Use olive oil to prepare candles for spells to manifest success, protection, and well-being for the family. Use olive oil or leaves in spells to increase abundance, luck, and money. Olive encompasses all things sexual: from attraction and lust to love and passion. To strengthen fidelity in any type of relationship, write the person's name on a picture of an olive tree and hold it while you meditate on the bond you have with that person. Dry three olive pits to use for a fertility charm.

Use olive oil as an offering for healing circles. Burn a few dried leaves to prepare sacred space. The olive's connection with spirituality and powers of purification make it ideal for consecrating anything used in ritual, magic, and divination. The olive tree also aids in contacting the spirit realm. Place a twig on your altar or eat three olives before working with spirits.

ORANGE

Seville Orange (*Citrus aurantium*); also known as bitter orange, sour
orange.

Sweet Orange (*C. sinensis* syn. *C. aurantium* var. *dulcis*); also known as
China orange.

The sweet orange tree grows between twenty to forty feet tall and is believed to have
originated in Southeast Asia. The bitter orange is smaller, ten to thirty feet tall, but har-
dier. It is believed to have come from northeastern India and the areas bordering Myanmar (Burma) and China. Both trees have shiny oval leaves. Their white five-petaled
flowers are fragrant and grow singly or in clusters.

The species name of the sweet orange, *sinensis*, is Latin meaning "of China."[118] The name *orange* evolved from the Sanskrit *nárangá-s* for "orange tree," through Persian, early medieval Latin, and then Old French *orenge*.[119]

The Moors, a nomadic people of North Africa, introduced the bitter orange into the Mediterranean region. They brought it with them in the eighth century when they invaded Spain. Italian merchant and explorer Marco Polo (1254–1324) saw oranges growing in Iran and referred to them as "apples of paradise."[120] Although it is often debated that an orange may have been the golden apple in Greek legend that Gaia presented to Hera, many scholars note that it was most likely the citron, the large gnarly cousin to the lemon, which was the citrus fruit well known to the ancient Greeks and Romans.

Introduced into the rest of Europe in the early fifteenth century, the bitter orange fruit was mainly used for medicinal purposes and the flowers for fragrance. The arrival of the sweet orange wasn't far behind its less palatable cousin. By the end of the fifteenth century, King Louis XIII of France (1601–1643) was giving the fruit as gifts.

Not long after it hit Europe, the sweet orange was adopted as an ingredient in mulled wine and by the seventeenth century, Europeans were crazy for oranges. With fragrant flowers and glossy leaves, the exotic orange was the must-have tree in royal gardens. Among the upper class, having an *orangerie*, a special greenhouse in which to grow citrus fruit, became a fashionable luxury and status symbol.

Neroli oil, made from orange blossoms, was named in honor of Princess Anne Marie Orsini (1642–1722) of Nerola, Italy, who adored the fragrance and made it all the rage throughout the Continent. Orange blossoms were used in love charms and became an important component in bridal bouquets where they symbolized purity, commitment, and fertility. Wedding cakes were decorated with orange blossom petals. Into the nineteenth century on the Italian island of Sardinia, the horns of oxen drawing a bridle couples' wagon were adorned with garlands of orange blossoms.

For love and marriage divination in England, oranges were sometimes used instead of apples. The peels were removed in a long strip from two oranges, and then tossed over the shoulders. The shapes they formed were supposed to reveal the initials of a future

118. Coombes, *Dictionary of Plant Names*, 56.

119. Barnhart, *The Barnhart Concise Dictionary of Etymology*, 525.

120. Staub, *75 Remarkable Fruits for Your Garden*, 153.

husband. According to Japanese legend, the scent of orange blossom reawakens forgotten love. As part of a marriage proposal in China, the future bride was given a gift of oranges.

Magical Connections

Elements:	Air, earth, fire, water
Astrological influence:	Sun; Aries, Leo, Sagittarius
Deities:	Fortuna, Gaia, Juno, Jupiter, Uranus, Zeus
Powers/attributes:	Abundance, awareness (enhance, heighten), clarity (enhance, foster), communication, concentration/focus, confidence, creativity, divination, dream work, emotions (deal with, support), family and home, fertility, growth, happiness, love, loyalty/fidelity, manifest (desires, dreams, will), money/prosperity, the otherworld, peace, protection, psychic abilities, purification, sex/sexuality, spirit guides/spirits, strength, success
Other associations:	Litha

Items to purchase when the tree is not available: fresh or dried oranges, orange juice, dried peel chopped or powdered from both sweet and bitter oranges, flower essence is made from the sweet orange. There are three essential oils: Orange is made from the peel of the sweet orange, neroli is made from the flowers of the bitter orange, and petitgrain is made from the leaves of the bitter orange.

Spellwork and Ritual

Oranges are excellent for preritual purification and as an aid for divination, dream work, and communicating with spirits. To stimulate creativity and focus your mind, place an orange in your workspace or use one of the essential oils to scent the air. Burn a piece of dried orange peel to boost the energy of a spell. Use a fresh peel or neroli essential oil in spells to attract love. Place dried orange seeds in the bedroom to enhance a fertility spell.

Prepare a candle with orange juice or essential oil to sharpen your focus and enhance clarity in psychic work. The scent of orange helps to awaken deep memories that foster personal growth. For spells to attract abundance and happiness to the home, peel an orange, separate the sections, and place them in a circle on your altar or in the kitchen. Leave them in place for three hours, and then eat them.

Use a whole orange on your altar at Litha to represent the warmth of the sun. Sprinkle dried orange peel around your property to invite peace and protection for you and your family.

PALM

Coconut Palm (*Cocos nucifera*)
Date Palm (*Phoenix dactylifera*); also known as common date palm.

Believed to have originated in the Malaysia and Indonesia region of Southeast Asia, the coconut palm is a slender tree that grows up to eighty feet tall. The leaves of its crown can grow fourteen to twenty feet long. The trunk is ringed with the bases of old leaves. Large clusters of coconuts turn brown as they mature and develop a thick fibrous husk over a hard shell. It takes about ten months for the fruit to mature. Growing to about seventy-five to eighty feet tall, the date palm trunk is also marked by old leaf bases. The leaves of its crown can grow up to sixteen feet in length. Long spikes of flowers produce clusters of fruit. Over one thousand dates can grow in a cluster. The date palm may have had its origin in India.

Both palm trees yielded the basics of life: food, medicine, timber, and fiber for weaving. The coconut aided the colonization of the Pacific Islands because it supplied all the basic needs for survival. Its nut was highly prized for milk and meat (the white lining inside the nut). The coconut has been likened to a monkey face because of its three indentations. Called *eyes*, they are marks left by the stem that attached the nut to the tree and through which a new tree can sprout. According to the mythology of the Maori of New Zealand, the indentations are the eyes and mouth of the eel that played a part in the tree's creation legend. The name *coconut* was derived from the late fifteenth century Portuguese word *coco* meaning "grimace," but also "goblin."[121]

In the South Pacific, coconut oil was used in women's purification rituals and in the ceremonial bathing of newborns. On the islands of Samoa, coconuts were not taken from the ground because it was believed that they belonged to magic spirits and doing so might result in the spirit taking revenge. In Malaysia, a coconut that lacked three eyes was considered a powerful charm against enemies.

In India, the coconut was regarded as a fruit of the gods. The act of breaking one open was used in place of sacrifice to Kali, the fierce manifestation of the Hindu mother goddess. This was also done in rituals when asking for blessings from Ganesh, the god of wisdom and luck. Coconuts were also believed to have the power to fulfill wishes. The coconut was a symbol of Shiva, one of the three supreme gods, and was sacred to Sarasvati, the goddess of learning. The leaves were used as decoration for important events such as weddings and Hindu religious ceremonies.

According to archeological evidence, date palms were being cultivated in Pakistan, Iran, and Egypt as early as 5000 BCE.[122] Regarded as the king of the oasis, this tree was revered by the Arabs. It was a holy tree to the Babylonians and Assyrians who frequently depicted it in their art. The Assyrians used date wine in prophecy rituals. The Greeks and Romans planted date palms around temples and shrines.

---

121. Mark Morton, *Cupboard Love 2: A Dictionary of Culinary Curiosities*, 2nd revised ed. (Toronto, Canada: Insomniac Press, 2004), 87.

122. Staub, *75 Remarkable Fruits for Your Garden*, 67.

Because of its high yield of fruit, the date palm was a symbol of fertility. This theme is evident in depictions of the goddess Diana with abundant dates as multiple breasts. The tree was also regarded as a phallic symbol. As a symbol of the sun, it was dedicated to Apollo and Helios. Because it was a symbol of life and rebirth, Swedish naturalist Carl Linnaeus (1707–1778), the founder of the structured botanical nomenclature, gave it the genus name of *Phoenix*.

Herbalists from Roman Dioscorides and Pliny the Elder in ancient times to English John Gerard and Flemish Rembert Dodoens in the Middle Ages, the date palm was a go-to tree for healing. Dates are still highly regarded for their health benefits. As for magic, a polished date seed was worn as an amulet against spells. On the Italian island of Sicily, three palm leaves and the proper incantation could ward off witches.

Magical Connections

Elements:	Air, fire
Astrological influence:	Jupiter, Mars, Moon, Sun; Leo, Sagittarius, Scorpio
Deities (coconut palm):	Ganesh, Hina, Kali, Sarasvati, Shiva, Vishnu
Deities (date palm):	Amun, Aphrodite, Apollo, Artemis, Asherah, Astarte, Diana, Dumuzi, Hecate, Helios, Hermes, Inanna, Ishtar, Isis, Leto, Mercury, Nike
Powers/attributes all palms:	Abundance, balance/harmony, banish, challenges/obstacles (overcome), consecrate/bless, courage, family and home, fertility, healing, hope, love, luck, negativity (remove, ward off), peace, prophecy, protection, purification, sex/sexuality, spirituality, strength, stress/anxiety (calm, release), success, wishes
Powers/attributes coconut palms:	Intuition
Powers/attributes date palms:	Happiness

Items to purchase when the trees are not available: dates; coconuts; coconut milk; dried coconut meat in slices, cubes, and flaked; copra, a ball of dried coconut meat; coconut shell beads; fibers from the coconut shell husk, known as coir, are used for a number of products.

Spellwork and Ritual

Use coconut milk as a libation for rituals. For fertility spells, prepare a candle with coconut oil and incorporate several dates into your ritual or a picture of a date palm. For success in any type of endeavor, wear a string of coconut shell beads or carry them in your pocket or purse. To attract abundance to your home, sprinkle a small handful of coconut flakes across the threshold of your front door. For protection, bury a date at each corner of your property or place a string of nine coconut beads as high as possible in your home.

Peach (*Prunus persica* syn. *Amygdalus persica*)

Reaching fifteen to twenty-five feet tall, the peach tree has drooping lance-shaped leaves and pink five-petaled flowers that grow singly or in pairs. The green fruit ripens to reddish orange. It is fleshy with a large hard seed, which is also known as a pit or stone. Native to China, cultivation of the peach tree began around 2000 BCE.[123]

According to Chinese mythology, a peach tree grew at the gate of the guardian spirits. Images of guardians carved of peach wood were used as amulets to repel demons. The flowers, fruit, and wood were highly regarded and believed to hold a great deal of spiritual power. The Chinese name for the peach is *tao*.[124]

123. Staub, *75 Remarkable Fruits for Your Garden*, 161.
124. Wells, *Lives of the Trees*, 251.

In Taoism (a Chinese philosophical and religious tradition also known as Daoism), the peach was regarded as sacred and a symbol of feminine sexuality. The peach also appears in Taoist myths associated with immortality. In addition to its connection with Chinese New Year celebrations, the peach blossom was a symbol of renewal and fertility. It was also associated with marriage. In Japan, the flower represented purity and fidelity. Both the tree and its fruit came to represent immortality and eternal youth. Peach tree bark was used to dye silk a popular brownish tea color.

The peach was also associated with protection. Tapestries featuring peaches were hung in homes to ward off evil spirits. At New Year, a figurine made of peach wood was placed above the front door to function as a guardian. Branches and woodcarvings were hung on porches to keep evil away. Peach branches were believed to have the power to exorcise evil. Peach stone pendants were placed on children to protect them from demons.

Greek botanist Theophrastus gave this tree the species name, *persica*, because he mistakenly thought it had originated in Persia. The fruit became commonly known as Persian plum and Persian apple. The Romans also referred to peaches as apples. Along with oranges, peaches vie for the mythological fruit referred to as Hera's golden apples. The Greeks used peaches for offerings to Harpocrates, the god of spring and silence. In Egypt, peach trees were often planted next to sepulchers that were used in the Mysteries of Osiris rituals and celebrations.

A laurel and peach tree in the garden of Roman emperor Alexander Severus (208/209–235 CE) were believed to predict the outcome of military actions. When the laurel sprouted branches higher than the peach tree, it was regarded as a sign that his army would defeat the Persians. As with many other plants, the Romans were responsible for spreading the peach tree into Europe and the British Isles. In addition to prophecy, magical healing became associated with it.

Included in ancient Chinese medicine, the peach was also mentioned in the writings of Pliny the Elder, Dioscorides, and Galen. It was used for healing and sympathetic magic. In the tenth century, burying peach leaves in the ground was believed to cure epilepsy and other ailments. In addition to treating ailments, herbalist Nicolas Culpeper noted that peaches fostered lust. Throughout Europe, the fruit was a symbol of female genitals and an ingredient in love potions. In England, the peach was regarded as a tree of prophecy. If it lost its leaves early, the owner's livestock would be afflicted with the plague. Peach branches were used as divining rods.

The peach was called *persicarius* in the tenth century and by the thirteenth century the name had evolved to *peske*, *peshe*, and eventually peach.[125] A cling peach is the type in which the flesh of the fruit holds tightly to the stone; a freestone peach separates easily from the stone. A nectarine (*P. persica* var. *nucipersica*) is a peach with smooth skin. It is so genetically similar to the peach that nectarines often show up on peach trees and vice versa.

Magical Connections

Elements:	Water
Astrological influence:	Sun, Venus
Deities:	Aphrodite, Asherah, Gaia, Harpocrates, Hera, Isis, Venus
Powers/attributes:	The afterlife, banish, death/funeral practices, fertility, happiness, healing, hexes (remove, ward off), love, loyalty/fidelity, luck, manifest (desires, dreams, will), negativity (remove, ward off), renewal, wisdom, wishes

Items to purchase when the tree is not available: fresh or dried fruit, peach juice, flower essence, peach kernel oil, dried leaves are sold as peach leaf tea.

Spellwork and Ritual

Prepare a candle with peach kernel oil or flower essence to use for love spells. Place a dried peach blossom in an organza bag and hang it in the bedroom as a fertility charm. To boost fidelity, sensually eat a peach with your lover. Use a leafy twig in ritual to manifest your dreams. Place a picture of three peaches in your kitchen to foster happiness. Hold a dried peach pit in meditation when seeking wisdom.

To release bottled-up emotions, drink a cup of peach leaf tea. To break a hex, crush a dried pit and throw the pieces in a river or fast-moving stream. If such water is not available, flushing it down the toilet will do. Burn a couple of dried leaves to remove any type of negativity or to symbolically banish something you no longer want in your life.

125. Wells, *Lives of the Trees*, 251.

Common Pear (Pyrus communis); also known as European pear.

Native to southern Europe and northwest Iran, the pear tree grows to a height of twenty-five to forty feet. It has glossy dark leaves that turn various shades of red and yellow in the autumn. The fragrant five-petaled flowers are creamy white and sometimes tinged with pink.

Found in sites stretching from the Middle East to Europe, archaeological evidence shows that Neolithic and Bronze Age people enjoyed wild pears. Botanists generally regard the common pear as a complex hybrid that developed over thousands of years of cultivation. The earliest written mention of pears comes from the Assyrian empire and dates to 2000 BCE; records of their cultivation come from Persia and date to 500 BCE.[126]

126. Joan Morgan, *The Book of Pears: The Definitive History and Guide to Over 500 Varieties* (White River Junction, VT: Chelsea Green Publishing, 2015), 12.

Both Theophrastus and Pliny the Elder wrote about the pear and poets sang its praises. The Greeks dedicated the tree to Hera and used pear wood for her statues. The Romans dedicated the tree to Juno. By the fourth century CE, a beverage of fermented pear juice called *castomoniale* was more popular than apple wine with the Romans.[127]

The pear tree was sacred to Germanic peoples and others in Europe. In the town of Auxerre, France, hunters made offerings to a venerated pear tree with the heads of their quarry. In other areas, the fruit was used as offerings in thanks for a good harvest and for help to ward off the plague. The Vainakh people of the North Caucasus region of Russia worshipped many trees, but especially the pear believing it was home to deities. The trees were also regarded as totems.

Pear trees were used for prophecy. An especially good crop of pears meant that many of the babies soon to be born would be girls. The pear tree was regarded as the female counterpart to the male apple and oak. Burying the afterbirth under a pear tree would bring a baby girl next time; burying it under an apple tree would bring a boy. On New Year's night, if a woman heard a dog bark as she shook a pear tree, her future husband would come from the place where the sound originated. The last pear of the season was often left on a tree as an offering to appease any spirit responsible for bad weather.

The pear was used for healing in sympathetic magic; hugging a pear tree and walking around it three times was believed to transfer an ailment to the tree. Objects pinned to the tree were also believed to alleviate illness. In Bavaria, Germany, the nail of a horseshoe hammered into a pear tree would cure the ailment of a female child; an oak was used for boys.

In England, some pear trees were believed to be sensitive and possess the ability to remember traumatic events. One such tree in Worcestershire at the location of the battle of Evesham in 1265 was said to bear fruit streaked blood red.

Witches were said to gather and dance at midnight underneath pear trees. Demons or evil spirits were believed to live in them and taunt or play pranks on passersby. In Ireland, taking pear blossoms into the house was regarded as unlucky with the potential of heralding a death in the family. This taboo was common to many plants with white flowers. Despite witches and demons, the pear became a symbol of prosperity.

---

127. Ben Watson, *Cider, Hard & Sweet: History, Traditions, and Making Your Own*, 3rd ed., (Woodstock, VT: The Countryman Press, 2013), 124.

Pears were associated with sex, representing both female and male genitalia. This sexual connotation was a common device used in medieval literature as was a woman wanting to eat raw pears a sign of pregnancy. Most types of pears during that period were unpalatable and hard if eaten uncooked. For this reason, they were often referred to as choke-pears.

During the seventeenth century in England, pears had the folk name *pyrrie*. It was derived from the name of a drink that was made from the perry pear; a small hard pear that was high in tannins. In a case of history repeating itself, long after the Roman *castomoniale* was forgotten, perry became as popular as apple cider and slightly more alcoholic. Today, with the rise of craft beer, wine, and cider, perry is making a comeback.

Magical Connections

Elements:	Air, earth, water
Astrological influence:	Jupiter, Moon, Sun, Venus
Deities:	Apollo, Aphrodite, Athena, Helios, Hera, Juno, Minerva, Pomona, Venus
Magical beings and woodland spirits:	Fairies
Powers/attributes:	Bind, consecrate/bless, creativity, healing, justice/legal matters, love, luck, manifest (desires, dreams, will), money/prosperity, protection, sex/sexuality, success, wisdom, wishes

Items to purchase when the tree is not available: fresh or dried fruit, pear juice, pear wine, perry pear cider, flower essence.

Spellwork and Ritual

Use a fresh pear in spells to attract love or heighten passion. Use the juice or flower essence to prepare a candle for meditation when dealing with sexuality issues. Sprinkle blossoms to consecrate an altar or ritual space or burn a couple of dried leaves. To stoke creativity, place a pear or hang a picture of one in your workspace.

Place a branch on your altar for wisdom when seeking justice. Hold a branch during ritual or meditation to manifest your dreams. Hang a branch over your front door for protection. The pear is also effective in binding spells and healing circles.

PINE

Eastern White Pine (*Pinus strobus*); also known as northern pine, soft
pine, white pine

Ponderosa Pine (*P. ponderosa*); also known as silver pine, western pitch
pine, western red pine

Scots Pine (*P. sylvestris*); also known as Scotch pine

Pines are cone-bearing evergreens with needles that grow in clusters. The cones have
rigid, woody scales and hang underneath the branches. Eastern white pine typically
grows seventy-five to one hundred feet tall. Its smooth gray bark breaks into small plates
as the tree matures. The soft, flexible needles are dark green. The eastern white and Ponderosa pines are native to eastern and western North America, respectively. Ponderosa
pine ranges between 150 to 200 feet tall. The scaly bark matures into irregular-shaped
plates and the yellow-green needles are stiff with sharp points. The slender cones turn
glossy and reddish brown. Typically growing thirty to sixty feet tall in parks and yards,

in the wild Scots pine can reach one hundred feet. It has distinctive, flaking, reddish-brown bark. The needles are blue green and cones gray or light brown. This pine is native to Europe, Siberia, and eastern Asia. Also see the section "Is That a Spruce, Pine, or Fir Tree?" in the profile for spruce.

The Assyrians and Egyptians revered pine. The Greeks and Romans dedicated it to many gods and goddesses. According to ancient texts, pines trees were planted around the temple of Poseidon because the wood was used extensively for shipbuilding. The resin or pitch was used to seal ships and wine amphoras. The genus *Pinus* is the Latin name for the tree, which was derived from the Greek *pitys*, meaning "pine" or "fir."[128] Through a type of misadventure common in mythology, the Greek nymph Pitys, who loved Pan, was turned into a pine tree. Pine is associated with Pan and other woodland deities and spirits. The species name of the Scots pine, *sylvestris*, means "of the woods or forests."[129] To the Romans, pine symbolized the power of male virility.

Germanic peoples also revered pine trees and believed that spirits lived in them. According to Roman historian Tacitus (c. 56–120 CE), the Teutonic tribes held an annual festival to celebrate this tree. Pine was popularly used as a Yule log and branches were hung in homes as festive decoration for Yuletide revels and to ward off evil spirits. Not only was pine used at the winter solstice, in the Harz Mountain area of Germany, it fueled summer solstice bonfires. Throughout the year, the resinous wood was commonly used as torches.

Like other evergreens, pine represented victory and immortality. In Corinth, Greece, the winners of athletic games held in honor of Poseidon were crowned with pine wreaths. Also used as a funerary emblem, pine boughs were placed in front of homes where people were in mourning for lost loved ones. Boughs were also placed on graves. To the Romans, this tree was a symbol of resurrection. In Japan, pine was a tree of good omen.

As symbols of permanence and fertility, pine sprigs and cones were commonly part of the décor for wedding ceremonies. To symbolize fertility, of the land and women, the Greeks threw pine seeds into the caves of Demeter during the Thesmophoria, a religious festival held in honor of the goddess and her daughter Persephone.

Although in some accounts, Merlin's shamanic tree was an apple, the pine that stood beside the fountain of Barenton in the forest of Brocéliande in Brittany, France, was also noted as the doorway for Merlin to leave this world. Brocéliande was the home

---

128. Small, *North American Cornucopia*, 525.

129. Bill Neal, *Gardener's Latin: Discovering the Origins, Lore & Meanings of Botanical Names* (Chapel Hill, NC: Algonquin Books of Chapel Hill, 1992), 120.

of the enchantress Viviane, the Lady of the Lake. According to legend, a magical cloud shielded the forest and made it appear as a lake. Prior to the mid-seventeenth century when the pineapple (*Ananas comosus*) was introduced into England, the pinecone had been known as a pine apple.

Magical Connections

Elements:	Air, earth, fire
Astrological influence:	Jupiter, Mars, Saturn; Aquarius, Aries, Cancer, Capricorn, Pisces, Scorpio
Deities:	Aphrodite, Artemis, Astarte, Attis, Bacchus, Ceres, Cybele, Demeter, Diana, Dionysus, Faunus, Ishtar, Isis, Neptune, Pan, Persephone, Poseidon, Rhea, Silvanus, Venus, Vulcan
Magical beings and woodland spirits:	Elves, faeries, Pitys (Greek mountain forest nymph), pixies, satyrs
Wildlife:	Crow, deer, jackdaw, lapwing, porcupine, raven
Ogham:	Ailm/Ailim + Ifin/Iphin ᚛ Amhancholl/Eamancholl/Emancoll/Mór ▦ Onn/Ohn ╫
Alternate tree calendar:	August 24 to September 2 and February 19 to 29

Runes:	Dagaz/Daeg/Dag ᛞ
	    Runic half month: June 14 to 28
	Kenaz/Kaun/Cen ᚲ
	    Runic half month: September 13 to 27

Powers/attributes:	Abundance, balance/harmony, banish, bind, communication, concentration/focus, confidence, consecrate/bless, courage, creativity, defense, determination/endurance, emotions (deal with, support), family and home, fertility, growth, happiness, healing, hexes (remove, ward off), hope, inspiration, intuition, justice/legal matters, knowledge (seek, acquire), manifest (desires, dreams, will), negativity (remove, ward off), peace, protection, psychic abilities, purification, release (let go, move on), renewal, spirit guides/spirits, spirituality, strength, support (provide, receive), transformation, wisdom
Other associations:	Beltane, Litha, Midsummer's Eve, Yule

Items to purchase when the tree is not available: dried pinecones, essential oil made from the needles and twigs of the Scots pine, flower essence is made from the Scots pine.

Spellwork and Ritual

The pine tree is well known for its purification properties and for dispelling negative energy. It is especially effective in public spaces. The same qualities also make it an ally in defensive magic and for protection from hexes, especially for the home. Burn a few dried needles for these purposes. Use the cones to represent blessings and to attract abundance. Also use them for spells that banish or bind.

The scent of pine can steady and focus the mind for psychic work and for communication with spirits. Also use the scent to stimulate the energy around you. On a spiritual level, pine aids in healing, inspiration, and access to ancient wisdom. Carry a few scales from a pinecone for confidence and courage, especially when dealing with legal matters.

POMEGRANATE

Pomegranate (*Punica granatum* syn. *Malum punicum*)

The pomegranate grows from six to twenty feet tall and has pointed, glossy leaves that turn yellow in the autumn in areas where the tree is deciduous. In the tropics, this tree is an evergreen. The orange-red, trumpet-shaped flowers grow singly or in clusters. The round fruit ripens to yellowish red. It is divided into compartments that contain juicy fleshy pulp surrounding the seeds. Technically, these are berries encased in a rind. The pomegranate is native to an area that stretches from Iran to northern India.

Pomegranate's older botanical name, *Malum punicum*, means "apple of Carthage"; *Punica* was the ancient Roman name for Carthage, a Phoenician city on the north coast of Africa.[130] The name *pomegranate* is derived from the Latin *pomum*, meaning "apple"

---

130. Small, *Top 100 Exotic Food Plants*, 477.

or more generally "fruit" and *granatum*, "having grains."[131] Cultivation began around 4000 BCE in northern Iran and Turkey and spread throughout the Mediterranean region.[132]

Pomegranates have been found in Egyptian tombs dating to 2500 BCE.[133] Leaves from several plants including pomegranate were woven into garlands as part of the grave goods for King Tutankhamun. In Egyptian art, pomegranates were frequently depicted in paintings of domestic gardens.

The Phoenicians associated the pomegranate with the sun. According to Islamic legend, each fruit holds a seed from paradise. For long journeys, thirst-quenching pomegranates were the ideal provision for desert caravans. They became so important as a trade commodity in Asia Minor that fines were levied against anyone who damaged a pomegranate tree.

In Greece, pomegranates were a symbol of fertility, regeneration, and transformation. The story of Demeter and Persephone is the most well-known myth involving the pomegranate.

Hades tricked Persephone into eating several pomegranate seeds while in the underworld, which bound her to spend part of the year in his realm. Her reemergence to join her mother in the spring represented eternal fruitfulness as well as the mysteries of death and rebirth.

In another myth, Aphrodite created the pomegranate from the blood of her dying lover Adonis. Becoming one of her symbols, she is attributed with planting the first pomegranate tree on the island of Cyprus. Another legend has pomegranates springing from the blood of Dionysus. The pomegranate competes for the role of a golden apple from Hera's garden given by Trojan prince Paris to Aphrodite.

In Roman art, pomegranates were depicted on the sides of altars and tombs to represent abundance. Ceramic containers fashioned into the shape of a pomegranate were used as funerary offerings. Pliny the Elder recommended pomegranate for several ailments as well as perfume. In addition to enjoying the fruit, the Romans used the juice to make wine.

---

131. Barnhart, *The Barnhart Concise Dictionary of Etymology*, 583.

132. Staub, *75 Remarkable Fruits for Your Garden*, 189.

133. De Cleene and Lejeune, *Compendium of Symbolic and Ritual Plants in Europe*, 583.

Believed to have magical power, a pomegranate tree was planted near a home to keep evil spirits away. The Persians made garlands from the twigs to ward off witches and demons. On the island of Sicily, the branches were used as diving rods to find hidden treasure. Pomegranate juice was placed on the horns of plow oxen in Morocco to boost the fertility of the land and ensure abundant crops.

Associated with fertility for humans, too, pomegranates were considered an aphrodisiac. In India, sap from the tree was used as a remedy for infertility. Pomegranates were also associated with prophecy. At weddings in parts of the Middle East, it was customary for a bride to toss one on the floor. The number of seeds that fell out indicated the number of children she would have. The gemstone name *garnet* was derived from the Latin *granatum* in reference to red garnet pebbles resembling pomegranate seeds.[134]

Magical Connections

Elements:	Earth, Fire
Astrological influence:	Mercury, Saturn, Venus; Gemini, Scorpio, Virgo
Deities:	Adonis, Aphrodite, Apollo, Astarte, Attis, Ceres, Cybele, Demeter, Dionysus, Hades, Hera, Hermes, Inanna, Ishtar, Mercury, Mithra, Persephone, Pluto, Sekhmet
Magical beings and creatures and woodland spirits:	Rhoea (Greek tree nymph), unicorn
Wildlife:	Myna bird, parakeet
Powers/attributes:	Abundance, the afterlife, balance/harmony, changes/transitions, clarity (enhance, foster), consecrate/bless, creativity, death/funeral practices, divination, family and home, fertility, hope, loss/sorrow (ease, recover from), love, luck, money/prosperity, the otherworld, protection, psychic abilities, renewal, security, sex/sexuality, success, wisdom, wishes
Other associations:	Samhain

134. Lance Grande and Allison Augustyn, *Gems and Gemstones: Timeless Natural Beauty of the Mineral World* (Chicago: The University of Chicago Press, 2009), 170.

Items to purchase when the tree is not available: the fruit, pomegranate juice, flower essence, dried seeds, pomegranate oil is made from the seeds.

Spellwork and Ritual

Typically placed on the altar at Samhain, pomegranate is effective at any time to honor the dead or to connect with the otherworld. Pomegranate serves as a reminder of the cycles of change and new beginnings. Prepare candles with pomegranate oil or juice when dealing with the loss of a loved one.

Eat pomegranate seeds before divination and other psychic work to foster clarity. Use the oil to consecrate divination and ritual tools. Pomegranate helps to ground energy and come into balance after ritual. Use pomegranate in spells as a symbol of boundless love that brings desires to life. Carry several dried seeds in a pouch as a good luck charm.

POPLAR

Balsam Poplar (*Populus balsamifera*); also known as balm of Gilead, cottonwood, tacmahac.

Black Poplar (*P. nigra* syn. *P. italica*, *P. nigra* var. *italica*); also known as Italian poplar, Lombardy poplar.

White Poplar (*P. alba*); also known as abele, lady poplar, silver poplar, silverleaf poplar.

In the early spring before the leaves appear, poplars sprout reddish male catkins and yellow-green female catkins on separate trees. When the leaf buds develop, they are covered with an aromatic yellowish resin. On the North American poplar, the resin has a pine-like balsam scent. The seeds of poplars become encased in white, cottony hairs called *seed wool* or *seed fluff*.

Native to Europe, northwestern Africa, and western Asia, the black poplar grows in a columnar shape and reaches sixty to ninety feet tall. Its dark green leaves turn yellow in the autumn. The white poplar is native to central and southern Europe. It reaches forty to eighty feet tall. Young twigs and buds are pale and silvery. Its leaves are dark green on top and whitish underneath. Native to North America, the balsam poplar reaches seventy-five to one hundred feet tall.

According to Greek mythology, the gods turned the Heliades, the daughters of sun god Helios, into black poplar trees when they could not stop mourning the death of their beloved brother Phaethon. The yellowish resin produced by the buds was said to be amber resulting from their tears. One of the Hesperides, who was charged with guarding the golden apples in Hera's garden, was turned into a poplar after losing them.

In another myth, Hades was in love with Leuce, the daughter of sea god Oceanus, and took her to the underworld with him. When she died, he turned her into a white poplar and placed it beside the River Acheron. Derived from the word *leukos*, "white," *leuce* is the Greek name for the tree.[135] Homer called the white poplar *acherois*. In other legends, black poplars line the way to the underworld, while white poplars grow in the underworld providing hope for those entering. Black poplars were also said to grow along the banks of the River Eridanos in the underworld. According to legend, it was the wood used for the funeral pyre of the first Roman Emperor Augustus (63 BCE – 14 CE). White poplars were often planted alongside graves.

Hercules is involved in a legend about the color of the white poplar leaves. His final task was to fetch Cerberus, the guard dog of Hell, from the underworld. He adorned himself with a garland of white poplar around his head to aid him in finding his way out. The sweat of his forehead turned one side of the leaves white. Because the upper and undersides of white poplar leaves are starkly different, it was regarded as a tree of duality symbolizing the inescapable connection of life and death. These leaves have been found in Sumerian graves dating to 4000 BCE.[136] Because of Hercules, the tree became a symbol of courage.

In many Greek sanctuaries, poplar was the only wood burned for offerings, especially white poplar for Zeus. White poplar was dedicated to Persephone and black poplar

---

135. Arthur Plotnik, *The Urban Tree Book: An Uncommon Field Guide for City and Town* (New York: Three Rivers Press, 2000), 165.

136. De Cleene and Lejeune, *Compendium of Symbolic and Ritual Plants in Europe*, 598.

to Hades. Because of their association with mourning, Demeter's sacred grove consisted of willows and black poplars. Dedicated to the moon, it was believed that the sap of the white poplar could increase a woman's fertility.

In Russia, a poplar twig was planted on the grave of anyone suspected of being a witch to keep him or her in place. Poplar leaves were said to be an ingredient in the medieval witch's flying ointment. In England, the catkins of the black poplar were known as devil's fingers and it was unlucky to pick up fallen ones. Their abundance on the tree foreshadowed problems or disaster. Believed to attract lightning in Germany, poplars were planted in the vicinity of farmyards to attract strikes away from the barn and house. In weather lore, if the pale undersides of white poplar leaves turned upward, it would rain.

Magical Connections

Elements:	Water
Astrological influence:	Moon (white poplar), Saturn
Deities:	Apollo, Asherah, Brahma, Chronos, Demeter, Hades, Hecate, Leuca, Luna, Persephone, Pluto, Selene, Zeus
Magical beings and woodland spirits:	Aigeiros (Greek tree nymph), Dryope (Greek tree nymph), hamadryads
Wildlife:	Beaver
Ogham (white poplar):	Edad/Eadha/Eadhadh ᚘ
Alternate tree calendar:	May 1 to 14, August 5 to 13, and February 4 to 8
Powers/attributes all poplars:	Ancestors, astral travel/journeying, challenges/obstacles (overcome), courage, death/funeral practices, defense, determination/endurance, divination, loss/sorrow (ease, recover from), money/prosperity, the otherworld, past-life work, spirit guides/spirits, spirituality, strength
Powers/attributes black poplars:	Prophecy
Powers/attributes white poplars:	Hope, renewal
Other associations:	Ostara, Beltane, Samhain

Items to purchase when the tree is not available: Essential oil is made from the buds and twigs of the balsam poplar and often marketed as balm of Gilead; flower essence is made from the balsam poplar and sometimes marketed as cottonwood bud.

Spellwork and Ritual

Place a poplar twig on your Samhain altar to honor and connect with ancestors. Use a few catkins on your Ostara altar to symbolize renewal. Any part of the white poplar can be used for esbat rituals. Place a leaf or two in a pouch to keep with you when journeying to other realms. Keep a pressed leaf in your wallet to stimulate prosperity. Prepare a candle with poplar essential oil or flower essence to enhance a divination session or deepen spiritual practices.

QUINCE

Common Quince (*Cydonia oblonga* syn. *C. vulgaris*, *Pyrus cydonia*);
also known as fruiting quince, true quince.

Growing twelve to fifteen feet tall, the quince is a gnarly, multi-trunked tree with crooked branches. It is thought to have originated in the Caucasus region of southern Russia, Georgia, and Azerbaijan between the Black and Caspian Seas. The tree has pale-green leaves that are gray and fuzzy underneath. Its five-petaled flowers are white with a tinge of pale pink. The slightly knobby fruit is round to pear-shaped and green with gray-white fuzz. It turns bright yellow when ripe. Unlike its close relatives the apple and pear, quince fruit has a tough rind. The seeds contain trace amounts of cyanide. The fruiting quince is the only species in the *Cydonia* genus. Although in the same botanical family rose (*Rosaceae*), the flowering quince (*Chaenomeles speciosa*) is grown as an ornamental rather than for its fruit.

Cultivation of the quince began in Mesopotamia and by the first century CE, it was grown on the island of Crete.[137] Imported from the city of Kydon (or Cydon), on mainland Greece the fruit became known as *mela Kydonia*, "apple from Kydonia".[138] According to Pliny the Elder, wild quince was common in hedges. Although it had been regarded as a type of apple, by the Middle Ages it was called a *quince pear*. Even Swedish naturalist Carl Linnaeus classified it as a pear.

Some scholars believe that the golden apple from Hera's garden given to Aphrodite by the Trojan prince Paris was actually a quince. It is also a contender for the forbidden fruit in the Garden of Eden. The quince was a fertility symbol in Greece and usually given to new brides. The earliest mention of its connection with marriage ceremonies comes from around 600 BCE in Greece.[139] Both the Greeks and Romans used quince boughs and fruit to decorate the nuptial bedchamber.

The fruit became an integral part of marriage ceremonies with the bride and groom partaking of honeyed quince. Eating the fruit was symbolic of consummating the marriage. Quince remained part of wedding celebrations into the 1700s in England with the custom of the groom presenting them as a gift to the bride. Outside of marriage, quince was a token of love when sent as a gift. The fruit also became a symbol of harmony and peace. In Croatia, quince was used as a birth tree, planted to celebrate the new infant.

The Romans dedicated the tree to Venus, who was often depicted holding a quince. Her temple on the island of Cyprus was decorated with quince trees. Depicted in Roman wall paintings, a couple of murals found at Pompeii portray a bear eating a quince. Any connection between bears and quince is unknown, however, they might be attracted to the fruit because of the custom of storing them in honey. The Latin name of quince, *melimelum*, "honey apple," comes from this practice.[140] Throughout the Mediterranean, honeyed quince was used to flavor food and to make jam. Derived from the Portuguese *marmelada* for quince preserves, marmalade evolved to include other fruit, most notably orange.[141]

---

137. Peter Blackburne-Maze, *Fruit: An Illustrated History* (London: Firefly Books, Ltd., 2003), 80.

138. Wells, *Lives of the Trees*, 274.

139. Alan Davidson, *The Oxford Companion to Food*, 3rd ed. Tom Jaine, ed. (Oxford, England: Oxford University Press, 2014), 664.]

140. Ibid.

141. Ibid.

Hard and acidic, raw quince fruit requires bletting, which is the practice of storing fruit until it is overripe and soft. In England, quince was often bletted by storing them among linens, which gave the fabric a pleasant scent. Storing them in honey or wine was the more common form of bletting.

Popular for espaliering along walls in medieval gardens, quince was a culinary favorite throughout Europe. A specialty of Orléans, France, quince jelly was given as a gift to Joan of Arc when she arrived in the city after the siege. For medicinal purposes, Nicolas Culpeper noted that quince's apple-like fragrance could counteract poison.

Herbalist John Gerard noted that if a pregnant woman ate quince, it would make her child wise. It was believed that quince syrup consumed after drinking wine would prevent drunkenness. Pliny the Elder noted that quince could be used as a love charm and for protection against the evil eye. Painting a picture of a quince on a house provided protection for it. Refer to the profile for mulberry for another belief regarding quince.

Magical Connections

Elements:	Earth
Astrological influence:	Moon, Saturn, Venus
Deities:	Aphrodite, Venus
Magical beings and woodland spirits:	Maliades (Greek tree nymph)
Wildlife:	Bear
Powers/attributes:	Balance/harmony, fertility, love, luck, money/prosperity, negativity (remove, ward off), peace, protection, sex/sexuality

Items to purchase when the tree is not available: fresh or dried fruit, seeds.

Spellwork and Ritual

As part of a handfasting ceremony, exchange gifts of quince to symbolize love and harmony in the marriage. Also place them in the bedroom on the first night of marriage. Use the fruit or leaves for fertility spells. Carry several dried seeds in a pouch for protective energy. Burn a small twig or several dried leaves to remove any form of negativity from your life. To foster a peaceful atmosphere, place a picture of a quince tree in a public area of your home.

REEDS, RUSHES, AND CATTAILS

Cattails (*Typha latifolia*); also known as cat-o-nine-tails, great reed mace, water torch.

Common Reed (*Phragmites australis* syn. *P. communis*); also known as common reed grass, Dutch reed, Norfolk reed, star-reed, water grass.

Common Rush (*Juncus effuses*); also known as bog rush, mat rush, soft rush.

Native to Europe and the British Isles, common reed has round, hollow stems that can reach a height of thirteen feet. Its long, bluish-green leaves are flat and blade-like. Plume-like flowers with tufts of silky hair grow on little spikelets. After the leaves break away in autumn, a bare stem is left standing through the winter. The common rush is a grass that reaches two to four feet tall and grows in dense, V-shaped clumps. In summer, tiny florets form on the sides of the round stems and develop into brown seed capsules. It is native to Africa, Asia, Europe, and North America. In some areas it has become invasive. Cattails usually grow four to eight feet tall and have flat blade-like leaves. Its brown, cylindrical, flowering spikes stay on the plant until autumn before breaking up into downy white fluff. Cattails are native to Europe, Africa, western Asia, and North and South America.

While reed does not seem like a prestigious enough plant to be ranked among trees, to the early people of the British Isles it was an extremely important component for warm, dry homes. Reeds and cattails are cousins that share the same botanical order, *Poales*, but are classified into different families and genera. The genus name for reed, *Phragmites*, comes from Greek and means "growing in hedges" or "fence-like," which describes how it can create a thick barrier.[142] Also from Greek, the genus name for cattails, *Typha*, means "bog" or "marsh" and describes the plant's habitat.[143] *Juncus* was derived from *iuncus*, the Latin name for rushes.[144]

Reeds were used for arrow shafts in Europe, Egypt, and the Americas. The Romans also used them as a writing instruments. Reeds, rushes, and cattails have been the source of material for roof thatching, musical instruments, and many domestic items. Nowadays, a thatched roof is an expensive status symbol with country charm, but thatch used to be cheap and plentiful. It was a perfect insulator to keep homes warm in winter and cool in summer. Thatch is excellent for keeping out rain, sleet, and snow as well as insects and vermin.

In addition to thatching, peasants in the Middle Ages used reeds and rushes for the walls of their homes. The timber framework was filled in with "wattle and daub", woven reeds or rushes that were covered in a plaster usually made by mixing mud, dung, and straw. The dirt floors were usually covered with reeds, rushes, or straw to minimize odors. As all-purpose plants, bundles of reeds or rushes soaked in fat provided a cheap alternative to candles. The downy fluff of cattail flowers was used to stuff pillows.

Fairies were said to turn rushes into beautiful horses with a magical word. In Ireland, cattails were known as fairy woman's spindle. In Portugal, a child was passed through a split reed in a midnight ritual on St. John's Eve to cure a hernia.

142. Sylvan T. Runkel and Dean M. Roosa, *Wildflowers and Other Plants of Iowa Wetlands,* 2nd ed. (Iowa City, IA: Iowa State University Press, 2014), 207.

143. Ibid, 105.

144. Quattrocchi, *Names, Eponyms, Synonyms, and Etymology: D–L,* vol. 2, 2141.

A number of plants vie for the pipes used in Greek god Pan's musical instrument and reed is one of them. According to one myth, Pan was in love with the water nymph Syrinx. When he tried to pull her from the water, he was left with a handful of reeds. Noticing the musical sound as a breeze passed through the hollow stems, he used them to make his pipes. There has been speculation that the Pied Piper of Hamelin played his magical tune on a reed flute.

Magical Connections

Elements:	Water
Astrological influence:	Mars, Pluto (reed); Pisces, Sagittarius, Scorpio
Deities:	Coventina, Geb, Inanna, Manannan, the Morrigan, Pan, Poseidon, Rhiannon, Spider Woman
Magical beings and woodland spirits:	Fairies, Turabug (Italian guardian or spirit of the reeds)
Wildlife:	Goose, kingfisher, owl
Ogham:	Ngetal/nGétal/nGéadal ╫ Celtic tree calendar: October 28 to November 24
Runes:	Algiz/Eolh/Elhaz ᛉ Runic half month: January 28 to February 11
Powers/attributes:	Abundance, ancestors, astral travel/journeying, awareness (enhance, heighten), balance/harmony, concentration/focus, confidence, determination/endurance, family and home, growth, healing, inspiration, loyalty/fidelity, prophecy, protection, security, sex/sexuality, spirit guides/spirits, spirituality
Other associations:	Imbolc, Samhain

Items to purchase when the plants are not available: dried cattails, rush mats. Check carefully if you buy reed or rush baskets as they are often made from other types of plants.

Spellwork and Ritual

For protection in ritual or spell work, cut six equal lengths of stalk from any of these plants, and then lay them out in two triangles to form a pentagram on your altar. Placing long stalks on or beside your altar aid in connecting with ancestors. Burn a piece of reed to honor any household spirit as well as to bring unity and loyalty to your family. Use any of these plants for meditation when seeking personal growth or to foster healing energy.

Pull a cattail flower spike apart to make a protective amulet to wear during journeys to other realms. It will also aid in expanding awareness. Hang a stalk of reed, rush, or cattails above your altar to strengthen concentration and focus and boost the energy of magic work. To enhance passion and sex, especially if there are issues in a relationship, place several long stalks of cattails in a tall vase in your bedroom.

ROSE

Dog Rose (*Rosa canina*); also known as beach rose, dagger rose, dog
   briar, wild briar, and witches' briar.

Sweet Briar Rose (*R. rubiginosa* syn. *R. eglanteria*); also known as briar
   rose, eglantine rose, mosqueta rose.

There are thousands of rose varieties and cultivars. The roses that we grow in our gardens are usually classified into three main groups: species roses, old-fashioned roses, and modern roses. The species roses have grown wild for hundreds if not thousands of years. They have simple flowers with five petals. The dog and sweet briar are species roses.

The flowers of the dog rose are white to pale pink; the sweet briar, pink with white centers. Both plants are thicket forming; the dog rose can reach six to eight feet tall, the sweet briar six to ten. Their arching stems are studded with thorns that help them cling onto and grow up anything nearby. Both plants produce scarlet rosehips in the autumn. A rosehip is the fruit of a rose, which is also known as a rose haw.

According to one Roman myth, a drop of Venus's blood gave the rose its color; another explains that Bacchus dropped some wine on a rose, which turned them all rosy red. The Greek god of love, Eros, was said to have presented a rose as a gift to Harpocrates, the god of silence. Using this as a cue, it became common practice to hang a rose over a dinner table when the conversation was to be confidential, which was the source of the term *sub rosa*, "under the rose."[145] However, a child that was "born under the rose" meant he or she had been born out of wedlock.

In the Roman ceremony of *Rosalia*, rose petals were scattered on the graves of loved ones, symbolizing the start of a new state of being. Rosalia evolved into a springtime feast to honor departed loved ones and offer their spirits food garnished with rose petals. The Greeks also strew petals over the graves of loved ones and made wreaths of rose canes (branches) to place on graves.

Pliny the Elder praised the dog rose for its use in treating a wide range of ailments. It is still popular for herbal remedies and as a refreshing tea. During the Middle Ages, a dried rosehip was carried as a charm against certain diseases and for protection against enchantment or sorcery. Enamored with roses in general, fairies are said to enjoy cavorting in dog rose thickets. In Scandinavia and Germany, roses were believed to be under the protection of elves and dwarves.

Like many plants, roses have been used for divination. To discover who she would marry, a woman would float a leaf for each suitor in a large bowl of water. The last one that sank would reveal her future husband. When placed under a pillow on Midsummer's Eve, a rose was said to bring dreams of one's future partner. Germanic tribes dedicated the rose to their goddess Frigg, queen of the Aesir and wife of Odin. In Hildesheim, Germany, a local name for the dog rose is still *Friggdorn*, "Frigg's thorn."[146]

145. Ernst Lehner and Johanna Lehner, *Folklore and Symbolism of Flowers, Plants and Trees* (New York: Dover Publications, Inc., 2003), 79.

146. Peter Harkness, The Rose: An Illustrated History (London: Firefly Books Ltd., 2003), 18.

Magical Connections

Elements:	Water
Astrological influence:	Venus; Cancer, Libra, Sagittarius, Taurus
Deities:	Adonis, Aphrodite, Athena, Cupid, Demeter, Eros, Flora, Freya, Frigg, Harpocrates, Hathor, Holle, Idunn, Isis, Odin, Venus
Magical beings and woodland spirits:	Dwarves, elves, fairies
Wildlife:	Bee, butterfly, nightingale
Powers/attributes:	The afterlife, attraction, balance/harmony, banish, bind, challenges/obstacles (overcome), clarity (enhance, foster), communication, confidence, consecrate/bless, courage, death/funeral practices, divination, dream work, emotions (deal with, support), family and home, happiness, healing, hexes (remove, ward off), love, loyalty/fidelity, luck, manifest (desires, dreams, will), the otherworld, peace, prophecy, protection, psychic abilities, secrets, sex/sexuality, spirit guides/spirits, spirituality, strength, wisdom
Other associations:	Midsummer's Eve

Items to purchase when the plant is not available: rosehip tea; rosehip seed oil; rose water; flower essences are made from the dog rose, which is usually marketed as wild rose, the rugosa or Japanese rose (*R. rugosa*), and the cluster rose (*R. pisocarpa*); essential oils are obtained from the Damask rose (*R. damascene*) and Maroc rose (*R. gallica* syn. *R. x centifolia*).

Spellwork and Ritual

Hold a rose leaf or flower petal between your hands to help ground and center your energy before a divination session. Also do this before bed to encourage prophetic dreams. Alternatively, drink a cup of rosehip tea. Sprinkle rosewater around your home to attract peace and aid in dealing with family issues. Rose is also instrumental in turning your dreams into reality.

Use rosehip seed oil or rosewater to consecrate amulets and charms and to prepare candles for spell work. Place a rose on your altar when engaging in clairvoyance, communicating with spirits, and psychic work in general. Use dried and crumbled rosehips to break hexes and in spells to banish unwanted things from your life. Carry a dried rosehip to attract luck.

With a heavy-duty needle and darning thread, string rosehips together to make a circlet. Make it large enough to place things within when you lay it on your altar for magic and ritual. Make a smaller circlet to wear as a bracelet when doing divination or psychic work. Use three thorns or make a small circle with a rose cane to use in protection spells.

Plant a dog rose to invite fairies to your garden. No matter where you find a dog rose, leave an offering underneath it for them.

ROWAN

American Mountain Ash (*Sorbus americana*); also known as dogberry, mountain sumac, and wild ash.

European Mountain Ash (*S. aucuparia*); also known as common mountain ash, quickbeam, roan tree, rowan, sorb apple, Thor's helper, witch beam, witch wood, witchen tree.

These trees have lance-shaped leaves and dense, flattened clusters of white flowers. Their orange-red berries ripen in late summer. Native to North America, the American mountain ash is a small, shrubby tree reaching fifteen to twenty-five feet tall. Its leaves are dark green and turn yellow in the autumn. Native to Europe and Asia, the European mountain ash grows twenty to forty feet tall. Its leaves turn yellow to reddish-purple in the fall.

Rowan is the prevalent name for these trees in the United Kingdom. Although the word *ash* is in their common names and their leaves resemble those of the ash, true ash trees are in the genus *Fraxinus*.

Germanic peoples dedicated the rowan to Thor. Regarded as extremely powerful, the wood was included in Norse ships as an amulet to calm ocean storms conjured by Ran, the mother goddess of the sea. Well into the twentieth century in Europe, bundles of rowan were placed in windows to ward off lightning. In India, rowan was also associated with lightening. According to Vedic myth, lightning striking a rowan tree created the first fire.

The name *rowan* may be associated with the Old Norse word *runa*, meaning "magic."[147] The wood was often used for rune sticks. It was believed that keeping a branch by the bed at night provided protection from witches and carrying a piece of rowan kept one safe from enchantment. In parts of England, rowan branches were carried in procession around the Beltane fire to prepare them for magical uses. Throughout the British Isles, rowan was associated with sacred wells and springs. On Beltane, it was used as part of the spring/well dressing (decoration) that also served as an offering. In Celtic myth, rowan berries eaten by the salmon of knowledge were responsible for its reddish spots.

Farmers in England either planted a rowan on their land or hung branches on their homes and barns for protection. Branches were used in charms to improve the fertility of the land and it was considered bad luck to cut down a rowan tree. Because witches were thought to access homes via the chimney, support beams around fireplaces were often made of rowan. Called *witch posts*, they were sometimes decorated with symbols to enhance their ability to ward off witches. In areas where rowan was regarded as mystical, it was believed to take away the power of witches. Oddly enough, witches were said to have used rowan branches as wands. Similarly, some legends advised that planting a rowan near the front door protected the occupants from evil spirits. Yet other legends noted that evil spirits lurked around rowan trees. A branch kept by the bed at night provided protection from witches and evil in general. In Scotland, rowan was said to protect against witches and fairies.

Small twigs were used as amulets for general protection; three tied into knots were used as charms. Wearing a sprig of rowan, usually on a hat, was said to keep bad fairies away. According to folklore, this tree was brought from the fairy realm. In other beliefs, horses that had been bewitched could only be controlled with a whip of rowan, and a rowan branch driven through a corpse would keep its ghost from wandering. In the

---

147. De Cleene and Lejeune, *Compendium of Symbolic and Ritual Plants in Europe*, 659.

weather lore of southern Germany, an abundance of berries meant a hard, snowy winter was ahead. According to another legend, dragons guarded these magical berries.

During the fifteenth and sixteenth centuries, rowan acquired a negative reputation. The berry was associated with witchcraft because it carries a five-pointed star, pentagram-like design at its base. Many herbalists avoided using it for fear of being labeled a witch by the Inquisition. Although it was avoided at times, from Pliny the Elder to Nicholas Culpeper, rowan was highly prized for healing. The berries and leaves are still used in herbal medicine.

Magical Connections

Elements:	Earth, fire
Astrological influence:	Moon, Saturn, Sun, Uranus; Aquarius, Capricorn, Sagittarius
Deities:	Aphrodite, Brigantia, Brigid, Cerridwen, the Dagda, Hecate, Luna, Pan, Ran, Selene, Thor, Vulcan
Magical beings and creatures and woodland spirits:	Dragons, elves, fairies, Pihlajatar (Finish tree fairy)
Wildlife:	Duck, quail, salmon
Ogham:	Luis ᚂ
Celtic tree calendar:	January 2 to February 17
Alternate tree calendar:	April 1 to 10 and October 4 to 13

Runes:	Algiz/Eolh/Elhaz ᛉ
	    Runic half month: January 28 to February 11
	Naudiz/Naudhr/Nyd ᚾ
	    Runic half month: November 13 to 27

Powers/attributes:	Astral travel/journeying, authority/leadership, balance/harmony, bind, challenges/obstacles (overcome), consecrate/bless, creativity, defense, divination, enchantment, family and home, fertility, healing, hexes (remove, ward off), inspiration, knowledge (seek, acquire), luck, prophecy, protection, psychic abilities, security, spirit guides/spirits, strength, stress/anxiety (calm, release), success, wisdom
Other associations:	Imbolc, Beltane, Lughnasadh

Items to purchase when the tree is not available: dried berries; flower essence is made from the European mountain ash.

Spellwork and Ritual

Rowan is a powerful ally for divination and when working with spirits. Hold a rowan branch to connect with your spirit guides, especially when seeking their advice. Burn a small piece of bark or twig to enhance psychic abilities. Write the name *rowan* or draw its ogham character on a candle for protection during ritual or astral travel.

Cut five branches to the same length and lay them out in a pentagram shape on your altar to boost the energy of sabbat rituals or in spells to remove hexes. Place a picture of the tree on your altar for healing rituals. To attract success, carry a dried rowan berry as an amulet. A rowan branch makes a good, magically protective walking stick. Enhance its power by carving its runes into the wood.

SPINDLETREE

Spindletree (*Euonymus europaeus*); also known as death alder, gatter
  tree, louse berry, lus-thorn, peg wood, prickwood, spindle wood,
  spindleberry.
Wahoo (*E. atropurpureus*); also known as burning bush, eastern wahoo, Indian arrow wood, purple spindletree.

Native to Europe and western Asia, the spindletree grows twelve to twenty feet tall with
a tangle of branches. Its oval leaves are dull green and turn orange to rusty red in the
autumn. The small, yellowish-green, four-petalled flowers bloom in early summer. The
reddish-pink berries ripen in late summer. Native to eastern North America, the wahoo
is more of a spreading shrub that grows to about fifteen feet tall. Its oval leaves are dark
green with a purple tinge and turn dull red or greenish red in autumn. Its flowers are
dark purple, and its fruit ripens to scarlet-red.

The name *wahoo* for the American tree comes from the Lakota Sioux *wanhu*, meaning "arrow shaft."[148] This name is also used for the American strawberry bush (*Euonymus americanus*) and the winged elm (*Ulmus alata*). Growing in woods and scrubland areas in the wild, the spindletree was commonly included in the hedgerows of England because its tangled branches created an effective barrier to keep domestic animals contained.

Although all parts of the tree are poisonous, Native Americans used it medicinally. For a time in the late nineteenth and early twentieth centuries, both the British and United States Pharmacopeia recognized the dried root bark of wahoo. The fruit of the European variety was used as a laxative; however, a little could be toxic and dangerous. John Gerard and later herbalists noted that all parts of the plant induce purging and vomiting. Ironically, the genus name, *Euonymus*, was derived from the Greek meaning "of good name."[149] According to Gerard, Greek philosopher Theophrastus had named the plant.

Gerard also noted that spindletree was a danger to goats, which earned it the name *gatter tree* from Old English *gat*, meaning "goat."[150] Notorious for eating anything, goats have been poisoned by the tree. The name *louse berry* comes from the practice of sprinkling powdered dried berries and leaves on the heads of children to rid them of lice. Whether this had any detrimental consequence to the children is unknown. The Old English name of *lus-thorn* is a reference to this practice. In parts of England, spindletree was called *death alder* and it was considered unlucky to bring any part of it into the home. According to Pliny the Elder, an abundance of flowers meant an outbreak of plague would soon strike.

First encountering the tree in Europe, English botanist William Turner (c. 1508–1568) mentioned in his notebook that the English did not have a name for it. Copying the Dutch, he suggested that it be called *spyndell tree* because the wood was commonly used to make spindles.[151] The Roma people favored the wood for knitting needles.

---

148. Michael A. Homoya, *Wildflowers and Ferns of Indiana Forests: A Field Guide* (Bloomington, IN: Indiana University Press, 2012), 78.

149. Hugh Glen, *Sappi What's in a Name: The Meanings of the Botanical Names of Trees* (Johannesburg, South Africa: Jacana Media (Pty) Ltd, 2004), 26.

150. Watts, *Elsevier's Dictionary of Plant Lore*, 362.

151. William Turner, *A New Herball* (London: Steven Mierdman, 1551) 313.

The spindle and the act of spinning are powerful female symbols. Various goddesses are credited with teaching humans this craft, which was vitally important for survival and comfort. Spinning was one form of woman's work that was highly prized because, prior to the industrial revolution, cloth was a valuable commodity. In addition to keeping her family clothed, an industrious woman could also provide for them by spinning enough to sell or trade. While the term *spinster* has come to have a negative connotation for an unmarried woman, the woman who was a skilled spinner would not be trapped as anyone's dependent. The spindle is a symbol of magic and manifestation. It was the tool of the Fates, daughters of the goddess Necessity, who fashioned the destiny of humans.

Magical Connections

Elements:	Water
Deities:	Athena, the Fates, Freya, Frigg, Holle, Minerva
Ogham:	Oir/Or ◇
Powers/attributes:	Challenges/obstacles (overcome), concentration/focus, courage, creativity, divination, family and home, healing, hexes (remove, ward off), inspiration, manifest (desires, dreams, will), purification, spirituality, success, wisdom
Other associations:	Imbolc

Items to purchase when the tree is not available: dried bark from the wahoo tree.

Spellwork and Ritual

Place any part of the tree on your altar to honor the Goddess. For spells, use a branch like a spindle and wrap a piece of yarn around it as you chant or recite an incantation. Place three berries in a small pouch to keep with you during divination sessions. To break a hex, hold a small twig between your hands as you visualize all the negative energy going into it, and then bury it in the ground. Press a leaf and when it's dry carry it with you when you need support in dealing with problems.

For a boost in creativity, draw the Oir ogham on the tools you use for self-expression or carve it into a branch from the tree and hang it in your work area. Use a small picture of the tree for a cleansing ritual to heal old emotional wounds. Write a few keywords on the picture, burn it in your cauldron, and then waft a little of the smoke over you.

SPRUCE

Black Spruce (*Picea mariana*); also known as American spruce, bog
spruce, swamp spruce.

Norway Spruce (*P. abies* syn. *P. excelsa*); also known as mountain
spruce, red fir, spruce fir, white fir.

White Spruce (*P. glauca*); also known as Black Hills spruce, cat spruce,
Canadian spruce, skunk spruce.

Black spruce is native to North America and usually grows forty-five to sixty feet tall.
Older trees have a spike-like crown. It has stiff, blue-green needles and purplish-brown,
egg-shaped cones that grow in clusters. Native to Europe, Norway spruce has a pyramid
shape and typically reaches between forty to sixty feet tall and occasionally one hundred. Its small branches droop from the upward-arching main branches. Its needles are
dark green. White spruce is native to North America. It usually grows sixty to eighty feet

tall but can reach over one hundred. Its blue-green needles have a waxy white coating, which is the source of its common and species names. When crushed, the needles have a pungent odor that earned it the nicknames *skunk spruce* and *cat spruce*.

The genus name *Picea* was derived from the Latin *pix*, which means "pitch," referring to the tree's resin.[152] Pitch was used as caulking for wooden sailing ships and small boats. The wood was used for framing ships and the trunks of black spruce were favored for masts. The sap was fermented with molasses and malt to make spruce beer. This brew originated with sailors during the sixteenth century to prevent scurvy.

Violin makers such as Stradivari and Amati valued spruce wood for its excellent resonance. Known as the Musical Woods, the forest in the Fiemme Valley of northern Italy where Stradivari and Amati found their trees is still the source of timber for some of the finest instruments.

In Bavaria, Germany, spruce was often used for Maypoles. Like pine, spruce was frequently used as a Yule log. Spirits were commonly believed to inhabit spruce trees. In the Tyrol region of Austria, branches were used on Walpurgis for protection against witches and evil spirits. Torches were made of spruce, blackthorn, hemlock, and rosemary to scare witches away. These were carried around town accompanied by the ringing of bells and beating of pans.

In Sweden, spruce branches were often used in burials to cover the deceased and sometimes placed underneath like bedding and a pillow. While birch was used in the same way, spruce had an added advantage of preventing the deceased from haunting the living.

Like other types of trees, spruce was used as a nail tree for sympathetic medicine, magic, and personal offerings. The remnant of one from the fifteenth century is on display behind glass on a busy street corner in Vienna. Known as the *stock-im-Eisen*, "staff in iron," the trunk is bound with pieces of iron and heavily studded with nails. First mentioned in the early sixteenth century, the tree once marked the edge of the much-loved Vienna Woods.

The Blue Mountains of Virginia were named for the bluish haze created by refracted light and caused by naturally occurring spruce resin droplets in the air. Black spruce was so named because from a distance its bark has a dark, charred appearance. Norway

---

152. Hageneder, *The Meaning of Trees*, 224.

spruce is sometimes known as red fir because of its reddish bark and because of the confusion over spruce and fir trees as well as pine.

Is That a Spruce, Pine, or Fir Tree?

While pine, fir, and spruce trees can be difficult to tell apart, you don't have to be a botanist to figure out which is which. The cones and needles provide clues to help identify them.

Pine, Spruce, and Fir Identification			
	Pine	Spruce	Fir
Cones	Hang pointing down; Flexible	Hang pointing down; Rigid with woody scales	Stand upright on branch
Needles	Grow individually; Roll easily between fingers	Grow in clusters	Grow individually; Flat, not easy to roll between fingers

Magical Connections

Elements:	Earth, water
Astrological influence:	Cancer, Capricorn, Sagittarius (black spruce)
Deities:	Attis, Cerridwen, Cybele, Danu, Poseidon
Wildlife:	Duck (mallard), grouse (spruce)
Alternate tree calendar:	July 5 to 14 and January 2 to 11
Runes:	Dagaz/Daeg/Dag ᛞ Runic half month: June 14 to 28
Powers/attributes:	Adaptability, awareness (enhance, heighten), balance/harmony, challenges/obstacles (overcome), clarity (enhance, foster), dream work, emotions (deal with, support), growth, healing, hope, inspiration, intuition, money/prosperity, protection, psychic abilities, renewal, security, spirit guides/spirits, spirituality, wisdom
Other associations:	Beltane, Yule

Items to purchase when the tree is not available: Essential oil is obtained from the needles and twigs of the black spruce.

Spellwork and Ritual

Burn spruce needles or pieces of bark to stimulate psychic abilities, especially for channeling and dream work. The scent of spruce helps develop intuition as well as to discern when to act on it. Use needles or cones to connect with the energy of forest spirits. Place a sprig on your altar for aid in finding inspiration, deepening spirituality, or strengthening trust. Holding a cone grounds and stabilizes energy after ritual or magic work and helps to transition back to the mundane realm. Hang a bough anywhere in your home to generate protective energy. Use needles or cones to raise and direct energy in healing circles.

When facing problems, write a few keywords on a picture of a spruce. Meditate on how to meet the challenges, and then burn the picture in your cauldron. Scatter the ashes outdoors as you visualize a resolution. Spruce can also point the way for renewal and personal growth.

SYCAMORE

American Sycamore (*Platanus occidentalis*); also known as American
  plane tree.

London Plane Tree (*P.* x *acerifolia*)

Oriental Sycamore (*P. orientalis*); also known as eastern plane tree,
  oriental plane tree.

All three trees are also known as buttonwood, ghost tree, great maple.

Indigenous to the southeastern United States, the American sycamore has the largest leaves of any native tree in North America reaching up to ten inches wide. Resembling maple leaves, they are dark green and turn yellow brown in autumn. The tree can
reach seventy-five to one hundred feet tall. Its brown bark peels off in irregular pieces
revealing the creamy inner bark. Small clusters of yellow and red flowers appear in early
spring. Fuzzy seed balls turn brown in autumn and stay on the tree into early winter.
The London plane tree is a hybrid between the American and oriental sycamores. Some-

times difficult to distinguish from the American sycamore, its leaves are smaller and have deeper indentations. Its seed balls grow in pairs. The London plane is thought to have been developed during the 1650s or 1660s in France or Spain.[153] Native to south-eastern Europe and western Asia, the oriental sycamore reaches sixty to eighty feet tall and sometimes one hundred. Its flaky bark is mottled brown, gray, and cream. Its seed balls grow in clusters of two to six.

The name *ghost tree* came about because of the sycamore's pale, mottled bark, which gives it a ghostly appearance, especially on foggy mornings and at dusk. The sycamore's twigs grow in a zigzag pattern from one bud to the next, which adds to its unusual appearance.

The sycamore is a valued shade tree, especially in cities, because of its resistance to pollution as well as the amount of pollutants it can remove from the air. Sycamores can live for 500 to 600 years. At around 200 to 300 years, it is fairly common for the trunks to become hollow. A new tree will grow from a stump if the original tree was at least ten feet tall when it was cut down.

In ancient Greece, this tree was regarded as a gift from the gods. According to legend, Hercules planted sycamores to honor his father Zeus. In Greek myth, soothsayer Calchas received an omen about the Trojan War as he stood under a sycamore. The city leaders of Athens frequently met in the shade of sycamores. Philosophers and other teachers held sessions under sycamores, giving the trees an association with knowledge and wisdom. Like the Greeks, the Romans found sycamores a convenient place to meet because their thick foliage offered shelter from the sun and rain.

The Romans prized these trees so much that they poured libations of wine on their roots and made sacrifices to them. Sycamore wood was used in the temple of Diana. According to legend, a giant sycamore on the Greek island of Corfu held the earth in place in the heavens. Representing harmony, lovers who had to part for a while each took half of a sycamore leaf to symbolize their love and their eventual reunion.

The sycamore was considered so beautiful by King Xerxes of Persia (c. 519–465 BCE) that he had gold ornaments hung from one and posted guards to keep watch over it. The king is said to have worn a gold amulet with an image of the tree. Until the late nineteenth century, amulets were often hung on sycamores in Syria.

A common medieval belief in the Netherlands was that bats hated these trees. This may have come from Pliny the Elder's assertion that a sycamore could neutralize a bat's venom. Although not poisonous, bats can carry rabies and other diseases. During the

---

153. Andrew Praciak, et al., comps. *The CABI Encyclopedia of Forest Trees* (Boston: CABI, 2013), 380.

Middles Ages, various parts of the sycamore were used for medicinal purposes. Having sycamore trees in a village was believed to keep the plague at bay.

Through misidentification, the Egyptian tree of life was called a sycamore even though it is a fig (*Ficus sycomorus*). Because of its leaf shape, sycamores are frequently misidentified as maples. It doesn't help that one type of maple (*Acer pseudoplatanus*) is known as sycamore maple and plane tree maple. The flower essence marketed as sycamore is made from this maple.

Magical Connections

Elements:	Air, water
Astrological influence:	Jupiter, Venus
Deities:	Artemis, Diana, Eros, Europa, Zeus
Magical beings and woodland spirits:	Genii
Wildlife:	Goldfinch
Powers/attributes:	Abundance, astral travel/journeying, balance/harmony, challenges/obstacles (overcome), communication, determination/endurance, divination, knowledge (seek, acquire), love, prophecy, protection, psychic abilities, purification, renewal, strength, stress/anxiety (calm, release), support (provide, receive), wisdom
Other associations:	Imbolc

Items to purchase when the tree is not available: Plane tree flower essence is made from the London plane tree.

Spellwork and Ritual

Before divination or any type of psychic work, crumble a piece of dried leaf and burn it to clear the energy of your workspace. Sycamore also aids in opening the mind to receive information and interpret messages. When engaging in astral travel, keep a twig or seed ball nearby for support. To bring harmony and stability to your life, hold a branch during meditation. This is especially helpful when seeking emotional shelter and comfort.

Collect a few seed balls to place on your Imbolc altar to represent renewal. Seed balls can also be used in spells to attract abundance and love.

TAMARISK

Athel Tamarisk (*Tamarix aphylla* syn *T. articulata*, *Thuja aphylla*); also
   known as athel pine, desert tamarisk, leafless tamarisk, salt cedar,
   salt tree.
French Tamarisk (*T. gallica* syn. *T. angelica*); also known as common
   tamarisk, English tamarisk, manna plant, salt cedar, sea cypress,
   tamarisk of Apollo.
Manna Tamarisk (*T. gallica* var. *mannifera* syn. *T. mannifera*)

Tamarisk trees were known as salt cedars because their scale-like leaves resemble cedar
foliage and they secrete salt. Slender, willowy branches and clouds of feathery white to
pale pink flowers give tamarisks an ethereal appearance. The triangular seed capsules
are tufted on top. Putting down long roots, tamarisks can grow in deserts and tolerate

saltwater. Native to southern Europe, Asia, and Africa, the French tamarisk is a deciduous, spreading tree that grows about fifteen feet tall and wide. Growing on short spikes, its pink flowers resemble little bottlebrushes. The evergreen athel tamarisk is native to Africa, the Middle East, western Asia, and India. It can grow up to fifty feet tall and wide. Its pale pink to whitish flowers grow in clusters near the tips of the branches.

This tree's common name comes from the Latin name for the tree *tamarix*, which may have been derived from the Sanskrit *tama* meaning "darkness" in reference to the bark.[154] Also from Latin, the genus name, *Aphylla* means "having no leaves."[155] The common name *athel* was derived from the Hebrew name for the tamarisk, *eshel*.[156]

In Egyptian mythology, the tamarisk was integral to the resurrection story of Osiris. In one version, when his sarcophagus came to rest in Phoenicia, a tamarisk tree grew around and encompassed it. The king and queen had the tree made into a pillar for their palace where Isis eventually found it. In another version of the legend, Osiris turned into a tamarisk when placed in the coffin. The Egyptian funerary deity, Wepwawet, whose name means "opener of the ways," was also associated with the tamarisk.[157] Wepwawet protected the dead as he led them through the underworld. In India, the tamarisk was considered a messenger of Yama, the god of death. Like the acacia, tamarisk was used as a funerary staff also known as the staff of the dead, which was placed in tombs with the deceased or depicted in murals on the walls. The tree was also believed to provide protection from bad spirits.

Egyptian priests wore sprigs of tamarisk and used the wood to make charcoal upon which to burn incense. The soot of burnt tamarisk wood was used to inscribe amulets for the dead. Persian priests used bundles of tamarisk branches to aid them in divination and prophecies. According to legend, only an arrow made of tamarisk wood could kill a Persian prince. Tamarisk was one of the sacred woods used in the Assyrian palace at Nimrud in what is now present-day Iraq. The Arabs also regarded the tree as sacred.

---

154. Wells, *Lives of the Trees*, 318.

155. Harrison, *Latin for Gardiners*, 28.

156. James A. Duke, *Duke's Handbook of Medicinal Plants of the Bible*, (Boca Raton, FL: CRC Press, 2008), 451.

157. Mark G. Boyer, *An ABeCeDarian of Sacred Trees: Spiritual Growth through Reflections on Woody Plants* (Eugene, OR: Wipf & Stock Publishers, 2016), 159.

In addition to providing shade for desert travelers, the tamarisk was important for its resin. The resin provided aromatic smoke for sacred rituals to communicate with deities and it was valuable for medicinal purposes. The resin was also used to make sweet cakes. Tamarisk is one of the contenders for the source of the manna from heaven that saved the Israelites during their sojourn in the desert. Manna is thought to be the white drops of honey-like resin that form on the tamarisk tree, the camel's thorn bush (*Alhagi maurorum*), and several other desert shrubs.

Symbolizing beauty and youth, the Greeks dedicated this tree to Aphrodite and Apollo, who was often depicted holding a tamarisk branch. The Greeks regarded it as a tree of prophecy. Although the Greeks used the name *myrica* for the tamarisk, it is now used for the false tamarisk (*Myricaria germanica*) and various types of myrtle. According to Pliny the Elder, the Romans used the fragrant, flexible branches of tamarisk as brooms, a practice also found in medieval England. Culpeper and other herbalists of the Middle Ages recommended tamarisk for a range of ailments. Cups made of tamarisk wood were thought to improve the flavor of ale. On the island of Guernsey in the British Channel, water diviners favored tamarisk rods. Although their names are similar, tamarisk should not be confused with the tamarind tree (*Tamarindus indica*).

Magical Connections

Element:	Water
Astrological influence:	Saturn
Deities:	Anu, Apollo, Cernunnos, Osiris, Pan, Wepwawet, Yama
Powers/attributes:	The afterlife, ancestors, banish, death/funeral practices, divination, hexes (remove, ward off), hope, negativity (remove, ward off), prophecy, protection, spirituality
Other associations:	Samhain

Items to purchase when the tree is not available: Flower essences are made from the French tamarisk and the pink tamarisk (*T. ramosissima*).

Spellwork and Ritual

Tamarisk's historical association with death makes it an appropriate tree to use at Samhain to honor ancestors and wish them well in the otherworld. Place sprigs on your altar or use the flower essence to prepare candles. To release negative energy or anything unwanted from your life, bundle a couple of branches together to use as a broom to symbolically sweep it away. For protection, place a small sprig or two over the exterior doors of your home. To remove a hex, burn a sprig in your cauldron and then bury the ashes in the ground or throw them in a stream of moving water.

American Blackberry (*Rubus villosus*); also known as bramble, high
   blackberry, shrub blackberry.

European Blackberry (*R. fruticosus*); also known as black heg, bramble,
   bramble thorn, brambleberry, wild blackberry.

Blackberry bushes are sprawling shrubs with woody, arching stems called *canes*. The
canes tend to take root where their tips rest on the ground. Blackberry leaves are comprised of three to five coarsely toothed leaflets. They are dark green on top and pale
underneath. White five-petaled flowers grow in clusters at the ends of the stems. Each
flower produces a berry, which is technically a cluster of little fruits. The berries change
from green to red to black as they ripen. They are fully ripe when dull black, not glossy.

   While the term *vine* has come to include the grapevine, in the Celtic ogham it refers
to the blackberry vines that populated the hedgerows in the British Isles and formed

thorny thickets. The name of the ogham character Muin comes from a Gaelic word meaning "thicket."[158] During the early Middle Ages, the word *bramble* originally referred to any thorny plant.[159] The common name *black heg* was derived from the Anglo-Saxon *hege* "hedge."[160] While the term *heg berry* could refer to fruit from a variety of hedge plants, black heg is specific to blackberries.

According to Celtic mythology, the divine people known as the Tuatha Dé Danann brought the bramble with them to Ireland. The interlacing patterns of Celtic design seem to indicate their admiration of the plant.

Since the time of the ancient Greeks, blackberries have been used to treat a range of ailments. In European folk medicine, the arching canes were believed to have magical properties. Creeping along the ground underneath the arches or passing children through gaps in a thicket were prescribed to cure various ailments. Blackberry bushes were also believed to protect against evil. In parts of England, they were sometimes planted on graves or canes laid across them to keep the dead in place.

In weather lore, cool weather in May after the flowers bloom was known as a blackberry winter. Warm weather at the end of September was a blackberry summer. In the American south, rain on June 2 meant there would be no blackberries that season.

In some areas of England, eating blackberries after the end of August was considered dangerous because witches poisoned them. In Derbyshire, September 30 was the date after which they should be avoided. According to similar legends, after Michaelmas (September 29 or October 11 on the old calendar) the devil was said to put a curse on blackberries. Michaelmas was when Lucifer was banished from heaven. In Ireland, they were not to be gathered after October 31 because the Pooka was said to have spat on them.

On the island of Guernsey in the English Channel, blackberry wreaths were hung in the rafters of barns to scratch any witches that might fly inside the building. Burning a sprig of leaves also offered protection. Since the bramble vine and holy wells were associated with Brigid, a cure for burns (she is also a fire goddess) was to dress the wound with nine bramble leaves dipped in water from a spring. This needed to be done three times to make it work.

---

158. Niall MacCoitir, *Irish Trees: Myths, Legends & Folklore* (Cork, Ireland: The Collins Press, 2003), 167.

159. Watts, *Elsevier's Dictionary of Plant Lore*, 44.

160. Frederick Edward Hulme, *Wild Fruits of the Country-Side* (London: Hutchinson & Co., 1902), 95.

Like ivy, blackberry vines grow in a spiral, which is a symbol of the Mother Goddess. According to some traditions, the full moon of September is called the *wine moon* and esbat rituals include blackberry wine. Imbolc is Brigid's sabbat and blackberry wine or juice is commonly used in that ritual, too.

Magical Connections

Elements:	Water
Astrological influence:	Moon, Venus; Aries, Scorpio, Taurus
Deities:	Brigid, the Dagda, Danu, Freya, Manannan
Magical beings and woodland spirits:	Ampelos (Greek tree nymph), fairies, Pooka (a type of Irish fairy or spirit)
Wildlife:	Eagle, titmouse, swan
Ogham:	Muin/Muinn ╈ 　　Celtic tree calendar: September 2 to 29
Runes:	Thurisaz/Thurs/Thorn ᚦ 　　Runic half month: July 29 to August 12 Wunjo/Wynn/Wyn ᚹ 　　Runic half month: October 13 to October 27
Powers/attributes:	Abundance, awareness (enhance, heighten), balance/harmony, challenges/obstacles (overcome), communication, death/funeral practices, enchantment, fertility, growth, happiness, healing, intuition, knowledge (seek, acquire), luck, money/prosperity, protection, purification, spirit guides/spirits
Other associations:	Imbolc, Beltane, Lughnasadh, Mabon, September full moon

Items to purchase when the plant is not available: blackberries, blackberry juice, blackberry wine, dried leaves, blackberry leaf tea.

Spellwork and Ritual

Grow a blackberry bush on your property to attract fairies or set out a small bowl of berries as a token of friendship. Eat a handful of blackberries before magic work to reach deeper levels of consciousness or when working with the fairy realm. Use the berry juice to prepare candles when communicating with spirits. Blackberries enhance and aid in developing intuition.

Burn dried leaves in spells to attract money and prosperity or sprinkle them around your property to attract luck. Blackberries are also instrumental for healing. Plant a bush on your property to foster happiness. Make a wreath with several prickly canes to hang above your altar or on your front door to stimulate protective energy. Place a blackberry cane alongside your altar to aid in grounding energy after ritual. Because blackberries are associated with Brigid, gather enough to make jam or wine and use it to honor her at Imbolc.

VINE/GRAPE

Common Grape (*Vitis vinifera*); also known as English grape, European grape, wine-bearing grape.

Fox Grape (*V. labrusca*); also known as Concord grape, wild grape.

Grapevines have thick, woody base stems and climb with the aid of tendrils. The leaves are deeply lobed and measure five to nine inches across. Spikes of small, greenish-white flowers grow in dense clusters. The fruit grows in inverted pyramidal clusters and ripen in early autumn. The common grape is native to Asia Minor and has green fruit. Native to eastern North America, the fruit of the fox grape is blue black and ripens to dark purple.

The name *Vitis* is Latin for "grape" and *vinifera*, "wine-bearing."[161] In Persia, Greece, and throughout Asia Minor, the grapevine was highly venerated to the point of cult status.

---

161. Neal, *Gardener's Latin*, 132.

Wine was regarded in many cultures as a gift from the gods or the blood of the gods. It was considered a gift because under certain circumstances grapes can ferment on the vine producing ready-made wine. For the Babylonians, Egyptians, Phoenicians, Greeks, and Romans, wine provided a means for communing with deities and for spiritual transcendence. Of course, the secular pleasures were well enjoyed too.

Wine was an important part of Greek culture and commerce as evidenced from the number of wine amphoras found in ancient shipwrecks. The Romans took wine production to a new level, and like many other plants, the grapevine was transported as the Roman Empire expanded. They established some of the finest wine-growing regions of France and Spain.

The Egyptians made offerings of wine to deities and used it widely in religious rituals. As a funerary offering, wine was placed in the tombs of the rich and royalty and even the graves of common people. The Greeks associated wine with the dead and the underworld.

In Athens, Dionysian festivals were held in March and December. Dionysus and Faunus were often depicted crowned with wreaths of grape leaves. Extremely fond of wine, the lusty woodland satyrs were said to wear garlands of grapevine with sprigs of ivy and pine. According to legend, Dionysus, the Greek god of wine and vineyards, favored grapes as a child because they were refreshing. Liber, a Roman god who presided over vegetation, was later identified with Dionysus and worshipped as Bacchus, whose name may have been derived from the Latin *bacca* meaning "berry."[162] Liber/Bacchus became the personification of the blessings of nature, especially autumn.

Offerings of wine and grapes were made to Silvanus, the Roman god of forests and fields. The Roman festival of *Vinalia* celebrated the start of the growing season in the spring and the *Vinalia Rustica* in late summer, the grape harvest. The *Meditrinalia* held in late autumn became a festival in which old and new stocks of wine were mixed. As part of this festival, offerings were made to deities as part of a ceremony asking for protection against disease.

From ancient times through the Renaissance, wine was included in herbal texts as a remedy for a range of ailments. Recommendations stressing its importance for good health by Greek physician Hippocrates and later Galen were based on the fact that wine was often safer to drink than water. Wine was also used to treat wounds because of its

---

162. E. M. Berens, *Myths and Legends of Ancient Greece and Rome* (Irvine, CA: Xist Publishing, 2015), 124.

antiseptic properties. While the people of ancient Egypt, India, Greece, and Rome sung praises about wine, they also acknowledged its darker side and its potential for bringing disaster.

Magical Connections

Elements:	Air, fire, water
Astrological influence:	Moon, Sun
Deities:	Ariadne, Athena, Bacchus/Liber, Bona Dea, Dionysus, Faunus, Hathor, Juno, Mabon, Rhea, Saturn, Silvanus, Thor
Magical beings and woodland spirits:	Ampelos (Greek tree nymph), fairies, satyrs
Wildlife:	Bee, hedgehog
Ogham:	Muin/Muinn ┼ Celtic tree calendar: September 2 to 29
Powers/attributes:	Abundance, balance/harmony, bind, changes/transitions, consecrate/bless, creativity, divination, fertility, growth, happiness, healing, inspiration, love, money/prosperity, prophecy, psychic abilities, sex/sexuality, transformation
Other associations:	Mabon

Items to purchase when the grapevine is not available: fresh fruit, raisins, grape juice, wine, grapeseed oil.

Spellwork and Ritual

Eat three grapes before divination or any type of psychic work to bring clarity to your sessions. Use a bunch of grapes in spells to attract abundance and prosperity. Use a short length of vine or several tendrils to boost the effectiveness of binding spells. Prepare a candle with grapeseed oil for spells to kindle romance or heighten sexual attraction.

Use grape juice as a libation for healing rituals. Meditate with a piece of vine or leaves for inspiration and to help find your best method for creative expression. When dealing with changes in your life, write your desired outcome on a picture of a grape vine. Keep it in a safe place until your goal has been achieved. Grapes are instrumental for attracting happiness.

WALNUT

Black Walnut (*Juglans nigra*); also known as American black walnut,
   eastern black walnut.
English Walnut (*J. regia*); also known as Persian walnut.
White Walnut (*J. cinerea*); also known as butternut walnut.

Walnut trees have lance-shaped leaves that turn dull yellow in the autumn. In the early spring, male and female catkins develop on the same tree. Reaching seventy-five to one hundred feet tall, the black walnut is native to eastern North America. Its round, edible nuts are encased in a yellow-green husk. Native to northeastern United States and southeastern Canada, the white walnut reaches forty to sixty feet tall. It is similar in appearance to the black walnut. The English walnut is native to Europe and central Asia. It reaches forty to sixty feet tall and produces the familiar nut sold in stores.

It was common practice for Romans to bury a coin beneath a walnut tree as an offering to Pomona, the goddess of fruit trees. Archaeologists have found that black walnuts were a popular snack for the Romans. The genus name *Juglan* comes from the Latin *Jovis glans*, "the fruit of Jove"; the species name *regia*, means "royal."[163] The Romans may have introduced the walnut into the British Isles. The Greeks dedicated the tree to Zeus and Persephone and associated it with prophecy. Germanic peoples dedicated the tree to Freyr and Thor.

The walnut was regarded as a magically protective tree. In France, walnut leaves that were gathered before dawn on St. John's Day, June 24, were believed to protect against lightning. A branch that was held while dancing around the Midsummer's Eve bonfire was often hung over the entrance to a cowshed to protect the animals. In the Middle East, powdered walnut root and bark combined with henna (*Lasonia intermis*) provided protection against supernatural forces.

In Italy, demons were said to live near walnut trees and witches to gather underneath them on St. John's Night. A venerated walnut tree in Benevento, Italy, later became known as the wizard walnut and a notorious gathering place for witches. It reputedly had the image of a snake in its bark, and, according to legend, when the tree was cut down, a large viper was discovered amongst its roots. Further legends claim that a phantom walnut tree appears on that spot whenever witches hold a sabbat.

As a nut with two distinctive halves, walnuts were a symbol of marriage. Scattered at Roman weddings, they were believed to protect any children that resulted from the union. According to Pliny the Elder, the association of walnuts with fertility and their use in marriage ceremonies was due to their resemblance to testicles. It was traditional to place a basket of walnuts beside the bridal bed. According to Spanish Catalan physician and alchemist Arnaud de Villeneuve (1235–1311), walnuts were an aphrodisiac and used in sexual magic.

In the fifteenth century, walnuts were believed to cure madness and trouble from "wicked spirits."[164] Another belief warned that sleeping under a walnut tree could result in madness. For this reason, throughout parts of Europe sitting in the shade of a walnut tree was considered risky behavior. In addition to being regarded as a cure for baldness, walnuts were also believed to be an antidote to poisonous herbs.

In weather lore, a heavy crop of walnuts meant a good corn harvest the following year. In some areas, an exceptionally large crop of walnuts indicated an icy winter ahead. If the first walnut opened on New Year's Day was black inside, a death or serious illness

163. De Cleene and Lejeune, *Compendium of Symbolic and Ritual Plants in Europe*, 706.
164. Watts, *Elsevier's Dictionary of Plant Lore*, 410.

would occur in the family. As a symbol of health and prosperity, walnuts were wrapped in silver paper and hung on Christmas trees in parts of Germany. In Switzerland, a small, perfectly formed walnut was carried for good luck.

Magical Connections

Elements:	Air, fire
Astrological influence:	Jupiter, Sun; Gemini, Leo, Virgo
Deities:	Aphrodite, Apollo, Artemis, Astarte, Diana, Dionysus, Freyr, Jove, Jupiter, Persephone, Pomona, Rhea, Thor, Zeus
Magical beings and woodland spirits:	Elves, Karya (Greek tree nymph)
Wildlife:	Eagle
Alternate tree calendar:	April 21 to 30 and October 24 to November 2
Powers/attributes:	Changes/transitions, clarity (enhance, foster), consecrate/bless, fertility, healing, inspiration, love, luck, manifest (desires, dreams, will), money/prosperity, prophecy, protection, purification, sex/sexuality, spirit guides/spirits, success, transformation, wishes
Other associations:	Midsummer's Eve, Yule

Items to purchase when the tree is not available: Nuts, which come mostly from the English walnut; flower essence is made from the English walnut; walnut oils are obtained from the black and English walnut trees.

Spellwork and Ritual

Use walnuts during ritual as an offering to deities. Carry a small walnut for luck. As part of a love spell, separate the halves of a walnut and write your name and the other person's name on each half. Tie them back together by wrapping red thread around them. Use a walnut in a protection spell and then place it near the front door of your home.

At Yule, wrap enough walnuts in silver paper for each member of the family. On the solstice, each person should hold theirs and make a wish before hanging it on the Yule tree. To provide clarity when making decisions, meditate while holding two walnut leaves. Burn a few dried leaves to clear the energy for a healing circle.

WILLOW

American Willow (*Salix discolor*); also known as pussy willow.
European Willow (*S. alba*); also known as European willow, withy.
Weeping Willow (*S. babylonica*)

All of these trees have narrow, lance-shaped leaves that are lighter underneath than on top. They turn greenish yellow in the autumn. The American willow is a shrubby, multi-trunked tree that reaches six to fifteen feet tall. Native to North America, it has the nickname pussy willow because of its fuzzy gray catkins that resemble the soft pads of cat's feet. Native to China, the weeping willow is widely loved for its long, graceful branches that sweep to the ground. It can grow thirty to fifty feet tall with a crown that can be just as wide. Reaching fifty to eighty feet tall, the white willow is native to Europe, central Asia, and northern Africa. The silky white undersides of its leaves give the tree a white appearance.

Usually found near water, willows are linked with sacred and mysterious powers as well as enchantment and death. Associated with in-between times and places, willows are often used in Beltane and Samhain rituals. Common throughout folklore, the willow was believed to contain an entrance to the otherworld.

The Greeks and Romans dedicated the willow to Circe, Hecate, Persephone, and Saturn. Demeter's sacred grove consisted of willows and black poplars. In Greek mythology, the poet and musician Orpheus carried a willow branch for protection when he descended to the underworld to retrieve his beloved Eurydice. Believed to hold special protective powers, willow branches were associated with the miraculous births of Diana and Osiris.

Although it is associated with death and grieving, the weeping willow also has a long association with dispelling sadness and recovering from emotional darkness. It was often planted in cemeteries and depicted on gravestones for the dual purpose of both expressing and relieving grief. Branches carried in funeral processions symbolized the sadness of the mourners as well as rebirth for the deceased. In England, the drape of weeping willow branches became a symbol of forsaken love.

Because it is often found in a swampy, misty habitat, the willow's proximity to water gave it a dark connotation. In parts of Germany, will-o-the-wisps, witches, and evil water spirits were believed to lurk in the vicinity of these trees. In the moors of southwest England, travelers told stories of being followed by willow trees, which is why walking passed one at night was usually avoided. In Ireland, harps were often made of willow wood because it was believed that the tree's soul would come through the music. In one type of traditional witches' besom broom, long pliable branches of willow were used to secure birch twigs to an ash handle. Long thin willow branches have been used for knot magic, too.

Beliefs swing like a pendulum; at one time willows were believed to suppress sexual urges and at other times to be an aphrodisiac. Long used in herbal medicine, in the late 1800s, the chemical compound acetylsalicylic acid was isolated from willow bark and the painkiller aspirin was born.

Magical Connections

Elements:	Fire, water
Astrological influence:	Moon, Venus; Aries, Capricorn, Pisces, Taurus
Deities:	Artemis, Athena, Bel/Belenus, Brigid, Ceres, Cerridwen, Circe, Danu, Demeter, Diana, Hecate, Hera, Hermes, Ishtar, Juno, Loki, Luna, Mercury, the Morrigan, Osiris, Persephone, Poseidon, Proserpina, Rhiannon, Saturn, Zeus
Magical beings and woodland spirits:	Elves, fairies, Helike (Greek tree nymph), water sprites
Wildlife:	Bee, crane, deer, dove, hare, hawk, owl (snowy)
Ogham:	Saille/Saile ⊤⊤⊤⊤ Celtic tree calendar: April 15 to May 12
Alternate tree calendar:	September 3 to 12 and March 1 to 10
Runes:	Laguz/Logr/Lagu ⌐ Runic half month: April 29 to May 13
Powers/attributes:	Adaptability, the afterlife, bind, communication, consecrate/bless, courage, death/funeral practices, divination, dream work, enchantment, fertility, healing, inspiration, intuition, knowledge (seek, acquire), loss/sorrow (ease, recover from), love, the otherworld, prophecy, protection, sex/sexuality, spirit guides/spirits, strength, wishes
Other associations:	Beltane, Samhain

Items to purchase when the tree is not available: dried bark in pieces or powdered from the white willow, willow baskets. Flower essence is made from the golden willow (*S. alba* var. *vitellina*), a cultivar of the white willow.

Spellwork and Ritual

Willow is allied with moon goddesses. Make a circle with pussy willow catkins and/or willow leaves on your esbat altar to aid in raising lunar energy.

To empower love spells and divination sessions, take a thin weeping willow branch, strip off the leaves, and wind it into a circle. Tie short pieces of yarn in several places to keep the circle intact, and then set it on your altar. Draw the willow ogham or rune on a pink or red candle for love spells or on a white candle for divination. Place the candle in the middle of the willow circle to aid in raising energy. Willow branches work well as the base for any size wreath.

Once you befriend this tree, it is very generous and will provide you with many wands and other gifts. Spirits that dwell in willows tend to be curious, sometimes shy, but always welcoming. They can aid you in contacting fairies and other nature spirits.

WITCH HAZEL

Common Witch Hazel (*Hamamelis virginiana*); also known as American witch hazel, fall-blooming witch hazel, snapping alder, snapping hazelnut, winterbloom.
Witch Hazel Hybrids (*H.* x *intermedia*)

Resembling crinkled ribbons, witch hazel's spidery-looking flowers bloom in the autumn or winter after the leaves have dropped. Sometimes tinged with red or orange, these yellow flowers on bare branches brighten a dull landscape and are especially stunning in the snow. The leaves are rounded, oblong, and coarsely toothed. Greenish little seed capsules form over a long period of time, extending into the following growing season. They become woody with age and mature to a light brown color. When ripe, the capsules explode open shooting seeds as far as twenty feet.

Common witch hazel is native to eastern and central North America and usually reaches ten to fifteen feet tall. Its leaves are bright green and turn greenish yellow to orange in the autumn. The hybrids are a cross between the Chinese (*H. mollis*) and Japanese (*H. japonica*) witch hazels and were created for winter blooming and for fragrance. Although the quintessential color of the flowers is yellow, some of these hybrids have orange or red flowers. The medium to dark green leaves turn orange to orange brown in autumn.

Witch hazel's genus name comes from the Greek *hama*, "together," and *mela*, "fruit," referring to the seeds and flowers.[165] The seeds take a year to mature, which is why they are on the tree at the same time as the flowers. Like the wych elm, the word *witch* in its common name comes from an Old English word meaning "to bend" because of its pliant branches.[166] The word *hazel* was applied because its leaves are very similar to the hazel tree. Early colonists in North America confused it with hazel and alder trees due to the resemblance of their leaves. Witch hazel was called *snapping alder* because of the loud sound the seed pods make when they pop open.

John Banister (1654–1692), an English missionary and naturalist, was the first European to take note of the witch hazel. Banister visited the colony of Virginia and collected plants that were unknown back home in Britain. The tree was included in the book *Almegestrum Botanicum* published in 1695 by English botanist Leonard Plukenet (1642–1706).[167] It was one of the earliest North American trees adopted and grown as an ornamental plant in Europe. In England and America, forked branches were used for dowsing to find water and mineral deposits. Witch hazel was also attributed with the ability to find buried pirate's treasure. The divining rods were sometimes called *witch brushes*.

Because of its name, the tree sometimes had a negative connotation. If the tree cast a shadow across a stream or pond, the water was considered unfit to drink. In Kentucky, it was regarded as unlucky to carry a leaf with you because witches were believed to use the tree for spells and conjuring.

Used medicinally by a number of Native American tribes, European settlers quickly adopted it for remedies. Witch hazel is best known for the distilled astringent extract that is made from the bark, leaves, and twigs. First sold as *Aqua Hamamelidis* in the 1800s, witch hazel extract was also marketed as Hawes Extract, Extract of Hamamelis, and Golden Treasure.

---

165. Glyn Church, *Trees and Shrubs for Fragrance* (Buffalo, NY: Firefly Books (U.S.) Inc., 2002), 74.

166. Martin, *The Folklore of Trees & Shrubs*, 207.

167. Peattie, *A Natural History of Trees of Eastern and Central North America*, 302.

Magical Connections

Elements:	Earth, fire, water
Astrological influence:	Saturn, Sun; Libra
Wildlife:	Deer, rabbit
Ogham:	Amhancholl/Eamancholl/Emancoll/Mór ⊞
Powers/attributes:	Ancestors, banish, challenges/obstacles (overcome), communication, courage, divination, healing, inspiration, knowledge (seek, acquire), loss/sorrow (ease, recover from), love, loyalty/fidelity, protection, release (let go, move on), sex/sexuality, strength, stress/anxiety (calm, release), wisdom
Other associations:	Samhain

Items to purchase when the tree is not available: witch hazel, witch hazel water, dried leaves in pieces or powdered, dried bark.

Spellwork and Ritual

Collect a few witch hazel flowers and tuck them into a sachet for love divination or place them in your work area when you want to give inspiration a boost. Sprinkle a little witch hazel water wherever you need to clear the energy for ritual and magic or anywhere around the home. Dry several flowers and then burn them for protection spells or banishing rituals; scatter the ashes outside. Use witch hazel flowers on your Samhain altar to honor loved ones who have passed.

Place a small witch hazel twig on your altar or table during divination sessions to help focus your mind and open psychic channels. Hold a branch during a ritual to aid in communicating with deities. Hanging a branch over the front door creates protective energy for your home.

Burn dried flowers, bark, or a twig to aid in recovering from loss. Sprinkle a handful of dried leaves in your favorite outdoor place as you visualize letting go of something or someone. After a relationship breakup, waft a little smoke from the bark in each room of the house to remove the presence of the person who left. Burn a few flowers for a healing circle or ritual to strengthen the energy you send out.

American Yew (*Taxus canadensis*); also known as Canada yew.

English Yew (*T. baccata*); also known as common yew.

Reaching only six feet tall, the American yew is an evergreen shrub with multiple trunks and reddish bark. The English yew is also an evergreen; however, it can reach almost fifty feet tall. Both have dark green needle-like leaves that are glossy on top and gray to pale green underneath. The needles of the American tree have a reddish-brown tint in the winter. The red, cup-shaped berry contains seeds, which ripen in the autumn. The seeds and foliage are toxic. The American yew is native to North America, the English yew to Europe, western Asia, and northern Africa.

The yew's association with death dates to the Greco-Roman period. The Latin genus name, *taxus* may have been derived from the Greek *toxon* meaning "bow" or *toxicon*, the poison used on arrows, which was most often from the yew.[168] According to Greek myth, Artemis used poison from the yew on the tips of her arrows. Yew wood was favored for the English and Welsh longbows because of its strength and flexibility. The Celts of Gaul also used the yew for bows and poison. According to archaeological evidence, the use of yew wood for spears dates to the Stone Age. A fire-hardened yew spear tip was found in the rib cage of a woolly mammoth.

The Greeks dedicated the yew to Hecate and regarded it as a magical tree. As mentioned in the profile for mistletoe, the yew has more recently become the candidate for the golden bough in Greek myth that was carried by Aeneas to gain access to the underworld. In addition to fitting the description of being used like a staff, on rare occasions a single branch on a yew tree can turn a golden-yellow hue. The Romans also associated the yew with death. According to Roman poet Ovid, the path along the River Styx in the underworld was lined with yews.

The yew can live for thousands of years and became a symbol of immortality and the afterlife. Eleusinian ritual wreaths made of yew and myrtle were worn to symbolize death and rebirth. Also used as a symbol of mourning, the practice of planting yews in cemeteries became widespread.

In Yorkshire, England, ancient burials contained yew charcoal. In medieval burials, sprigs of yew were often placed within the shroud. In France, funeral mourners carried yew branches. Sprigs of yew were placed in the grave and on it. The wood was used for a wide range of votive objects in Britain, France, and Switzerland.

Germanic peoples associated the yew with rune magic. In Germany, it was believed that the tree offered protection from witches and a twig nailed to the inside of a door would keep them from entering a house. In northern England, a twig was used as a dowsing rod to find lost items. According to French philosopher and historian Jean Markale, Druids used yew wands for divination.[169] In Wales, fairies could be seen when under a yew and in the Highlands of Scotland, they often lived under them. Near the village of Llanwrin in north Wales, a magical yew was said to grow at the center of the woods known as the Forest of the Yew. While there were said to be a number of fairy circles in the forest, the one under the great yew at the center was known as the Dancing Place of the Goblin and associated with legends of people being whisked into fairyland.

---

168. Wells, *Lives of the Trees*, 346.

169. Markale, *Merlin Priest of Nature*, 160.

In England, the yew was one of the trees under which courts and moots were held. According to legend, the great Arkenwyke Yew at Runnymede along the River Thames was the place where Magna Carta was signed in 1215 and a trysting place of King Henry VIII and Anne Boleyn in the 1530s.[170]

Magical Connections

Elements:	Air, fire, water
Astrological influence:	Jupiter, Mars, Saturn; Capricorn
Deities:	Artemis, Badb, Banba, Cailleach Bheur, the Dagda, Dionysus, Dôn, the Furies, Hecate, Hermes, Holle, Loki, Lugh, Odin, Saturn
Magical beings and woodland spirits:	Elves, fairies
Wildlife:	Deer, eaglet (young eagle), hummingbird
Ogham:	Ioho/Idho/Iodho/Iodahdh ᚎ
Alternate tree calendar:	November 3 to 11

Runes:	Algiz/Eolh/Elhaz ᛉ
	    Runic half month: January 28 to February 11
	Iwaz/Eoh/Eihwaz ᛇ
	    Runic half month: December 28 to January 12
	Hagalaz/Hagall/Haegl ᚼ
	    Runic half month: October 28 to November 12
	Yr (Younger Futhark) ᛦ

Powers/attributes:	Adaptability, the afterlife, ancestors, changes/transitions, communication, death/funeral practices, divination, dream work, enchantment, hexes (remove, ward off), justice/legal matters, knowledge (seek, acquire), loss/sorrow (ease, recover from), negativity (remove, ward off), the otherworld, protection, psychic abilities, renewal, spirit guides/spirits, strength
Other associations:	Ostara, Samhain, Yule

170. Marissa Fessenden, "Legend Says the Ankerwycke Yew Witnessed the Magna Carta's Signing," *Smithsonian Magazine*, February 20, 2015, https://www.smithsonianmag.com/smart-news/legend-says-ankerwycke-yew-witnessed-signing-magna-carta-180954373/.

Items to purchase when the tree is not available: Boxes and other small objects are made from yew wood; flower essence is made from the English yew.

Spellwork and Ritual

Place yew sprigs with berries on your altar during divination sessions to heighten psychic abilities. Hang a sachet of dried berries on a bedpost or place it on a bedside table to soothe bad dreams. Place three berries on your altar to aid in turning inward during the dark of the year to nurture yourself, and then burn them at Yule. Yew sprigs on the Samhain altar aid in drawing close to ancestors.

If you have a spirit in your house that troubles you, hang sachets with yew leaves and berries or sprigs of yew in active areas on the dark moon. As you do this, suggest that the spirit follow the energy of the yew to find peace and rest in the otherworld. On the full moon, take the sprigs or sachets down and burn them.

CONCLUSION

Go for walks in the woods, a park, or around your neighborhood. Look at the trees and be aware of their energy as well as their spirits. Feel the sense of awe and wonder that the ancients experienced. Find a special place with trees that is sacred to you. Spend time, meditate, and leave offerings.

Over time, particular trees that you see often become like acquaintances and neighbors. Acknowledge them when you pass by; thank them for all they provide. Getting to know trees does more than boost the energy of magic and ritual, it deepens our connection with the green world and enhances many aspects of our lives. Listen for the whispers from the woods and the wisdom of trees that will speak to your soul.

APPENDIX A
MAGICAL POWERS AND ATTRIBUTES

This listing provides a quick reference to help you find trees and plants to suit your purposes.

Abundance: Acacia, almond, apple, beech, birch, cedar, cherry, chestnut, crabapple, elder, fig, gorse, hackberry, hazel, juniper, laurel, lemon, maple, myrtle, oak, olive, orange, palm, pine, pomegranate, reeds/rushes/cattails, sycamore, vine/blackberry, vine/grape

Adaptability: Bamboo, hackberry, heath/heather, spruce, willow, yew

The Afterlife: Acacia, apple, cedar, cypress, myrtle, oak, peach, pomegranate, rose, tamarisk, willow, yew

Ancestors: Acacia, apple, aspen, beech, box, crabapple, cypress, eucalyptus, fig, hawthorn, oak, poplar, reeds/rushes/cattails, tamarisk, witch hazel, yew

Astral Travel/Journeying: Ash, aspen, birch, frankincense, hawthorn, maple, poplar, reeds/rushes/cattails, rowan, sycamore

Attraction: Almond, apple, cherry, elm, frankincense, ivy, linden, olive, rose

Authority/Leadership: Alder, blackthorn, cedar, frankincense, heath/heather, myrtle, oak, rowan

Awareness (Enhance, Heighten): Acacia, almond, ash, birch, cypress, fig/Bodhi fig, fir, frankincense, hazel, heath/heather, laurel, lemon, oak, orange, reeds/rushes/cattails, spruce, vine/blackberry

Balance/Harmony: Acacia, almond, apple, ash, aspen, bamboo, cedar, cherry, eucalyptus/lemon eucalyptus, fig, fir, frankincense, hazel, holly, ivy, juniper, locust, maple, olive, palm, pine, pomegranate, quince, reeds/rushes/cattails, rose, rowan, spruce, sycamore, vine/blackberry, vine/grape

Banish: Alder, birch, blackthorn, cedar, chestnut/horse chestnut, cypress, dogwood, elder, eucalyptus, frankincense, hazel, holly, hornbeam, juniper, laurel, lemon, lilac, mistletoe, palm, peach, pine, rose, tamarisk, witch hazel

Bind: Apple, cypress, ivy, locust, pear, pine, rose, rowan, vine/grape, willow

Challenges/Obstacles (Overcome): Acacia, birch, blackthorn, cedar, cherry, elder, hawthorn, hazel, ivy, juniper, laurel, lemon, lilac, locust, mistletoe, mulberry, oak, palm, poplar, rose, rowan, spindletree, spruce, sycamore, vine/blackberry, witch hazel

Changes/Transitions: Almond, ash, birch, cypress, elder, elm, fir, hackberry, hawthorn, hazel, heath/heather, hornbeam, linden, mistletoe, pomegranate, vine/grape, walnut, yew

Clarity (Enhance, Foster): Alder, birch, cedar, cypress, fir, frankincense, heath/heather, laurel, lemon, orange, pomegranate, rose, spruce, walnut

Communication: Almond, ash, aspen, cedar, eucalyptus, fir, hazel, lemon, linden, maple, myrtle, orange, pine, rose, sycamore, vine/blackberry, willow, witch hazel, yew

Concentration/Focus: Ash, birch, cedar, cypress, eucalyptus, frankincense, lemon, lilac, orange, pine, reeds/rushes/cattails, spindletree

Confidence: Cedar, cypress, heath/heather, lemon, oak, orange, pine, reeds/rushes/cattails, rose

Consecrate/Bless: Acacia, almond, apple, birch, cedar, chestnut, cypress, elder, eucalyptus, frankincense, hawthorn, holly, lemon, mistletoe, mulberry, myrtle, oak, olive, palm, pear, pine, pomegranate, rose, rowan, vine/grape, walnut, willow

Courage: Aspen, bamboo, cedar, frankincense, holly, laurel, oak, palm, pine, poplar, rose, spindletree, willow, witch hazel

Creativity: Almond, apple, ash, beech, birch, cherry, dogwood, elder, fig, fir, hackberry, hawthorn, hazel, laurel, lilac, maple, mistletoe, mulberry, myrtle, orange, pear, pine, pomegranate, rowan, spindletree, vine/grape

Death/Funeral Practices: Acacia, alder, apple, aspen, box, crabapple, cypress, elder, fig, fir, frankincense, holly, mistletoe, myrtle, oak, olive, peach, pomegranate, poplar, rose, tamarisk, vine/blackberry, willow, yew

Defense: Birch, blackthorn, box, cypress, dogwood, elder, fir, frankincense, gorse, hawthorn, hazel, heath/heather, holly, juniper, laurel, lilac, linden, locust, mistletoe, oak, pine, poplar, rowan

Determination/Endurance: Aspen, birch, cedar, elm, eucalyptus, gorse, hornbeam, laurel, locust, myrtle, oak, pine, poplar, reeds/rushes/cattails, sycamore

Divination: Acacia, alder, almond, apple, ash, aspen, bamboo, birch, box, cedar, cherry, chestnut/horse chestnut, crabapple, cypress, elm, fir, frankincense, gorse, hazel, heath/heather, holly, ivy, juniper, laurel, lemon, lilac, linden, maple, mistletoe, mulberry, olive, orange, pomegranate, poplar, rose, rowan, spindletree, sycamore, tamarisk, vine/grape, willow, witch hazel, yew

Dream Work: Acacia, alder, almond, apple, ash, bamboo, cedar, elder, elm, eucalyptus, frankincense, heath/heather, holly, juniper, laurel, lilac, linden, maple, mistletoe, mulberry, myrtle, orange, rose, spruce, willow, yew

Emotions (Deal With, Support): Cedar, cypress, eucalyptus, fir, frankincense, hawthorn, juniper, lemon, lilac, myrtle, orange, pine, rose, spruce

Enchantment: Apple, aspen, crabapple, hawthorn, holly, oak, rowan, vine/blackberry, willow, yew

Family and Home: Cedar, chestnut, eucalyptus, gorse, hawthorn, heath/heather, holly, juniper, laurel, lilac, mistletoe, myrtle, oak, olive, orange, palm, pine, pomegranate, reeds/rushes/cattails, rose, rowan, spindletree

Fertility: Almond, apple, ash, beech, birch, box, cedar, cherry, crabapple, fig, gorse, hawthorn, hazel, ivy, juniper, mistletoe, myrtle, oak, olive, orange, palm, peach, pine, pomegranate, quince, rowan, vine/blackberry, vine/grape, walnut, willow

Growth: Ash, birch, cedar, cypress, eucalyptus/lemon eucalyptus, fir, frankincense, hawthorn, heath/heather, ivy, juniper, myrtle, oak, orange, pine, reeds/rushes/cattails, spruce, vine/blackberry, vine/grape

Happiness: Almond, apple, bamboo, box, cherry, crabapple, eucalyptus, fir, frankincense, hawthorn, juniper, lemon, lilac, linden, orange, palm/date palm, peach, pine, rose, vine/blackberry, vine/grape

Healing: Acacia, alder, apple, ash, aspen, beech, birch, cedar, chestnut, crabapple, cypress, dogwood, elder, elm, eucalyptus, fir, frankincense, hackberry, hazel, heath/heather, holly, ivy, juniper, larch, laurel, mistletoe, myrtle, oak, olive, palm, peach, pear, pine, reeds/rushes/cattails, rose, rowan, spindletree, spruce, vine/blackberry, vine/grape, walnut, willow, witch hazel

Hexes (Remove, Ward off): Ash, aspen, bamboo, blackthorn, box, cedar, chestnut, elder, fir, gorse, holly, juniper, laurel, lilac, peach, pine, rose, rowan, spindletree, tamarisk, yew

Hope: Almond, fir, gorse, hawthorn, olive, palm, pomegranate, pine, poplar/white poplar, spruce, tamarisk

Inspiration: Acacia, ash, birch, cedar, dogwood, fir, frankincense, hackberry, hazel, ivy, laurel, lilac, mulberry, oak, pine, reeds/rushes/cattails, rowan, spindletree, spruce, vine/grape, walnut, willow, witch hazel

Intuition: Alder, almond, ash, birch, elm, hazel, holly, larch, laurel, palm/coconut palm, pine, spruce, vine/blackberry, willow

Justice/Legal Matters: Cedar, chestnut, cypress, elm, frankincense, larch, laurel, linden, oak, pear, pine, yew

Knowledge (Seek, Acquire): Alder, almond, apple, ash, aspen, beech, birch, cherry, cypress, elder, eucalyptus, fig/Bodhi fig, frankincense, hazel, heath/heather, ivy, juniper, larch, lemon, oak, pine, rowan, sycamore, vine/blackberry, willow, witch hazel, yew

Loss/Sorrow (Ease, Recover From): Cypress, eucalyptus, fir, hackberry, hazel, maple, myrtle, pomegranate, poplar, willow, witch hazel, yew

Love: Acacia, almond, apple, ash, birch, box, cedar, cherry, chestnut, crabapple, elder, elm, fig, frankincense, gorse, hawthorn, heath/heather, hornbeam, ivy, juniper, lemon, lilac, linden, locust, maple, mistletoe, myrtle, olive, orange, palm, peach, pear, pomegranate, quince, rose, sycamore, vine/grape, walnut, willow, witch hazel

Loyalty/Fidelity: Blackthorn, cedar, dogwood, elder, elm, ivy, laurel, linden, locust, myrtle, oak, olive, orange, peach, reeds/rushes/cattails, rose, witch hazel

Luck: Alder, almond, apple, ash, bamboo, beech, box, cedar, cherry, chestnut, hawthorn, hazel, heath/heather, holly, ivy, larch, lilac, linden, mistletoe, mulberry, myrtle, oak, olive, palm, peach, pear, pomegranate, quince, rose, rowan, vine/blackberry, walnut

Manifest (Desires, Dreams, Will): Beech, cherry, dogwood, elm, hackberry, hazel, heath/heather, juniper, laurel, lemon, oak, olive, orange, peach, pear, pine, rose, spindletree, walnut

Money/Prosperity: Acacia, almond, apple, ash, aspen, beech, box, cedar, chestnut, crabapple, elder, fig, fir, gorse, hawthorn, hazel, hornbeam, juniper, laurel, maple, mistletoe, myrtle, oak, olive, orange, pear, pomegranate, poplar, quince, spruce, vine/blackberry, vine/grape, walnut

Negativity (Remove, Ward off): Acacia, alder, ash, aspen, bamboo, birch, blackthorn, cedar, elm, eucalyptus, frankincense, gorse, hackberry, hawthorn, hornbeam, ivy, juniper, laurel, lilac, linden, locust, mistletoe, oak, palm, peach, pine, quince, tamarisk, yew

The Otherworld: Apple, aspen, crabapple, cypress fir, hawthorn, hazel, mistletoe, myrtle, oak, orange, pomegranate, poplar, rose, willow, yew

Past-life Work: Cypress, eucalyptus, frankincense, hazel, lilac, poplar

Peace: Almond, apple, ash, aspen, bamboo, cedar, cherry, chestnut, cypress, fig, fir, hawthorn, heath/heather, laurel, lilac, linden, mistletoe, myrtle, olive, orange, palm, pine, quince, rose

Prophecy: Acacia, alder, ash, beech, box, elm, ivy, laurel, lilac, linden, maple, oak, palm, poplar/black poplar, reeds/rushes/cattails, rose, rowan, sycamore, tamarisk, vine/grape, walnut, willow

Protection: Acacia, alder, almond, ash, aspen, bamboo, beech, birch, blackthorn, box, cedar, chestnut, crabapple, cypress, dogwood, elder, elm, eucalyptus, fig, fir, frankincense, gorse, hackberry, hawthorn, hazel, heath/heather, holly, hornbeam, ivy, juniper, larch, laurel, lilac, linden, locust, mistletoe, mulberry, myrtle, oak, olive, orange, palm, pear, pine, pomegranate, quince, reeds/rushes/cattails, rose, rowan, spruce, sycamore, tamarisk, vine/blackberry, walnut, willow, witch hazel, yew

Psychic Abilities: Acacia, almond, beech, cedar, elm, eucalyptus, fig, fir, frankincense, hazel, heath/heather, juniper, laurel, lemon, lilac, mulberry, myrtle, orange, pine, pomegranate, rose, rowan, spruce, sycamore, vine/grape, yew

Purification: Acacia, ash, birch, blackthorn, cedar, elder, eucalyptus, fir, frankincense, gorse, hawthorn, heath/heather, juniper, laurel, lemon, lilac, mistletoe, myrtle, oak, olive, orange, palm, pine, spindletree, sycamore, vine/blackberry, walnut

Release (Let Go, Move On): Almond, birch, cedar, cypress, elder, eucalyptus, frankincense, hazel, hornbeam, juniper, laurel, lilac, maple, myrtle, pine, witch hazel

Renewal: Alder, almond, apple, ash, aspen, beech, birch, box, cedar, cherry, cypress, elder, elm, fir, frankincense, gorse, holly, ivy, lilac, mistletoe, oak, olive, peach, pine, pomegranate, poplar/white poplar, spruce, sycamore, yew

Secrets: Hazel, ivy, juniper, lemon, locust, mistletoe, mulberry, oak, rose

Security: Acacia, apple, birch, cedar, cypress, elder, eucalyptus, fir, hawthorn, hazel, holly, ivy, juniper, lilac, mistletoe, oak, olive, pomegranate, reeds/rushes/cattails, rowan, spruce

Sex/Sexuality: Acacia, almond, apple, hawthorn, mistletoe, myrtle, oak, olive, orange, palm, pear, pomegranate, quince, reeds/rushes/cattails, rose, vine/grape, walnut, willow, witch hazel

Shamanic Work: Apple, ash, birch, hazel, larch, oak

Spirit Guides/Spirits: Alder, almond, apple, ash, birch, cedar, crabapple, eucalyptus, fir, frankincense, heath/heather, holly, juniper, lemon, lilac, mistletoe, oak, olive, orange, pine, poplar, reeds/rushes/cattails, rose, rowan, spruce, vine/blackberry, walnut, willow, yew

Spirituality: Acacia, almond, cedar, cherry, elder, eucalyptus, fig/Bodhi fig, fir, frankincense, heath/heather, holly, ivy, juniper, larch, laurel, lemon, lilac, olive, palm, pine, poplar, reeds/rushes/cattails, rose, spindletree, spruce, tamarisk

Strength: Alder, apple, ash, bamboo, blackthorn, cedar, chestnut, cypress, eucalyptus, fir, frankincense, hazel, holly, hornbeam, juniper, laurel, lemon, linden, locust, myrtle, oak, orange, palm, pine, poplar, rose, rowan, spruce, sycamore, willow, witch hazel, yew

Stress/Anxiety (Calm, Release): Apple, aspen, birch, cypress, frankincense, lemon, linden, palm, spruce, sycamore, witch hazel

Success: Apple, aspen, cedar, elder, frankincense, hawthorn, juniper, larch, laurel, lemon, mistletoe, mulberry, myrtle, oak, olive, orange, palm, pear, pomegranate, rowan, spindletree, walnut

Support (Provide, Receive): Birch, fir, hazel, holly, lemon, linden, maple, pine, sycamore

Transformation: Alder, beech, cherry, cypress, fig/Bodhi fig, fir, frankincense, holly, ivy, juniper, linden, maple, mistletoe, pine, vine/grape, walnut

Wisdom: Acacia, almond, apple, ash, bamboo, beech, birch, cedar, cherry, crabapple, cypress, elder, elm, eucalyptus, fig/Bodhi fig, hawthorn, hazel, laurel, lilac, maple, mulberry, oak, peach, pear, pine, pomegranate, rose, rowan, spindletree, spruce, sycamore, witch hazel

Wishes: Bamboo, beech, chestnut, dogwood, elm, hawthorn, hazel, holly, juniper, laurel, palm, peach, pear, pomegranate, walnut, willow

APPENDIX B
MAGICAL CONNECTIONS

This section is another quick reference to help when coordinating astrological and elemental energy with trees.

Trees by Associated Zodiac Sign

Aquarius: Almond, apple, aspen, cherry, crabapple, cypress, frankincense, hawthorn, lemon, olive, pine, rowan

Aries: Alder, blackthorn, cedar, cherry, fir, frankincense, gorse, hawthorn, holly, juniper, locust, olive, orange, pine, vine/bramble, willow

Cancer: Alder, apple, chestnut, crabapple, eucalyptus, holly, lemon, maple, oak, pine, rose, spruce

Capricorn: Ash, aspen, birch, cypress, elm, holly, pine, rowan, spruce, willow, yew

Gemini: Almond, beech, chestnut, hawthorn, hazel, ivy, laurel, lemon, linden, mulberry, oak, pomegranate, walnut

Leo: Frankincense, hazel, holly, juniper, laurel, mistletoe, oak, olive, orange, palm, walnut

Libra: Apple, ash, aspen, cherry, crabapple, hazel, lilac, maple, rose, witch hazel

Pisces: Alder, ash, cypress, eucalyptus, laurel, lemon, pine, reeds/rushes/cattails, willow

Sagittarius: Beech, birch, cedar, chestnut, frankincense, holly, juniper, linden, myrtle, oak, orange, palm, reeds/rushes/cattails, rose, rowan, spruce (black spruce)

Scorpio: Blackthorn, heath/heather, ivy, palm, pine, pomegranate, reeds/rushes/cattails, vine/bramble

Taurus: Apple, ash, cedar, cherry, crabapple, cypress, hawthorn, heath/heather, hornbeam, lilac, linden, myrtle, rose, vine/bramble, willow

Virgo: Almond, ash, beech, chestnut, cypress, hazel, maple, mulberry, oak, pomegranate, walnut

Trees by Associated Planets

Jupiter: Almond, birch, cedar, chestnut, dogwood (cornelian cherry dogwood), fig, fir, larch, linden, maple, oak, olive, palm, pear, pine, sycamore, walnut, yew

Mars: Acacia, alder, almond, blackthorn, box, dogwood, fir, gorse, hawthorn, holly, juniper, palm, pine, reeds/rushes/cattails, yew

Mercury: Almond, ash, aspen, cedar, cherry, elder, elm, eucalyptus, hazel, juniper, lemon, lilac, linden, mistletoe, mulberry, olive, pomegranate

Moon: Birch, dogwood, eucalyptus, frankincense, hackberry, juniper, lemon, lilac, myrtle, olive, palm, pear, poplar (white poplar), quince, rowan, vine/bramble, vine/grape, willow

Neptune: Ash

Pluto: Cypress, reeds

Saturn: Aspen, beech, blackthorn, cypress, elm, eucalyptus, fir, holly, hornbeam, ivy, pine, pomegranate, poplar, quince, rowan, sycamore, witch hazel, yew

Sun: Acacia, almond, ash, bamboo, birch, cedar, chestnut, eucalyptus, frankincense, gorse, hazel, juniper, laurel, linden, mistletoe, oak, olive, orange, palm, peach, pear, rowan, vine/grape, walnut, witch hazel

Uranus: Ash, fir, rowan

Venus: Alder, almond, apple, aspen, birch, cherry, crabapple, elder, fig, heath/heather, ivy, lilac, mulberry, myrtle, peach, pear, pomegranate, quince, rose, sycamore, vine/bramble, willow

Trees by Associated Elements

Air: Acacia, alder, almond, apple, ash, aspen, bamboo, cedar, chestnut, crabapple, dogwood, elder, elm, eucalyptus, fig, fir, frankincense, hawthorn, hazel, holly, ivy, laurel, lemon, linden, maple, mistletoe, mulberry, oak, olive, orange, palm, pear, pine, sycamore, vine/grape, walnut, yew

Earth: Ash, blackthorn, box, cedar, cypress, dogwood, elder, elm, eucalyptus, fir, holly, ivy, juniper, lemon, locust, maple, oak, olive, orange, pear, pine, pomegranate, quince, rowan, spruce, witch hazel

Fire: Alder, almond, ash, beech, blackthorn, cedar, cherry, chestnut, elder, fir, frankincense, gorse, hackberry, hawthorn, hazel, holly, hornbeam, juniper, larch, laurel, oak, olive, orange, palm, pine, pomegranate, rowan, vine/grape, walnut, willow, witch hazel, yew

Water: Alder, apple, ash, aspen, beech, birch, cedar, cherry, chestnut, crabapple, cypress, elder, elm, eucalyptus, fig, frankincense, hackberry, hazel, heath/heather, hornbeam, ivy, juniper, lemon, lilac, locust, myrtle, olive, orange, peach, pear, poplar, reeds/rushes/cattails, rose, spindletree, spruce, sycamore, tamarisk, vine/bramble, vine/grape, willow, witch hazel, yew

APPENDIX C
TREES BY DATE

The following pages contain the trees associated with each day of the year.

JANUARY

	1 Apple, birch, fig, juniper, lilac, peach, pear, yew	**2** Birch, fir, lilac, spruce, yew	**3** Birch, fir, lilac, spruce, yew	**4** Birch, fir, lilac, spruce, yew	**5** Birch, fir, lilac, spruce, yew
6 Birch, fir, holly, juniper, lilac, mistletoe, spruce, yew	**7** Birch, fir, lilac, spruce, yew	**8** Birch, fir, lilac, spruce, yew	**9** Birch, fir, lilac, spruce, yew	**10** Birch, fir, lilac, spruce, yew	**11** Birch, fir, lilac, spruce, yew	**12** Birch, elm, lilac, yew
13 Apple, aspen, beech, birch, elm	**14** Apple, aspen, beech, birch, elm	**15** Apple, aspen, beech, birch, elm	**16** Apple, aspen, beech, birch, elm	**17** Apple, aspen, beech, birch, elm	**18** Apple, aspen, beech, birch, elm	**19** Apple, aspen, beech, birch, elm
20 Apple, aspen, beech, birch, elm	**21** Apple, aspen, beech, elm, rowan	**22** Apple, aspen, beech, elm, rowan	**23** Apple, aspen, beech, elm, rowan	**24** Apple, aspen, beech, elm, rowan	**25** Apple, aspen, beech, cypress, rowan	**26** Apple, aspen, beech, cypress, rowan
27 Apple, aspen, beech, cypress, rowan	**28** Cypress, reed and cattail, rowan, yew	**29** Cypress, reed and cattail, rowan, yew	**30** Cypress, reed and cattail, rowan, yew	**31** Cypress, reed and cattail, rowan, yew	

FEBRUARY		**1** Cypress, ivy, reed and cattail, rowan, yew	**2** Cypress, ivy, reed and cattail, rowan, yew	**3** Cypress, reed and cattail, rowan, yew	**4** Aspen, poplar, reed and cattail, rowan, yew	**5** Aspen, poplar, reed and cattail, rowan, yew
6 Aspen, poplar, reed and cattail, rowan, yew	**7** Aspen, poplar, reed and cattail, rowan, yew	**8** Aspen, poplar, reed and cattail, rowan, yew	**9** Cedar, hackberry, larch, reed and cattail, rowan, yew	**10** Cedar, hackberry, larch, reed and cattail, rowan, yew	**11** Cedar, hackberry, larch, reed and cattail, rowan, yew	**12** Cedar, hackberry, juniper, larch, laurel, mistletoe, rowan
13 Cedar, hackberry, juniper, larch, laurel, mistletoe, rowan	**14** Cedar, hackberry, juniper, larch, laurel, mistletoe, rowan	**15** Cedar, hackberry, juniper, larch, laurel, mistletoe, rowan	**16** Cedar, hackberry, juniper, larch, laurel, mistletoe, rowan	**17** Cedar, hackberry, juniper, larch, laurel, mistletoe, rowan	**18** Ash, cedar, hackberry, juniper, larch, laurel, mistletoe	**19** Ash, juniper, laurel, mistletoe, pine
20 Ash, juniper, laurel, mistletoe, pine	**21** Ash, juniper, laurel, mistletoe, pine	**22** Ash, juniper, laurel, mistletoe, pine	**23** Ash, juniper, laurel, mistletoe, pine	**24** Ash, juniper, laurel, mistletoe, pine	**25** Ash, juniper, laurel, mistletoe, pine	**26** Ash, juniper, laurel, mistletoe, pine
27 Ash, oak, pine	**28** Ash, oak, pine	**29** Ash, oak, pine	**Sabbat Imbolc:** Birch, blackthorn, cedar, reed and cattail, rowan, spindletree, sycamore, vine/bramble			

MARCH

1	Ash, oak, willow
2	Ash, oak, willow
3	Ash, oak, willow
4	Ash, oak, willow
5	Ash, oak, willow
6	Ash, oak, willow
7	Ash, oak, willow
8	Ash, oak, willow
9	Ash, oak, willow
10	Ash, oak, willow
11	Ash, linden, oak
12	Ash, linden, oak
13	Ash, linden, oak
14	Ash, birch, fir, linden
15	Ash, birch, fir, linden
16	Ash, birch, fir, linden
17	Ash, birch, fir, linden
18	Alder, birch, fir, linden
19	Alder, birch, fir, linden
20	Alder, birch, fir, linden
21	Alder, birch, fir, oak
22	Alder, birch, fir, hazel
23	Alder, birch, fir, hazel
24	Alder, birch, fir, hazel
25	Alder, birch, fir, hazel
26	Alder, birch, fir, hazel
27	Alder, birch, fir, hazel
28	Alder, birch, fir, hazel
29	Alder, birch, fir, hazel, maple (field), oak
30	Alder, ash, aspen, lilac, hazel, oak
31	Alder, ash, aspen, lilac, hazel, oak

Sabbat Ostara: Alder, almond, ash, birch, box, dogwood, gorse, linden, maple, mulberry, myrtle, oak, poplar, yew

APRIL

1	2	3	4	5	6	7
Alder, ash, aspen, lilac, oak, rowan	Alder, ash, aspen, lilac, oak, rowan	Alder, ash, aspen, lilac, oak, rowan	Alder, ash, aspen, lilac, oak, rowan	Alder, ash, aspen, lilac, oak, rowan	Alder, ash, aspen, lilac, oak, rowan	Alder, ash, aspen, lilac, oak, rowan
8	**9**	**10**	**11**	**12**	**13**	**14**
Alder, ash, aspen, lilac, oak, rowan	Alder, ash, aspen, lilac, oak, rowan	Alder, ash, aspen, lilac, oak, rowan	Alder, ash, aspen, lilac, maple, oak	Alder, ash, aspen, lilac, maple, oak	Alder, ash, aspen, lilac, maple, oak	Alder, ash, elm, holly, maple
15	**16**	**17**	**18**	**19**	**20**	**21**
Alder, ash, elm, holly, maple, willow	Alder, ash, elm, holly, maple, willow	Alder, ash, elm, holly, maple, willow	Alder, ash, elm, holly, maple, willow	Alder, ash, elm, holly, maple, willow	Alder, ash, elm, holly, maple, willow	Alder, ash, elm, holly, maple, walnut, willow
22	**23**	**24**	**25**	**26**	**27**	**28**
Alder, ash, elm, holly, maple, walnut, willow	Alder, ash, elm, holly, maple, walnut, willow	Alder, ash, elm, holly, maple, walnut, willow	Alder, ash, elm, holly, maple, walnut, willow	Alder, ash, elm, holly, maple, walnut, willow	Alder, ash, elm, holly, maple, walnut, willow	Alder, ash, elm, holly, maple, walnut, willow
29	**30**	**Walpurgis:** Ash, birch, blackthorn, elder, gorse, hawthorn, heath and heather, juniper, larch, linden, oak				
Walnut, willow	Walnut, willow					

MAY

Sun	Mon	Tue	Wed	Thu	Fri	Sat
	1 Aspen, blackthorn, box, chestnut, hornbeam, poplar, willow	**2** Aspen, poplar, willow	**3** Aspen, poplar, willow	**4** Aspen, blackthorn, hawthorn, poplar, willow	**5** Aspen, poplar, willow	**6** Aspen, poplar, willow
7 Aspen, poplar, willow	**8** Aspen, poplar, willow	**9** Aspen, poplar, willow	**10** Aspen, poplar, willow	**11** Aspen, blackthorn, chestnut, poplar, willow	**12** Aspen, poplar, willow	**13** Aspen, hawthorn, poplar, willow
14 Apple, aspen, crabapple, hawthorn, poplar	**15** Apple, chestnut, crabapple, hawthorn	**16** Apple, chestnut, crabapple, hawthorn	**17** Apple, chestnut, crabapple, hawthorn	**18** Apple, chestnut, crabapple, hawthorn	**19** Apple, chestnut, crabapple, hawthorn	**20** Apple, chestnut, crabapple, hawthorn
21 Apple, chestnut, crabapple, hawthorn	**22** Apple, chestnut, crabapple, hawthorn	**23** Apple, chestnut, crabapple, hawthorn	**24** Apple, chestnut, crabapple, hawthorn	**25** Apple, ash, crabapple, hawthorn	**26** Apple, ash, crabapple, hawthorn	**27** Apple, ash, crabapple, hawthorn
28 Apple, ash, crabapple, hawthorn	**29** Ash, hawthorn	**30** Ash, hawthorn	**31** Ash, hawthorn	**Sabbat Beltane:** Apple, ash, birch, blackthorn, box, cedar, chestnut, crabapple, dogwood, elder, fir, gorse, hawthorn, hazel, ivy, lilac, linden, oak, pine, poplar, rowan, spruce, vine/bramble, willow		

JUNE		1 Ash, hawthorn	2 Ash, hawthorn, vine/bramble	3 Ash, hawthorn	4 Hawthorn, hornbeam	5 Hawthorn, hornbeam
6 Hawthorn, hornbeam	7 Hawthorn, hornbeam	8 Hawthorn, hornbeam	9 Hawthorn, hornbeam	10 Hawthorn, hornbeam, oak	11 Hawthorn, hornbeam, oak	12 Hawthorn, hornbeam, oak
13 Hawthorn, hornbeam, oak	14 Fig, oak, pine, spruce	15 Fig, oak, pine, spruce	16 Fig, oak, pine, spruce	17 Fig, oak, pine, spruce	18 Fig, oak, pine, spruce	19 Fig, oak, pine, spruce
20 Fig, oak, pine, spruce	21 Fig, oak, pine, spruce	22 Fig, oak, pine, spruce	23 Fig, oak, pine, spruce	24 Birch, oak, pine, spruce	25 Apple, oak, pine, spruce	26 Apple, oak, pine, spruce
27 Apple, oak, pine, spruce	28 Apple, oak, pine, spruce	29 Apple, elder, hornbeam, oak	30 Apple, elder, hornbeam, oak	**Sabbat Litha:** Beech, birch, elder, heath and heather, holly, laurel, linden, mistletoe, myrtle, oak, orange, pine **Midsummer's Eve:** Beech, birch, dogwood, elder, holly, linden, oak, pine, rose, walnut		

JULY

1	2	3	4	5
Apple, elder, hornbeam, oak	Apple, elder, hornbeam, oak	Apple, elder, hornbeam, oak	Apple, elder, hornbeam, oak	Fir, elder, hornbeam, oak, spruce
6 Fir, elder, hornbeam, oak, spruce	**7** Fir, elder, hornbeam, oak, spruce			

8	9	10	11	12
Fir, elder, holly, hornbeam, spruce	Fir, elder, holly, hornbeam, spruce	Fir, elder, holly, hornbeam, spruce	Fir, elder, holly, hornbeam, spruce	Fir, elder, holly, hornbeam, spruce
13 Fir, elder, holly, hornbeam, spruce	**14** Birch, fir, holly, spruce			

15	16	17	18	19
Birch, elm, holly	Birch, elm, holly	Birch, elm, holly	Birch, elm, holly	Birch, elm, holly
20 Birch, elm, holly	**21** Birch, elm, holly			

22	23	24	25	26
Birch, elm, holly	Birch, elm, holly	Birch, elm, holly	Birch, elm, holly	Birch, cypress, holly
27 Birch, cypress, holly	**28** Birch, cypress, holly			

29	30	31
Blackthorn, cypress, hawthorn, holly, oak, vine/bramble	Blackthorn, cypress, hawthorn, holly, oak, vine/bramble	Blackthorn, cypress, hawthorn, holly, oak, vine/bramble

AUGUST

		1 Blackthorn, cypress, hawthorn, holly, oak, vine/bramble	**2** Blackthorn, cypress, hawthorn, holly, oak, vine/bramble	**3** Blackthorn, cypress, hawthorn, holly, oak, vine/bramble	**4** Blackthorn, cypress, hawthorn, holly, oak, vine/bramble	**5** Aspen, blackthorn, hawthorn, hazel, oak, poplar, vine/bramble
6 Aspen, blackthorn, hawthorn, hazel, oak, poplar, vine/bramble	**7** Aspen, blackthorn, hawthorn, hazel, oak, poplar, vine/bramble	**8** Aspen, blackthorn, hawthorn, hazel, oak, poplar, vine/bramble	**9** Aspen, blackthorn, hawthorn, hazel, oak, poplar, vine/bramble	**10** Aspen, blackthorn, hawthorn, hazel, oak, poplar, vine/bramble	**11** Aspen, blackthorn, hawthorn, hazel, oak, poplar, vine/bramble	**12** Aspen, blackthorn, hawthorn, hazel, oak, poplar, vine/bramble
13 Ash, aspen, hazel, linden, poplar	**14** Ash, cedar, hackberry, hazel, larch, linden	**15** Ash, cedar, hackberry, hazel, larch, linden	**16** Ash, cedar, hackberry, hazel, larch, linden	**17** Ash, cedar, hackberry, hazel, larch, linden	**18** Ash, cedar, hackberry, hazel, larch, linden	**19** Ash, cedar, hackberry, hazel, larch, linden
20 Ash, cedar, hackberry, hazel, larch, linden	**21** Ash, cedar, hackberry, hazel, larch, linden	**22** Ash, cedar, hackberry, hazel, larch, linden	**23** Ash, cedar, hackberry, hazel, larch, linden	**24** Ash, hazel, linden, pine	**25** Ash, hazel, linden, pine	**26** Ash, hazel, linden, pine
27 Ash, hazel, linden, pine	**28** Ash, hazel, linden, pine	**29** Hazel, oak, pine	**30** Hazel, oak, pine	**31** Hazel, oak, pine	**Sabbat Lughnasadh:** Apple, crabapple, gorse, myrtle, oak, rowan, vine/bramble	

SEPTEMBER

1	2	3	4	5	6	7
Hazel, oak, pine	Oak, pine, vine/bramble	Oak, vine/bramble, willow	Oak, vine/bramble, willow	Oak, vine/bramble, willow	Oak, vine/bramble, willow	Oak, vine/bramble, willow
8	**9**	**10**	**11**	**12**	**13**	**14**
Oak, vine/bramble, willow	Oak, vine/bramble, willow	Oak, vine/bramble, willow	Oak, vine/bramble, willow	Oak, vine/bramble, willow	Linden, pine, vine/bramble	Chestnut, hazel, linden, oak, pine, vine/bramble, walnut
15	**16**	**17**	**18**	**19**	**20**	**21**
Linden, pine, vine/bramble	Linden, pine, vine/bramble	Linden, pine, vine/bramble	Linden, pine, vine/bramble	Linden, pine, vine/bramble	Linden, pine, vine/bramble	Linden, pine, vine/bramble
22	**23**	**24**	**25**	**26**	**27**	**28**
Linden, pine, vine/bramble	Olive, pine, vine/bramble	Hazel, pine, vine/bramble	Hazel, pine, vine/bramble	Hazel, pine, vine/bramble	Hazel, pine, vine/bramble	Ash, elm, hazel, vine/bramble
29	**30**	**Sabbat Mabon:** Aspen, cedar, hackberry, hazel, ivy, locust, maple, myrtle, oak, olive, vine/bramble, vine/grape **Full moon:** Vine/bramble				
Ash, crabapple, elm, hazel, vine/bramble	Ash, elm, hazel, ivy, vine/bramble					

OCTOBER

1 Ash, elm, hazel, ivy	**2** Ash, elm, hazel, ivy	**3** Ash, elm, hazel, ivy	**4** Ash, elm, ivy, rowan	**5** Ash, elm, ivy, rowan
6 Ash, elm, ivy, rowan	**7** Ash, elm, ivy, rowan	**8** Ash, elm, ivy, rowan	**9** Ash, elm, ivy, rowan	**10** Ash, elm, ivy, rowan	**11** Ash, elm, ivy, rowan, vine/bramble	**12** Ash, elm, ivy, rowan

| **13** Ash, blackthorn, ivy, rowan, vine/bramble | **14** Ash, blackthorn, ivy, maple, vine/bramble | **15** Ash, blackthorn, ivy, maple, vine/bramble | **16** Ash, blackthorn, ivy, maple, vine/bramble | **17** Ash, blackthorn, ivy, maple, vine/bramble | **18** Ash, blackthorn, ivy, maple, vine/bramble | **19** Ash, blackthorn, ivy, maple, vine/bramble |

| **20** Ash, blackthorn, ivy, maple, vine/bramble | **21** Ash, blackthorn, ivy, maple, vine/bramble | **22** Ash, blackthorn, ivy, maple, vine/bramble | **23** Ash, blackthorn, ivy, maple, vine/bramble | **24** Ash, blackthorn, ivy, vine/bramble, walnut | **25** Ash, blackthorn, ivy, vine/bramble, walnut | **26** Ash, blackthorn, ivy, vine/bramble, walnut |

| **27** Ash, blackthorn, ivy, vine/bramble, walnut | **28** Ash, reed and cattail, walnut, yew | **29** Ash, reed and cattail, walnut, yew | **30** Ash, reed and cattail, walnut, yew | **31** Ash, crabapple, reed and cattail, vine/bramble, walnut, yew | **Sabbat Samhain:** Acacia, apple, beech, blackthorn, box, crabapple, cypress fig, hazel, locust, pomegranate, poplar, reed and cattail, tamarisk, willow, witch hazel, yew |

NOVEMBER

		1	2	3	4	5
		Ash, blackthorn, crabapple, gorse, reed and cattail, walnut, yew	Ash, gorse, reed and cattail, walnut, yew	Ash, reed and cattail, yew	Ash, reed and cattail, yew	Ash, reed and cattail, yew
6	**7**	**8**	**9**	**10**	**11**	**12**
Ash, reed and cattail, yew	Ash, reed and cattail, yew	Ash, reed and cattail, yew	Ash, reed and cattail, yew	Ash, reed and cattail, yew	Ash, blackthorn, reed and cattail, yew	Ash, chestnut, reed and cattail, yew
13	**14**	**15**	**16**	**17**	**18**	**19**
Beech, chestnut, reed and cattail, rowan	Beech, chestnut, reed and cattail, rowan	Beech, chestnut, reed and cattail, rowan	Beech, chestnut, reed and cattail, rowan	Beech, chestnut, reed and cattail, rowan	Beech, chestnut, reed and cattail, rowan	Beech, chestnut, reed and cattail, rowan
20	**21**	**22**	**23**	**24**	**25**	**26**
Beech, chestnut, reed and cattail, rowan	Beech, chestnut, reed and cattail, rowan	Ash, beech, reed and cattail, rowan	Ash, beech, reed and cattail, rowan	Ash, beech, reed and cattail, rowan	Ash, beech, elder, rowan	Ash, beech, elder, rowan
27	**28**	**29**	**30**			
Ash, beech, elder, rowan	Alder, ash, elder	Alder, ash, elder	Alder, ash, elder			

	DECEMBER	**1** Alder, ash, elder	**2** Alder, elder, hornbeam	**3** Alder, elder, hornbeam	**4** Alder, elder, hornbeam	**5** Alder, elder, hornbeam
6 Alder, elder, hornbeam	**7** Alder, elder, hornbeam	**8** Alder, elder, hornbeam	**9** Alder, elder, hornbeam	**10** Alder, elder, hornbeam	**11** Alder, elder, hornbeam	**12** Alder, elder, fig
13 Elder, fig, oak	**14** Elder, fig, oak	**15** Elder, fig, oak	**16** Elder, fig, oak	**17** Elder, fig, ivy, laurel, oak	**18** Elder, fig, ivy, laurel, oak	**19** Elder, fig, ivy, laurel, oak
20 Elder, fig, ivy, laurel, oak	**21** Elder, fig, ivy, laurel, oak	**22** Apple, beech, elder, ivy, laurel, oak	**23** Apple, elder, ivy, laurel, mistletoe, oak	**24** Apple, birch, elder, oak	**25** Apple, birch, elder, oak	**26** Apple, birch, elder, ivy, oak
27 Apple, birch, elder, oak	**28** Apple, birch, lilac, yew	**29** Apple, birch, lilac, yew	**30** Apple, birch, elder, lilac, yew	**31** Apple, birch, box, lilac, yew	**Sabbat Yule:** Apple, beech, birch, cedar, chestnut, crabapple, elm, fir, frankincense, holly, ivy, mistletoe, oak, pine, spruce, walnut, yew **Saturnalia:** Holly, ivy, laurel	

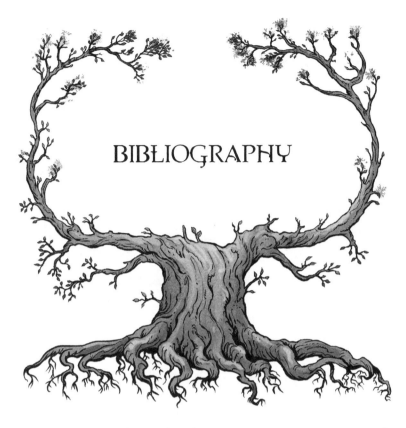

BIBLIOGRAPHY

Adamson, Melitta Weiss. *Food in Medieval Times*. Westport, CT: Greenwood Press, 2004.

Alcock, Joan P. *Food in the Ancient World*. Westport, CT: Greenwood Press, 2006.

Altman, Nathaniel. *Sacred Trees: Spirituality, Wisdom & Well-Being*. New York: Sterling Publishing Company, Inc., 2000.

Anthon, Charles. *A Dictionary of Greek and Roman Antiquities*. Edited by William Smith. New York: Harper & Brothers, 1843.

Balog, James. *Tree: A New Vision of the American Forest*. New York: Sterling Publishing Co., Inc. 2004.

Barker, Hugh. *Hedge Britannia: A Curious History of a British Obsession*. London: Bloomsbury Publishing Plc., 2012.

Barker, Margaret. *The Mother of the Lord: Volume 1 The Lady in the Temple*. New York: Bloomsbury T&T Clark, 2012.

Barnhart, Robert K., ed. *The Barnhart Concise Dictionary of Etymology*. New York: HarperCollins, 1995.

Berens, E. M. *Myths and Legends of Ancient Greece and Rome*. Irvine, CA: Xist Publishing, 2015.

Bevan-Jones, Robert. *The Ancient Yew: A History of Taxus Baccata*, 3rd ed. Havertown, PA: Windgather Press, 2017.

Bincsik, Monika. *Japanese Bamboo Art: The Abbey Collection*. New York: The Metropolitan Museum of Art, 2017.

Blackburne-Maze, Peter. *Fruit: An Illustrated History*. London: Firefly Books, Ltd., 2003.

Bosworth, Joseph. *A Dictionary of the Anglo-Saxon Language*. London: Longman, Rees, Orme, Brown, Green, and Longman, 1838.

Botterweck, G. Johannes, Helmer Ringgren, and Heinz-Josef Fabry, eds., *Theological Dictionary of the Old Testament*, vol. 7. Translated by David E. Green. Grand Rapids, MI: William B. Eerdmans Publishing Company, 1995.

Boyce, Charlotte, and Joan Fitzpatrick. *A History of Food in Literature: From the Fourteenth Century to the Present*. New York: Routledge, 2017.

Boyer, Mark G. *An ABeCeDarian of Sacred Trees: Spiritual Growth through Reflections on Woody Plants*. Eugene, OR: Wipf & Stock Publishers, 2016.

Briggs, Katherine. *The Fairies in Traditions and Literature*. New York: Routledge, 1967.

Budge, E. A. Wallis. *The Gods of the Egyptians: Studies in Egyptian Mythology*, vol. 1. New York: Dover Publications, Inc., 1969.

Carroll, Maureen. *Earthly Paradises: Ancient Gardens in History and Archaeology*. London: The British Museum Press, 2003.

Chevalier, Jean, and Alain Gheerbrant. *The Penguin Dictionary of Symbols*. Translated by John Buchanan-Brown. New York: Penguin Books, 1996.

Chevallier, Andrew. *The Encyclopedia of Medicinal Plants: A Practical Reference Guide to Over 550 Key Herbs and Their Medicinal Uses*. New York: Dorling Kindersley Publishing, 1996.

Chormaic, Sanas. *Cormac's Glossary*. Translated by John O'Donovan. Edited by Whitley Stokes. Dublin, Ireland: The Irish Archaeological and Celtic Society, 1868.

Church, Glyn. *Trees and Shrubs for Fragrance*. Buffalo, NY: Firefly Books (U.S.) Inc., 2002.

Clay, Horace F., and James C. Hubbard. *Tropical Shrubs*. Honolulu, HI: The University Press of Hawaii, 1987.

Coogan, Michael D., ed. *The Illustrated Guide to World Religions*. New York: Oxford University Press, 2003.

Coombes, Allen J. *Dictionary of Plant Names*. Portland, OR: Timber Press, Inc., 1985.

Cullina, William. *Native Trees, Shrubs and Vines: A Guide to Using, Growing, and Propagating North American Woody Plants*. New York: Houghton Mifflin, 2002.

Cumo, Christopher, ed. *Encyclopedia of Cultivated Plants: From Acacia to Zinnia*, vol. 3. Santa Barbara, CA: ABC-CLIO, 2013.

Cusack, Carole M. *The Sacred Tree: Ancient and Medieval Manifestations*. Newcastle upon Tyne, England: Cambridge Scholars Publishing, 2011.

Daniels, Cora Linn, and C. M. Stevans, eds. *Encyclopedia of Superstitions, Folklore, and the Occult Sciences of the World*, vol. 2. Honolulu, HI: University Press of the Pacific, 2003.

Daniels, Peter T., and William Bright, eds. *The World's Writing Systems*. New York: Oxford University Press, 1996.

Danver, Steven L., ed. *Popular Controversies in World History: Investigating History's Intriguing Questions. Prehistory and Early Civilizations*, vol. 1. Santa Barbara, CA: ABC-CLIO, LLC, 2011.

Darvill, Timothy. *Prehistoric Britain*, 2nd ed. New York: Routledge, 2010.

Davidson, Alan. *The Oxford Companion to Food*, 3rd ed. Edited by Tom Jaine. Oxford, England: Oxford University Press, 2014.

Davis, Jennifer R., and Michael McCormick, eds. *The Long Morning of Medieval Europe: New Directions in Early Medieval Studies*. New York: Routledge, 2016.

De Cleene, Marcel, and Marie Claire Lejeune. *Compendium of Symbolic and Ritual Plants in Europe, Vol. I: Trees and Shrubs*. Ghent, Belgium: Man & Culture Publishers, 2003.

Dobelis, Inge N., ed. *Magic and Medicine of Plants: A Practical Guide to the Science, History, Folklore, and Everyday Uses of Medicinal Plants*. Pleasantville, NY: The Reader's Digest Association, Inc., 1986.

Duke, James A. *Duke's Handbook of Medicinal Plants of the Bible*. Boca Raton, FL: CRC Press, 2008.

Dundes, Alan, ed. *The Evil Eye: A Casebook*. Madison. WI: The University of Wisconsin Press, 1992.

Dutton, Joan Parry. *Plants of Colonial Williamsburg: How to Identify 200 of Colonial America's Flowers, Herbs, and Trees*. Williamsburg, VA: The Colonial Williamsburg Foundation, 1994.

Eastman, John. *The Book of Forest and Thicket: Trees, Shrubs, and Wildflowers of Eastern North America*. Mechanicsburg, PA: Stackpole Books, 1992.

Editorial Staff, *Webster's Third New International Dictionary*, Unabridged, vol. 3. Chicago: Encyclopedia Britannica, Inc., 1981.

Edworthy, Niall. *The Curious World of Christmas: Celebrating All That is Weird, Wonderful and Festive*. New York: Penguin Group (USA) Inc., 2007.

Ellis, Peter Berresford. *The Chronicles of the Celts*. New York: Carrol and Graf Publishers Inc., 1999.

———. *A Brief History of the Druids*. New York: Carroll & Graf Publishers, 2002.

Elwes, Henry John, and Augustine Henry. *The Trees of Great Britain and Ireland*, vol. 2. New York: Cambridge University Press, 2014.

Evans, Erv. "Benefits of Trees," North Carolina State University, Department of Horticulture Science, Raleigh, NC. Accessed May 24, 2019. https://projects.ncsu.edu /project/treesofstrength/benefits.htm.

Ferber, Michael. *A Dictionary of Literary Symbols*, 3rd ed., New York: Cambridge University Press, 2017.

Fessenden, Marissa. "Legend Says the Ankerwycke Yew Witnessed the Magna Carta's Signing." *Smithsonian Magazine*, February 20, 2015. https://www.smithsonianmag .com/smart-news/legend-says-ankerwycke-yew-witnessed-signing-magna -carta-180954373.

Flynn, Paula. "Witches' Brooms on Trees." Iowa State University Extension and Outreach. Last updated February 23, 2005. https://hortnews.extension.iastate .edu/2005/2-23-2005/witchesbroom.html, accessed 3/11/19.

Fogel, Edwin Miller. *Beliefs and Superstitions of the Pennsylvania Germans*. Philadelphia: American Germanica Press, 1915.

Folkard, Richard. *Plant Lore, Legends, and Lyrics: Embracing the Myths, Traditions, Superstitions, and Folklore of the Plant Kingdom*, 2nd ed. London: Sampson, Low, Marston & Company, 1892.

Foster, Steven, and Rebecca L. Johnson. *National Geographic Desk Reference to Nature's Medicine*. Washington, DC: National Geographic Society, 2008.

Frances, Peter, ed. *Natural Wonders of the World*. New York: DK Publishing, 2017.

Franklin, Anna. *The Illustrated Encyclopedia of Fairies*. London: Vega, 2002.

Friend, Hilderic. *Flowers and Flower Lore*, vol. 2. London: W. Swan Sonnenschein and Company, 1892.

Fry, Susan Leigh. *Burial in Medieval Ireland 900–1500: A Review of the Written Sources*. Dublin, Ireland: Four Courts Press, 1999.

Garside, Rachael. "On the Trail of the Ancient Yew." *BBC Radio Wales*, September 2, 2018. https://www.bbc.co.uk/programmes/p065bs1h/p065bqks.

Gerard, John. *The Herball or Generall Historie of Plantes*. London: John Norton, 1597.

Giesecke, Annette. *The Mythology of Plants: Botanical Lore from Ancient Greece and Rome*. Los Angeles: Getty Publications, 2014.

Gledhill, David. *The Names of Plants*, 4th ed. New York: Cambridge University Press, 2008.

Glen, Hugh. *Sappi What's in a Name: The Meanings of the Botanical Names of Trees*. Johannesburg, South Africa: Jacana Media (Pty) Ltd, 2004.

Gordh, Gordon, comp. *A Dictionary of Entomology*, 2nd ed. Cambridge, MA: CABI Publishing, 2011.

Gordon, Lesley. *Green Magic: Flowers, Plants & Herbs in Lore & Legend*. New York: The Viking Press, 1977.

Grady, Wayne. *The Great Lakes: The Natural History of a Changing Region*. Vancouver, Canada: Greystone Books, 2007.

Grande, Lance, and Allison Augustyn. *Gems and Gemstones: Timeless Natural Beauty of the Mineral World*. Chicago: The University of Chicago Press, 2009.

Graves, Charles. "On the Ogham Character." *Archaeologia Cambrensis, The Journal of the Cambrian Archaeological Association* vol. 2, 3rd series. London: J. Russell Smith, 1856.

Graves, Robert. *The White Goddess: A Historical Grammar of Poetic Myth*. New York: The Noonday Press, 1997.

Green, Miranda Jane. *Celtic Myths*, 3rd ed. Austin, TX: University of Texas Press, 1998.

Grimm, Jacob. *Teutonic Mythology*, vol. 4, 4th ed. Translated by James Steven Stally-brass. London: George Bell & Sons, 1888.

Gupta, Shakti M. *Plant Myths and Traditions in India*. Leiden, The Netherlands: E. J. Brill, 1971.

Hageneder, Fred. *The Meaning of Trees: Botany, History, Healing, Lore*. San Francisco: Chronicle Books, LLC, 2005.

Hallowell, Barbara G. *Mountain Year: A Southern Appalachian Nature Notebook*. Winston-Salem, NC: John F. Blair, Publisher, 1998.

Hancock, James F. *Plant Evolution and the Origin of Crop Species*, 3rd ed. Cambridge, MA: CABI, 2012.

Harkness, Peter. *The Rose: An Illustrated History*. London: Firefly Books Ltd., 2003.

Harrison, Lorraine. *Latin for Gardeners: Over 3,000 Plant Names Explained and Explored*. Chicago: University of Chicago Press, 2012.

Hartman, John R., Thomas P. Pirone, and Mary Ann Sall. *Pirone's Tree Maintenance*, 7th ed. New York: Oxford University Press, 2000.

Hazlitt, Willian Carew. *Faiths and Folklore: A Dictionary of National Beliefs*, vol. 2. New York: Charles Scribner's Sons, 1905.

Healy, John F. *Pliny the Elder on Science and Technology*. New York: Oxford University Press, 1999.

Hemery, Gabriel, and Sarah Simblet. *The New Sylva: A Discourse of Forest and Orchard Trees for the Twenty-First Century*. London: Bloomsbury Publishing Plc., 2014.

Homoya, Michael A. *Wildflowers and Ferns of Indiana Forests: A Field Guide*. Bloomington, IN: Indiana University Press, 2012.

Hood, Karen Jean Matsko. *Coconut Delights Cookbook: A Collection of Coconut Recipes*. Spokane Valley, WA: Whispering Pine Press International, Inc., 2014.

Hooke, Della. *Trees in Anglo-Saxon England: Literature, Lore and Landscape*. Woodbridge, England: The Boydell Press, 2010.

Hulme, Frederick Edward. *Wild Fruits of the Country-Side*. London: Hutchinson & Co., 1902.

Jaimoukha, Amjad. *The Chechens: A Handbook*. New York: RoutledgeCurzon, 2005.

Janick, Jules, and James N. Moore, eds. *Fruit Breeding: Tree and Tropical Fruits*, vol. 1. New York: John Wiley & Sons, Inc., 1996.

Jashemski, Wilhelmina Feemster, and Frederick G. Meyer, eds. *The Natural History of Pompeii*. New York: Cambridge University Press, 2002.

Johns, Charles Alexander. *The Forest Trees of Britain*, vol. 2. London: Forgotten Books, 2018.

Jones, Julia, and Barbara Deer. *Cattern Cakes and Lace: A Calendar of Feasts*. London: Dorling Kindersley Ltd., 1987.

_____. *The Country Diary of Garden Lore*. London: Dorling Kindersley Ltd., 1989.

Kennedy, Ezra J., ed. "The Witch Hazel Industry" *The Pharmaceutical Era*, vol. 35 (January 18, 1906): 62–65. New York: D. O. Haynes & Co.

Khan, Iqrar. ed. *Citrus Genetics, Breeding and Biotechnology*. Cambridge, MA: CABI International, 2007.

Kieckhefer, Richard. *Magic in the Middle Ages*, 2nd ed. New York: Cambridge University Press, 2014.

Kittel, Gerhard, and Gerhard Friedrich, eds. *Theological Dictionary of the Old Testament*, vol. 7. Translated and edited by Geoffrey W. Bromiley. Grand Rapids, MI: William B. Eerdmans Publishing Company, 1995.

Koshy, Thomas. *Fibonacci and Lucas Numbers with Applications*. New York: John Wiley & Sons, Inc., 2001.

Larson, Jennifer. *Greek Nymphs: Myth, Cult, Lore*. New York: Oxford University Press, 2001.

Lawrence, Robert Means. *The Magic of the Horse-shoe: With Other Folk-lore Notes*. New York: Houghton, Mifflin and Company, 1898.

Lehmann, Ruth P. M. "Ogham: The Ancient Script of the Celts." *The Origins of Writing*. Edited by Wayne M. Senner, 159–170. Lincoln, NE: University of Nebraska Press, 1989.

Lehner, Ernst, and Johanna Lehner. *Folklore and Symbolism of Flowers, Plants and Trees*. New York: Dover Publications, Inc., 2003.

Lewis, C. S. *The Magician's Nephew*. New York: HarperCollins, 2005.

Leyel, C. F. *Herbal Delights: Tisanes, Syrups, Confections Electuaries, Robs, Juleps, Vinegars, and Conserves*. Redditch, England: Read Books Ltd., 2013.

Liese, Walter, and Michael Köhl, eds. *Bamboo: The Plant and its Uses*. New York: Springer, 2015.

Lindow, John. *Norse Mythology: A Guide to Gods, Heroes, Rituals, and Beliefs*. New York: Oxford University Press, 2002.

Littleton, C. Scott. *Gods, Goddesses, and Mythology, Druids-Gilgamesh, Epic of,* vol. 4. New York: Marshall Cavendish, 2005.

Looijenga, Tineke. *Texts and Contexts of the Oldest Runic Inscriptions*. Boston: Brill, 2003.

Loudon, John Claudius. *Arboretum Et Fruticetum Britannicum: Or, The Trees and Shrubs of Britain*, vol. 2, 2nd ed, London: Henry G. Bohn, 1854.

Lukacs, Paul. *Inventing Wine: A New History of One of the World's Most Ancient Pleasures*. New York: W. W. Norton & Company, Inc., 2013.

Mac Coitir, Niall. *Ireland's Trees: Myths, Legends & Folklore*. Wilton, Cork, Ireland: The Collins Press, 2003.

Macalister, R. A. Stewart. *The Secret Languages of Ireland*. New York: Cambridge University Press, 2014.

MacKillop, James. *Oxford Dictionary of Celtic Mythology*. Oxford, England: Oxford University Press, 2000.

Markale, Jean. *Merlin Priest of Nature*. Translated by Belle N. Burke. Rochester, VT: Inner Traditions, 1995.

Martimort, A. G., I. H. Dalmais, and P. Jounel, eds. *The Liturgy and Time: The Church at Prayer: An Introduction to the Liturgy,* vol.4. Collegeville, MN: Liturgical Press, 1986.

Martin, Laura C. *The Folklore of Trees & Shrubs*. Chester, CT: The Globe Pequot Press, 1992.

MacKillop, James. *Oxford Dictionary of Celtic Mythology*. New York: Oxford University Press, 1998.

McGovern, Patrick E., Stuart J. Fleming, and Solomon H. Katz, eds. *The Origins and Ancient History of Wine*. Amsterdam, The Netherlands: Taylor & Francis, 2005.

Mehl-Madrona, Lewis. *Coyote Medicine: Lessons from Native American Healing*. New York: Fireside, 1998.

Molinari, Mario. *Divided by Words: A Case for a New Literacy*. Bury St. Edmonds, England: Arena Books, 2009.

Morgan, Joan. *The Book of Pears: The Definitive History and Guide to Over 500 Varieties*. White River Junction, VT: Chelsea Green Publishing, 2015.

Morton, Mark. *Cupboard Love 2: A Dictionary of Culinary Curiosities*, 2nd revised ed. Toronto, Canada: Insomniac Press, 2004.

Musselman, Lytton John. *Figs, Dates, Laurel, and Myrrh: Plants of the Bible and the Qu'ran*. Portland, OR: Timber Press Inc., 2007.

Nayar, N. Madhavan. *The Coconut: Phylogeny, Origins, and Spread*. Cambridge, MA: Academic Press, 2017.

Neal, Bill. *Gardener's Latin: Discovering the Origins, Lore & Meanings of Botanical Names*. Chapel Hill, NC: Algonquin Books of Chapel Hill, 1992.

Newberg, Andrew, Eugene G. D'Aquili, and Vince Rause. *Why God Won't Go Away: Brain Science and the Biology of Belief*. New York: Ballantine Books, 2001.

Nicholson, Paul T., and Ian Shaw, eds. *Ancient Egyptian Materials and Technology*. New York: Cambridge University Press, 2000.

Ó Broin, Tomá. "Lia Fáil: Fact and Fiction in the Tradition." *Celtica 21* (393–401, 1990) Dublin, Ireland: Dublin Institute for Advanced Studies.

Ollhoff, Jim. *South Pacific Mythology*. Edina, MN: ABDO Publishing Company, 2012.

Page, R.I. *Runes*. Berkeley, CA: University of California Press, 1987.

_____. *An Introduction to English Runes*, 2nd ed. Woodbridge, England: The Boydell Press, 2006.

Pakenham, Thomas. *The Company of Trees: A Year in a Lifetime's Quest*. London: Weidenfeld & Nicolson, 2015.

Peattie, Donald Culross. *A Natural History of Trees of Eastern and Central North America*. New York: Houghton Mifflin, 1966.

_____. *A Natural History of North American Trees*. San Antonio, TX: Trinity University Press, 2007.

Peck, Alice. *The Green Cure: How Shinrin-Yoku, Earthing, Going Outside, or Simply Opening a Window Can Heal Us*. New York: CICO Books, 2019.

Pennant, Thomas. *A Tour in Scotland and Voyage to the Hebrides 1772*. Cambridge, England: Cambridge University Press, 2014.

Pennick, Nigel. *The Pagan Book of Days: A Guide to the Festivals, Traditions, and Sacred Days of the Year*. Rochester, VT: Destiny Books, 1992.

Pliny the Elder. *The Natural History of Pliny*, vol.3. Translated by John Bostock and H. T. Riley. London: Henry G. Bohn, 1857.

Plotnik, Arthur. *The Urban Tree Book: An Uncommon Field Guide for City and Town*. New York: Three Rivers Press, 2000.

Porteous, Alexander. *The Forest in Folklore and Mythology*. Mineola, NY: Dover Publications, Inc., 2002.

_____. *The Lore of the Forest*. New York: Cosimo Inc., 2005.

Power, Daniel. *The Norman Frontier in the Twelfth and Early Thirteenth Centuries*. New York: Cambridge University Press, 2004.

Praciak, Andrew, Nick Pasiecznik, Douglas Sheil, Miriam van Heist, Marieke Sassen, Cristina Sousa Correia, Christopher Dixon, George E. Fyson, Keith Rushforth, and Claire Teeling, comps. *The CABI Encyclopedia of Forest Trees*. Boston: CABI, 2013.

Pratt, Anne. *Flowering Plants, Grasses, Sedges, and Ferns of Great Britain*, vol. 2. Revised by Edward Step. London: Frederick Warne & Co., 1899.

Quattrocchi, Umberto. *CRC World Dictionary of Plant Names: Common Names, Scientific Names, Eponyms, Synonyms, and Etymology: D-L*, vol. 2. Boca Raton, FL: CRC Press, LLC, 2000.

_____. *CRC World Dictionary of Plant Names: Common Names, Scientific Names, Eponyms, Synonyms, and Etymology: M-Q*, vol. 3. Boca Raton, FL: CRC Press, LLC, 2000.

_____. *CRC World Dictionary of Plant Names: Common Names, Scientific Names, Eponyms, Synonyms, and Etymology: R-Z*, vol. 4. Boca Raton, FL: CRC Press, LLC, 2016.

Radford, Mona A., and Edwin Radford. *Encyclopaedia of Superstitions: A History of Superstition*. New York: Philosophical Library, 1949.

Raphael, Ray. *More Tree Talk: The People, Politics, and Economics of Timber*. Washington, DC: Island Press, 1994.

Rodd, Tony, and Jennifer Stackhouse, *Trees: A Visual Guide*. Berkeley, CA: University of California Press, 2008.

Rosengarten, Jr., Frederic. *The Book of Edible Nuts*. Mineola, NY: Dover Publications, 2004.

Rosenthal, Bernard. *Salem Story: Reading the Witch Trials of 1692*. New York: Cambridge University Press, 1999.

Roud, Steve. *The Penguin Guide to the Superstitions of Britain and Ireland*. New York: Penguin Group (USA) Inc., 2003.

Runkel, Sylvan T., and Dean M. Roosa. *Wildflowers and Other Plants of Iowa Wetlands*, 2nd ed. Iowa City, IA: Iowa State University Press, 2014.

Scheick, Bill. *Adventures in Texas Gardening*. College Station, TX: Texas A&M University Press, 2017.

Seager, Herbert West. *Natural History in Shakespeare's Time: Being Extracts Illustrative of the Subject as He Knew It*. London: Elliot Stock, 1896.

Skeat, Walter W. *The Concise Dictionary of English Etymology*. New York: Cosimo, Inc., 2005.

Skinner, Charles M. *Myths and Legends of Flowers, Trees, Fruits, and Plants, in All Ages and in All Climes*. Philadelphia: J. B. Lippincott Company, 1925.

Slavin, Michael. *The Ancient Books of Ireland*. Montreal, Canada: McGill-Queen's University Press, 2005.

Small, Ernest. *Top 100 Food Plants: The World's Most Important Culinary Crops*. Ottawa, Canada: NRC Press, 2009.

_____. *North American Cornucopia: Top 100 Indigenous Food Plants*. Boca Raton, FL: CRC Press, 2014.

Sonneman, Toby. *Lemon: A Global History*. London: Reaktion Books Ltd., 2012.

Soyer, Alexis. *Food, Cookery, and Dining in Ancient Times: Alexis Soyer's Pantropheon*. Mineola, NY: Dover Publications, Inc., 2004.

Stahl, Paul H. *Romanian Folklore and Art*. Bucharest, Romania: Meridiane Publishing House, 1969.

Staub, Jack. *75 Remarkable Fruits for Your Garden*. Layton, UT: Gibbs Smith, Publisher, 2007.

Stetkevych, Jaroslav. *Muhammad and the Golden Bough: Reconstructing Arabian Myth*. Bloomington, IN: Indiana University Press, 1996.

Stevenson, Angus, ed., *Oxford Dictionary of English*, 3rd ed. New York: Oxford University Press, 2010.

Stobart, Anne. *Household Medicine in Seventeenth-Century England*. New York: Bloomsbury Academic, 2016.

Stone, Damien. *Pomegranate: A Global History*. London: Reaktion Books, Ltd., 2017.

Sumner, Esther Yu. "A Date is a Date is a Date" *Ancestry Magazine*, vol. 25, no. 2, March-April 2007. Provo, UT: Ancestry, Inc.

Suttie, Jill. "Why Trees Can Make You Happier," *Greater Good Magazine*, April 26, 2019. https://greatergood.berkeley.edu/article/item/why_trees_can_make_you_happier.

Suzuki, David. *David Suzuki: The Autobiography*. Vancouver, Canada: Greystone Books, 2006.

_____. *The Sacred Balance: Rediscovering Our Place in Nature*. Updated and expanded. Vancouver, Canada: Greystone Books, 2007.

Taylor, Raymond L. *Plants of Colonial Days*. Mineola, NY: Dover Publications Inc., 1996.

Thomas, Daniel Lindsey, and Lucy Blayney Thomas. *Kentucky Superstitions*. Princeton, NJ: Princeton University Press, 1920.

Turner, William. *A New Herball*. London: Steven Mierdman, 1551.

Vescoli, Michael. *The Celtic Tree Calendar: Your Tree Sign and You*. Translated by Rosemary Dear. London: Souvenir Press, 1999.

Vickery, Roy, ed. *Oxford Dictionary of Plant-Lore*. Oxford, England: Oxford University Press, 1997.

_____. *Garlands, Conkers and Mother-Die: British and Irish Plant-lore*. New York: Continuum US, 2010.

_____. *Vickery's Folk Flora: An A-Z of the Folklore and Uses of British and Irish Plants*. London: Weidenfeld & Nicolson, 2019.

Walker, Barbara G. *The Woman's Dictionary of Symbols and Sacred Objects*. San Francisco: HarperSanFrancisco, 1988.

Watson, Ben. *Cider, Hard & Sweet: History, Traditions, and Making Your Own*, 3rd ed. Woodstock, VT: The Countryman Press, 2013.

Watts, D. C. *Elsevier's Dictionary of Plant Names and their Origin*. Amsterdam, The Netherlands: Elsevier Science B.V., 2000.

_____. *Elsevier's Dictionary of Plant Lore*. Burlington, MA: Academic Press, 2007.

Wells, Diana. *Lives of the Trees: An Uncommon History*. Chapel Hill, NC: Algonquin Books of Chapel Hill, 2010.

White, Newman Ivey, ed. *The Frank C. Brown Collection of North Carolina Folklore*, vol. 7. Durham, NC: Duke University Press, 1977.

Wilkinson, Gardner. *The Manners and Customs of the Ancient Egyptians*, vol. 5, 3rd ed. London: John Murray, 1847.

Wohlleben, Peter. *The Hidden Life of Trees: What They Feel, How They Communicate*. Berkeley, CA: Greystone Books, Ltd., 2016.

Wood, Michael. *In Search of England: Journeys into the English Past*. Berkeley, CA: University of California Press, 2001.

Ziedrich, Linda. *The Joy of Jams, Jellies, and Other Sweet Preserves*. Boston: The Harvard Common Press, 2009.

Zolar. *Zolar's Encyclopedia and Dictionary of Dreams*. New York: Fireside, 1992.

Zohary, Daniel, Maria Hopf, and Ehud Weiss. *Domestication of Plants in the Old World*, 4th ed. New York: Oxford University Press, 2012.

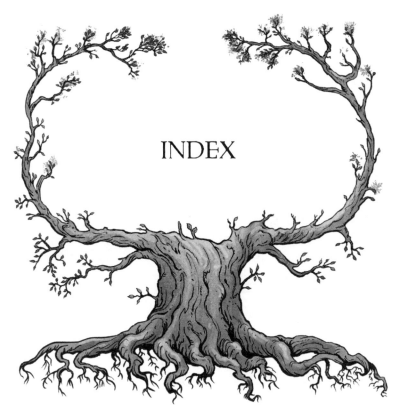

INDEX

To Write to the Author

If you wish to contact the author or would like more information about this book, please write to the author in care of Llewellyn Worldwide Ltd. and we will forward your request. Both the author and publisher appreciate hearing from you and learning of your enjoyment of this book and how it has helped you. Llewellyn Worldwide Ltd. cannot guarantee that every letter written to the author can be answered, but all will be forwarded. Please write to:

Sandra Kynes
℅ Llewellyn Worldwide
2143 Wooddale Drive
Woodbury, MN 55125-2989
Please enclose a self-addressed stamped envelope for reply,
or $1.00 to cover costs. If outside the U.S.A., enclose
an international postal reply coupon.

Many of Llewellyn's authors have websites with additional information and resources. For more information, please visit our website at http://www.llewellyn.com